second edition

TWENTIETH-CENTURY
MUSIC:
AN INTRODUCTION

ERIC SALZMAN
Composer

PRENTICE-HALL, INC., ENGLEWOOD CLIFFS, NEW JERSEY

Library of Congress Cataloging in Publication Data

SALZMAN, ERIC.
    Twentieth-century music.

    (Prentice-Hall history of music series)
    Includes bibliographies.
    1. Music—History and criticism—20th century.
I. Title.
ML197.S17 1974   780′.904   73-17211
ISBN 0-13-935015-2
ISBN 0-13-935007-1 (pbk.)

Printed in the United States of America

10 9 8 7 6 5 4 3 2

Cover photo: Albert Gleize's cubist portrait "IGOR STRAVINSKY," 1914.
Collection of Richard S. Zeisler.

Music: from Stravinsky's *Le Sacre du Printemps*. Copyright by Edition Russe de Musique. Copyright assigned 1947 to Boosey and Hawkes for all countries of the world. Reprinted by permission.

PRENTICE-HALL INTERNATIONAL, INC., *London*
PRENTICE-HALL OF AUSTRALIA, PTY. LTD., *Sydney*
PRENTICE-HALL OF CANADA, LTD., *Toronto*
PRENTICE-HALL OF INDIA PRIVATE LIMITED, *New Delhi*
PRENTICE-HALL OF JAPAN, INC., *Tokyo*

FOREWORD

Students and informed amateurs of the history of music have long needed a series of books that are comprehensive, authoritative, and engagingly written. They have needed books written by specialists—but specialists interested in communicating vividly. The Prentice-Hall History of Music Series aims at filling these needs.

Six books in the series present a panoramic view of the history of Western music, divided among the major historical periods—Medieval, Renaissance, Baroque, Classic, Romantic, and Contemporary. The musical culture of the United States, viewed historically as an independent development within the larger western tradition, is discussed in another book, and forthcoming will be similar books on the music of Latin America and Russia. In yet another pair, the rich yet neglected folk and traditional music of both hemispheres is treated. Taken together, the eleven volumes of the series will be a distinctive and, we hope, distinguished contribution to the history of the music of the world's peoples. Each vol-

Foreword continued

ume, moreover, may be read singly as a substantial account of the music of its period or area.

The authors of the series are scholars of national and international repute—musicologists, critics, and teachers of acknowledged stature in their respective fields of specialization. In their contributions to the Prentice-Hall History of Music Series their goal has been to present works of solid scholarship that are eminently readable, with significant insights into music as a part of the general intellectual and cultural life of man.

H. WILEY HITCHCOCK, *Editor*

PREFACE

Any consideration of the music of the twentieth century must begin with the reminder that a good deal of it has not yet been written. Fortunately, twentieth-century music can reasonably be said to have begun somewhere about 1900; it is one of our few clear-cut chronological realities.

The history of culture can be thought of in many ways: as a succession of events (the way we tend to think about ancient history), as the movement of great historical forces (the way we think about the Renaissance and Reformation), in terms of social, political, and economic realities (our view of the Middle Ages and of the Baroque and Rococo-Classical periods as well) or in terms of creative personalities (the Romantic view). As this series of books itself can testify, these conceptions need not be mutually exclusive and none of them need preclude an understanding of cultural history as a history of ideas. Without, I hope, entirely forgetting any of the former, it is the last-named that I have tried to write: the creative development of musical ideas in the last sixty-five years understood against and as distinct from the past, in the variety and unity of its own growth and in its potential for the future.

It is my hope and belief that a book of this kind can bring the reader towards the musical experience itself, in terms of the greatest variety and richness of ideas and expression, a richness itself characteristic of the twentieth-century musical experience. Towards this end, certain sacrifices have consciously been made. Detailed biographical information will have to be sought elsewhere (such things are, except in the cases of the very youngest composers, available in standard reference works). Analytic material has been relegated to an appendix consisting of a few indicative examples—it is always to be assumed that, on every page of this book, the reader is being actually referred to the music itself. No attempt has been made to achieve the illusory goal of completeness, and long lists of also-rans have been avoided. I am well aware that Schmitt, Schreker, Ghedini, Grainger and Glière, Weiner and Weinberger, Alfven, Zemlinsky, and a host of greater and lesser lights do not appear and that others, particularly—but not exclusively—composers of only national or local significance, receive brief consideration. I am also conscious of the fact that the work of certain composers—particularly since World War II —inevitably receives a certain emphasis because it lends itself easily to verbal analysis or description, qualities which do not necessarily correspond to artistic values. The deficiencies of this book with respect to American music are, fortunately, compensated for by the inclusion in this series of a volume of H. Wiley Hitchcock devoted entirely to the subject: *Music in the United States.* It is the intention here to treat the development of American music in our century in terms of the general development of twentieth-century ideas everywhere; it is, surprisingly enough (and limited as it is), one of the first such attempts. In any case, I can only hope that, in a book intended to be devoted to essentials, the essentials are there.

Although the first edition of this book was published in 1967, the bulk of it was written on a boat to Europe in the spring of 1964. This moment had more than symbolic value for me; it marked a change in direction for me as a composer beginning with my *Foxes and Hedgehogs*, on texts from John Ashbery's "Europe." The culture change—the clash in values from Old World to New—scored out in that piece as the structure of a music drama came to serve as a metaphor for the vast upheavals and changes of the 1960's and 1970's.

Change has continued to overtake music and the arts as it has the whole of society; new forces have been set in motion and the outcome is hardly in sight. Of necessity, one's own work and thought has also evolved. The decade that has elapsed is difficult to write about, not only because the events set in motion are still in progress, but also because the author himself has played a part in their unfolding.

The first version of this book marked off a distinct period; we can, with certain neatness, refer to it as the period of modern music. There were loose ends, of course, and even certain ideas that were clearly prophetic of what was to come. Approaching a second edition, I had two obvious choices; leave the book as it was or rewrite it completely, reflecting the state of the art and the currency of my own thought. However, I have chosen a third course. The earlier parts of the book have been left essentially intact. There are minor revisions—corrections, emendations, a few rephrasings and clarifications, an occasional re-evaluation —and the specimen analyses have been relegated to an appendix. However, the final section of the book has been rather substantially rewritten. It was my aim not merely to bring the book "up-to-date"—although the events of the past decade have been sketched and an attempt made to assess their significance—but also to establish a firmer conceptual framework for the whole post-war period.

Inevitably, certain differences of approach in this final section will become apparent. There is a much greater emphasis on social and technological change as a background for understanding the artistic events, and there is a greater emphasis on the interactions between the arts. This in part reflects the evolution of my own ideas, in part our closeness to the events (musical synthesis takes greater time and distance), and in part the nature of the period. On the other hand, many pages of the original still seem valid and have been retained.

One or two additional points need to be amplified here. The problem of providing dates for works is not always as simple as it might appear. Dates given in reference works, programs, chronologies, biographies, or scores often differ and may (when accurate) refer to the date of completion, copyright, publication, or first performance. The attempt here has been to give, as closely as possible, the actual dates of composition. Hopefully, any factual errors or imprecisions which remain undiscovered do not affect the basic premises of the book.

The intent in organizing the musical examples as an appendix is to make the book more continuously readable and less forbidding to the general, non-specialist reader. The examples are, in any case, only intended to suggest approaches for the reader who wishes to pursue more analytical studies. The illustrations—including Gleize's cubist portrait of Stravinsky reproduced on the cover of the volume—have been chosen with the idea of bringing together a series of portraits which are themselves works of art.

It is not possible to acknowledge more than a very few of the many intellectual and spiritual debts incurred in writing a book like this. Among those which cannot be omitted, I would like to include H. Wiley Hitchcock, the understanding and skillful editor of this series and the author of the volume on American music without which any grasp of the twentieth-century is necessarily incomplete; my principal teachers, Roger Sessions and Milton Babbitt; Edgard Varèse, who never taught but was, in the true sense, always a teacher; Ross Parmenter, former Music Editor of *The New York Times,* who was almost entirely responsible for my writing career in music; and, finally, that extraordinary younger generation of performers and creators—in music and the other performing arts—who have made possible the beginnings of a new, vital cultural life.

ERIC SALZMAN

CONTENTS

part one

Introduction

ONE

TWENTIETH-CENTURY
MUSIC AND THE PAST

The music of the twentieth century seems so fundamentally different from the music of the past and so varied and wide-ranging in itself
that it is difficult to realize that it has deep roots in what came before
and, at the same time, a pervasive unity that distinguishes it from its past.

The creative history of Western music since 1900 is inconceivable
without the evolution of Western culture in the preceding centuries; our
musical institutions and, indeed, our whole way of thinking about music
are inheritances from the recent and not-so-recent past, and in certain fundamental ways the tradition has continued to exert its influence
even on the greatest innovators.[1] Nevertheless we can also attempt to define a distinctly twentieth-century viewpoint when we recognize that

---

[1] When traditional historians talk about "modern" European history, they
mean "since the French Revolution." Similarly, "modern art" surveys used to begin
with David and Goya. Only in music has there been general agreement not to treat
this time span as one period.

1

nearly all the creative musical thinking of our century—even that which is described as "conservative"—has participated in the search for new forms. The old forms, the old expressive structures, can be implied by the term "functional tonality" understood in its broadest traditional sense, embracing ideas and "expression" on the one hand and underlying structural, organizing principles on the other. After 1900 the old propositions ceased to function as *a priori* assumptions; related to the tradition or not, tonal or non-tonal, conservative or revolutionary, all twentieth-century musical art has had to establish its own expressive and intellectual premises.

In spite of technological, social, and esthetic upheaval, contemporary musical ideals are still communicated in the context of a musical life whose structure, means, and institutions are largely derived from the late eighteenth and nineteenth centuries.[2] This is true of our concert and operatic institutions, of our instruments (even the old violins have been so largely rebuilt that they can be considered nineteenth-century instruments), and of instrumental technique. It is true of the modern orchestra, of our chamber music ensembles, of our operatic forms, of the virtuoso soloist, and of the solo recital. Similarly, the bulk of our musical repertory, our techniques of teaching the practice and theory of music (and the institution of the conservatory itself), as well as most of our artistic and esthetic notions and assumptions about what music is ànd what it ought to do—all these things reached their full development between 1700 and 1900 and have been bequeathed to us surprisingly intact.

Some of our most fundamental ways of thinking about music and musical creation are also inheritances from the recent past. Indeed, our whole notion of "art" and artistic creation as a unique and separable human activity is a relatively modern Western idea, by no means universal in human experience, and one which strongly links the "Romantic" era with the twentieth century. The notion of the creation and experience of music for its own sake is one that entered Western musical culture at a relatively recent date, and in spite of many attempts in the last decades to modify this rather special conception of the role of music in our society, we still tend to think of the highest forms of music-making as the purest—that is, the most isolated and detached from other forms of human activity. Like our nineteenth-century forebears, we think of the composer

---

[2] This is not a book that deals with the development of musical ideas in relationship to general history. Clearly, however, two world wars and the social, political, technological, and scientific revolutions of the twentieth century have had a meaning for contemporary culture parallel to the impact that the fall of the *ancien régime,* Napoleon, the Industrial Revolution, and the new bourgeois society had on the life and thought of the nineteenth. Attempts will be made now and then—particularly in the final section—to annotate the as yet unwritten social history of new music.

as a creative individual communicating personal, original, and unique thoughts with a distinctive style and a particularized point of view and expression. This concept of the composer—derived from the Romantic idea of the artist as a culture hero—has led us to place greater emphasis than ever on creative individuality, originality, and freedom. Finally, the nineteenth century taught us to understand the work of art as conditioned by its historical and cultural context and, at the same time and without contradiction, as an individual expression of artistic uniqueness. The very notion of "the avant-garde" as it is usually understood is a nineteenth-century, Romantic conception.[3]

We can expect then to comprehend a great deal of what has happened in the twentieth century in terms of the past. Just as the historical personalities of Beethoven and Wagner remain decisive in the formation of our conceptions of the role of the composer in society, so does the music of Beethoven and Wagner suggest the development of ideas and techniques which evolved into characteristic twentieth-century modes of musical thought. The modulatory freedom in Beethoven's music stands in a direct relationship to the chromatic freedom and incipient "atonality" of *Tristan und Isolde*. In turn, Wagner's expanded palette of orchestral, harmonic, and contrapuntal techniques can be clearly traced in the music of composers like Richard Strauss, Gustav Mahler, and even César Franck, Gabriel Fauré, and Claude Debussy. The revival and refinement of classical organizational principles and the close relation of these to modern structural ideas of a music that is totally organic and interrelated are already basic in the music of Brahms. The resources of harmonic and melodic patterns that lie outside of the major-minor functional tonality system are suggested by the music of composers like Mussorgsky and even Dvořák. The "back-to-Bach" movement and the rediscovery of "pre-Bach" music and musical forms were accomplished facts long before 1900. In short, chromaticism; the extended and freer use of dissonance; the establishment of harmonic and melodic freedom; the use of harmonic, melodic, and structural ideas derived from folk music and early Western music; the concept of the structural interrelationships between all the parts of a musical composition; the discovery of the distant past and of non-Western music; the vast expansion of instrumental technique and color; the new freedom, complexity, and independence of rhythm, dynamics, and tone color—all these modern ideas have roots deep in the last century.

Less obvious, perhaps, but equally important is the persistence of

[3] *Gebrauchsmusik* and the social ideals of the 1930's represented significant attempts to break with these Romantic notions. And the traditional view of art has again been challenged in the last years; see the final chapter of this book.

certain underlying modes of musical thought, especially those dealing with large statement and structure—complex and subtle ideas built up over the course of many generations and not easily dissipated even by revolutionary changes on the surface. There is a central development of musical thinking that connects Haydn directly with Mahler in a line of structural conceptions that constantly increase in size and scope. This kind of thinking remains surprisingly operative in the twentieth century —in the many attempts to revive and renew "sonata form," for example, or, in a more profound way, in the development of chromatic and twelve-tone structures in the work of the Viennese, the direct inheritors of the "main line" tradition.

More than anything else, however, the Romantic notion of the artist as an individualist has helped to form the modern impulse towards originality and uniqueness. In a sense, the vast and swift changes in all modern art can be seen as an intensification of a historical process of change that has long been operative in Western culture. But even if we accept the premise that the vast expansion of vocabulary and means in this century is part of an over-all process that has taken place over the past centuries, there is reason to believe that, after a point, the character of the process itself changed and quantitative distinctions became clearly qualitative. For our purposes, we can define that point as the moment when traditional tonality ceased to provide the fundamental expressive and organizational foundation of musical thought and was replaced by other modes of musical expression and organization. This change actually occurred in the years around 1900 and it is this fact that enables us to speak distinctively of the music of the twentieth century.

Western music between about 1600 and 1900 was distinguished by the developing and characteristic kind of musical thinking that we have termed "functional tonality." The word "tonality" can be defined in a rough way as a representation of a basic scale formation within which certain hierarchies prevail—expressed as points of stability and instability. Certain tones and combinations of tones represent goals and suggest stability and rest, while others imply motion to or away from these goals. Tonality, then, in its traditional form, presents a principle of order in musical thought which implies that every formation of horizontal and vertical (that is, melodic and harmonic) tones has a definable relationship to every other such formation. To express the idea in another way, every musical event has a "function" or a functional role which relates it to what has come before and what will happen next. The basic psychological principle here is expectation; the basic musical technique is that of direction and motion. Out of this grow the characteristic ways in which musical lines will rise and fall and the ways in which simultaneous musical lines will relate to one another in harmonic patterns. The idea of expectation suggests the use of resolution and non-resolution; of so-called dissonance and consonance; of intensity and relaxation; of cadence, accent, and articulation; of phrase and punctuation; of rhythm and dynamic; even of tempo and tone color.

Out of these apparently simple psychological and musical facts evolved one of the most complex and sophisticated modes of artistic expression that man has ever developed. The concept of primary goals suggested the possibility of secondary goals, the idea of "modulation," in which musical motion could turn away from its primary centers of gravity to secondary centers which could then serve to reinforce the. motion back to the primary ones. This made possible the complex structures of eighteenth- and nineteenth-century music, with their web of relationships which, unfolding in time, tie every note of a piece firmly to every other note. When we say that Beethoven's "Eroica" Symphony is in E♭, we are saying much more than the fact that its first and last harmonies are E♭ major triads; we are implying a whole way of thinking about the organization of sound which determines every aspect of our experience of the music.[4]

Characteristic forms of tonal expression, contrast, interrelationship, and structure guided musical thinking for three centuries. Except to a limited degree in certain forms of folk and popular music, they are no longer operative; since the opening years of this century, composers have ceased to accept the unquestioned validity of these concepts. Wagner's extreme chromatic freedom, "atonal" as it may seem at times, is still based on the listener's expectation that one musical event implies another— much of *Tristan* is built on the very idea of the defeat of expectation. The music of Debussy, Schoenberg, and Stravinsky, however, no longer depends on that expectation but sets forth new kinds of definitions and relationships. Even the most conservative twentieth-century music establishes forms of motion and rest with new means. When Beethoven uses the familiar dominant-tonic cadence, it has a formal and expressive significance that is inseparable from the entire fabric and structure of the musical thought; when the same musical event occurs in Prokofiev, it is a local incident whose significance must be understood in other terms. It is true that certain underlying universal principles have retained force and validity, but since 1900 there has no longer been any necessity and prior assumption—any generally accepted premise preceding the fact of musical composition—that would strictly imply that any one musical realization must follow or be derived from any other.

---

[4] The vexed question of "classical" tonality is obviously not so simple; the foregoing is intended to be suggestive rather than definitive. Most modern views about the encompassing function of the old tonality derive from the writings of the Austrian theorist Heinrich Schenker.

The development of creative musical thought since 1900 has been rich and complex, full of remarkable achievements, remarkable and unremarkable failures, enormous and continuing promise, and seemingly endless contradiction. There is some reason to believe that the developments of the last few years, particularly with respect to electronic means, instrumental and vocal techniques, music theater, and multi-media, mark a more definitive break with the past—for better or for worse—than anything accomplished up until now. But all twentieth-century music can be comprehended as a unity if it is understood against the background of the past and the dominating tonal ideas of the past. Once this unity, essentially negative in its nature, has been grasped, we can begin to understand the positive ways in which contemporary creative thought has redefined its intellectual, expressive, and creative aims.

The history of music in the twentieth century can be understood in terms of two great cycles: first, the abandonment of functional tonality after 1900, the explorations of vast new materials before and after World War I, and the new tonal and twelve-tone syntheses that followed; and second, the very different but parallel set of rejections, new beginnings, explorations, analyses, and syntheses following World War II. The bond that connects all of twentieth-century music grows out of the fact that each composer—and each piece—has had to establish new and unique forms of expressive and intellectual communication. To understand the music of this century, we must examine these forms.

BIBLIOGRAPHICAL NOTES

The general literature in English on the music and musical ideas of the twentieth century is neither large nor particularly distinguished. Out of fewer than a dozen surveys that can be found on the library shelves only one must necessarily be cited here—William Austins's *Music in the 20th Century* (New York, 1966)—and it is, in fact, limited largely to the period before World War II. Somewhat more specialized studies include *European Music in the Twentieth Century*, ed. Howard Hartog (New York and London, 1957; re-ed. Arthur Cohn, New York 1965); *Contemporary Music in Europe* (New York, 1963); and Wilfred Mellers's *Music in a New Found Land* (London, New York, 1964). Donald Mitchell's *The Language of Modern Music* (London, 2nd ed., 1966) concerns itself with major figures and ideas. Mention should be made of two important source collections: *Contemporary Composers on Contemporary Music*, eds. E. Schwartz and B. Childs (New York, 1967), and *The American Composer Speaks*, ed. Gilbert Chase (Baton Rouge, 1966). Nicolas Slonimsky's astonishing year-by-year documentary *Music Since 1900* is now in its fourth edition (New York, 1971). Slonimsky has also revised *Baker's Biographical Dictionary of Musicians* (New York, 1971) to include a wide range of twentieth-century composers, even some of the younger figures; a new, sixth edition of *Grove's Dictionary of Music and Musicians* scheduled for publication in 1976 will do the same on a still wider scale.

Several attempts have been made to produce generalized studies of twentieth-century materials and methods to serve as theoretical statements or teaching matter; only one or two of these, connected with the work of particular composers, will concern us (see the relevant chapters of this book). The following specialized periodicals—several of them no longer in existence—contain all sorts of matter pertaining to the history, criticism, documentation, esthetics, theory, and practice of twentieth-century music: *Modern Music* (New York); *Melos* (Mainz, Germany); *The Score* (London); *Die Reihe* (Vienna; Eng. tr. Bryn Mawr, Pa.); *Perspectives of New Music* (Princeton); *Journal of Music Theory* (New Haven); *Darmstädter Beiträge zur Neuen Musik* (Mainz, Germany); *Source* (Davis, Calif.).

part two

The Breakdown
of Traditional Tonality

TWO

THE SOURCES

More than anything else, the expansion of the use and meaning of chromatic inflection led to the development of the large tonal canvases of the eighteenth and nineteenth centuries. The structural use of modulation produced the large instrumental forms that are the great intellectual achievement of traditional tonality. Chromaticism pre-dates classical tonality, of course, but through the pattern of changing key relationships it came to play a particular structural role in the growth of tonal forms. In the evolution of things, it was modulation and chromaticism—and their local allies, secondary dominants and altered chords—that ultimately undermined that very tonality. Modulation, aided by the universal acceptance of equal temperament, helped create convincing, dramatic structures of large scope by delaying and ultimately reinforcing the musical motion of a piece towards home base. In the Classic and Romantic symphony, modulation and chromaticism were essential in the formation of large structures. With many of the romantic composers,

Chopin and Liszt for example, chromaticism played its major role in matters of expressive detail; in Brahms and, especially, in the gigantic structures of the Wagnerian music drama, it functioned both as detail and as the basis for structural prolongation. *Tristan und Isolde* is still part of the Classic-Romantic tradition in that its extreme chromaticism is still based on expectation defeated by "false" and evasive resolution, harmonic delay, and long-range suspension. Nevertheless, in parts of *Tristan* and *Parsifal* we are at the point where a quantitative development is very nearly a qualitative one, where the distinction between "tonal" and "atonal" chromaticism becomes a fine psychological line.

Tristan und Isolde* was first performed in 1865, but, in a way, its influence did not become decisive until the end of the century. None of the direct heirs of the Wagner tradition—Bruckner, Strauss, even Mahler —was primarily concerned with the development of Tristanesque chromatic procedures, although each of them employed the new harmonic, melodic, and modulatory freedom as the basis for a late-Romantic, tonal style. The only post-Wagnerian who used a complex chromatic idiom was Max Reger (1873–1916), but Reger's chromaticism is carefully systematized and based on eighteenth-century forms and procedures derived from Bach and Mozart. Reger had a certain influence—mainly theoretical —on Hindemith; otherwise his significance for the twentieth century is small.

The composer who most directly and completely connects late Wagner and the twentieth century is Arnold Schoenberg (1874–1951). The inventor of twelve-tone music began his career in perfect Tristanesque Wagnerianism, and in works like *Verklärte Nacht* (1899), the *Gurrelieder* cycle (1901; orchestrated 1910), *Pelleas und Melisande* (1902–1903), and the First and Second String Quartets (1905, 1907) the implications of *Tristan* and *Parsifal* are carried forward, eventually beyond the realm of tonal expectation and tonal form. By contrast, Richard Strauss (1864–1949) and Gustav Mahler (1860–1911) absorbed *Tristan* into their composing equipment along with the entire Wagnerian arsenal of new techniques.

Strauss developed few new techniques and, essentially, he found no new universal forms. His style up to and perhaps including *Der Rosenkavalier* (1909–1910) suggests not so much a development from as a thorough exploration of the implications of the Wagnerian revolution. It is impossible to deny the impact of works like *Salome* (1903–1905) and *Elektra* (1906–1908) on the early development of twentieth-century music, but it is difficult today to appreciate and assess the significance of that impact. Perhaps the relationship is clearest on the dramatic-psychological plane; we would call it Freudian and trace its influence on the development of "expressionist" musical theater in works like Schoenberg's

Erwartung and Berg's *Wozzeck* and *Lulu*. Musically, we can see two important contributions. In the small, Strauss finds it possible—in a way that Wagner never did—to delay or even omit the resolution of harmonic and melodic "dissonance"; in the large, he extends this principle of free, "dissonant" motion to produce "free association" forms which often defeat the natural and expected phrase-motion with breaks in the continuity of thought and with abrupt confrontations and juxtapositions which obviously derive from dramatic-psychological considerations. However, Strauss never really abandons functional tonality; it is somehow still operative, and, at the very moment when he seemed to be on the point of destroying it, he turned—first in *Der Rosenkavalier* and then definitively in *Ariadne auf Naxos* (1912)—to classical forms and techniques in a clear attempt to reinstate it. *Ariadne* is, in effect, the first piece of neo-classicism; it predates Stravinskyian neo-classicism by a number of years. But, as we shall see, Stravinsky's neo-tonality is synthetic; Stravinsky actually had to go through the process of destroying functional tonality and then inventing a new kind of tonality to replace it. Strauss never went that far; he went to the edge of the abyss and then turned back. He redefined his own limits as those of functional tonality. Strauss lived through nearly half of the twentieth century, long enough to become the only significant composer who still fully accepted and believed in those limitations.[1]

The case of Mahler is still more complex. To some extent, he can be said to have duplicated the Wagnerian revolution in symphonic music, partly by adapting the symphonic tradition to a vocal and lyric-dramatic conception of musical discourse (achieved, to a great extent, through the intermediate forms and techniques of the late-Romantic lied as represented, for example, in the work of a composer like Hugo Wolf). Mahler's basic language is the common practice of the nineteenth century—securely tonal, even fundamentally diatonic. Through the long, long extension of lyric, melodic lines, an ever-extended delay of the cadence, a magnificent long-range harmonic motion, careful planning and pacing of dynamic and rhythmic curves, and extensive and skillful modulation, he extended relatively simple and apparently limited ideas into enormous and powerful structures. Mahler, in fact, built entire structures on a complex interrelationship of tonal areas to the point where, although detail is always clearly set forth in terms of tonal function, the long-range motion builds up in new tonal shapes; these large-scale compositions move successively through wider and wider ranges of tonal areas and often resolve in tonal regions far from those in which they have set out. Mahler's work, con-

---

[1] Conscious "classicism" can be found in many Strauss works after *Der Rosenkavalier;* a good case can be made for a kind of new tonal synthesis in some of the composer's late works, parallel in some important respects to Schoenberg's "nontonal" synthesis; see especially the *Metamorphosen* for 23 solo strings of 1945.

Bust of Gustav Mahler by Rodin, which is on display in Philharmonic Hall, Lincoln Center for the Performing Arts. © 1965, Lincoln Center for the Performing Arts. Photographed by Bob Serating Photo, New York.

sisting almost entirely of symphonies and orchestral songs, makes extensive use of folk song and, in fact, synthesizes many aspects of nineteenth-century style. In a certain sense, Mahler orchestrated the crisis of traditional values in terms of large-scale, multi-faceted works whose very range is contemporary. Like Charles Ives, he articulated a crisis and a world-view which become widely understood only later through the massive intervention of technology in cultural life. The essentially new view of tonal form, the remarkable expansion of phrase-structure, the use and expansion of modulation and color, the very scope and range of the music, and its simultaneous character of involvement and detachment all have had an important influence in the twentieth century. Mahler seems at first to have escaped the tonal upheavals of the early years of the century, but the underlying spiritual crisis is nonetheless explicit in his work. Indeed, it is Mahler's achievement that he made this crisis his subject matter; this itself has kept his music alive and relevant in the latter part of the century.[2]

One important late-Romantic remains to be mentioned here: the enigmatic Ferruccio Busoni (1866–1924). In his teaching and writing about music, notably in the *Sketch of a New Esthetic of Music* published in 1907, the famous piano virtuoso anticipated part of the development of contemporary ideas with visionary clarity. But his own vast output escapes the late nineteenth century only occasionally: in the use of chromatic, expressive dissonance in a few late works like the *Elegies* for piano of 1907 and in the intense contrapuntal chromaticism of some of the other keyboard works. Busoni's chromatic practice, like Reger's, was as much a return to eighteenth-century ideals as a derivation from Wagner; however, the idea of a "neo-classical" chromaticism seems to have had no important development (except for a few works of Schoenberg, to be discussed later).

The tonal tradition in its most typical forms is Italo-German, and it can be said to have declined in Central Europe by virtue of its own inner, contrapuntal, chromatic development. Elsewhere this tonal tradition was much weaker, and once the overwhelming domination of Italian and German style had been shaken off, other, older traditions could rise to the surface and lead to new ideas. In Eastern Europe, for example, the Romantic rediscovery of folk music had a decided impact on tonal ideas. While the folk music of Germany, Austria, and Italy[3] actually seems to have accommodated itself over the years to classical tonal organization, the traditional music of Hungary and the Slavic countries always main-

[2] Mahler had, of course, a more direct and superficial influence, most notably on the modern Russian symphony.

[3] For pre-tonal forms in German folk music, see early chorale settings; in Italy, a pre-tonal folk music has persisted outside of the main urban centers.

tained its modal independence, and even the so-called Hungarian-Gypsy music of Liszt and Brahms[4] suggests certain melodic usages (and a harmonic carry-over) at variance with common diatonic tonal usage. Eastern modal ideas show up in the work of composers like Dvořák and the Russian "Five" (although tonally accommodated); in the case of a Mussorgsky, such ideas were decisive in forming a melodic and harmonic style which often contradicted prevailing contrapuntal-tonal notions. (The performing editions of Rimsky-Korsakov and other well-wishers were designed to eliminate or smooth out such "crudities.")

One highly developed Western art-music tradition has consistently remained somewhat outside the central development: that of France. Although the classical abstract formulation of tonal usage derives from the theoretical writings of Rameau, the actual evolution of French practice has taken place quite independently of the Italian-German tonal evolution. Characteristic of this independence is a metrical, rhythmic, and phrase flexibility closely related to the free, non-accentual character of the French language. This relative freedom from "tonic" accent confers on French music a quality of fluid, poetical prose as opposed to the metrical "verse" construction of Italian and German music; in turn, French music often seems much less directional and much more coloristic. The independence was very persistent in the eighteenth century; it was less noticeable in the nineteenth, when French composers—Berlioz was a notable exception—tended to accept classical Italian and German rhythmic and structural forms. The influence of Wagner was as decisive in the latter part of the century as that of the classical masters had been earlier, but Wagner at least could suggest fluid prose and expressive color, and the French version of Wagnerian chromaticism is a very distinct if minor development with consequences for the twentieth century. One characteristic form of Wagnerian chromaticism came to France by way of Belgium through the work and influence of César Franck. Franck and the Franckophiles, Vincent d'Indy and Ernest Chausson (d'Indy's pupil, Albert Roussel, carried the line into still another generation), used extensive schemes of chromatic modulation combined with a flexible, asymmetrical sense of line and a tendency for rich, chromatic harmonies to shade off into color inflections in a very French way. Henri Duparc (who corresponds somewhat to Hugo Wolf), Guillaume Lekeu (another Belgian), and Emmanuel Chabrier (at different times the most Wagnerian

---

[4] Both of these composers had, of course, a direct influence on posterity. Schoenberg has written eloquently of the intellectual impact of Brahms on modern musical thought; Liszt, who was an innovator in practically every musical domain, has been said to have prefigured nearly everyone from Wagner to Berg but, ironically, his late music, innovative to the point of atonality, seems to have had no direct influence.

and the most anti-Wagnerian of French composers) all made their Bay-reuth pilgrimages. Equally important, the literary influence of Wagner, particularly as transmitted through the work of the "symbolist" poets, played no small role in creating the rather special esthetic and intel-lectual atmosphere of *fin-de-siècle* Paris.

The tendency towards a flexible melodic style joined to a rich, sensuous, subtle harmonic palette is most highly developed (and most free of Wagnerianism) in the work of Gabriel Fauré (1845–1924), a com-poser who developed his poetic, evanescent chromaticism within the bounds of a complex, refined sense of tonal structure. Fauré, like Reger and Mahler, never left the confines of functional tonality, and his influ-ence on later developments was only peripheral, but the freedom and subtlety of his style represent the artistic climate in France in the late nineteenth century and suggest, in a way parallel to Debussy's, the com-ing tonal revolutions.

BIBLIOGRAPHICAL NOTES

The sources of contemporary music—unlike the origins of modern art—have received little serious attention. One of the few important studies in this field, Ernst Kurth's *Romantische Harmonik und ihrer Krise in Wagner's "Tristan"* (Berlin, 1921), has never been translated into English. Elliott Zuckerman's *The First Hundred Years of Wagner's "Tristan"* (New York, 1964) is stronger on literary than musical matters. On the French background there is Martin Cooper's *French Music from the Death of Berlioz to the Death of Fauré* (London, 1951). More specialized books in-clude Dika Newlin's *Bruckner, Mahler, Schoenberg* (New York, 1947), Kurt Blaukopf's *Gustav Mahler* (New York, 1973), and three multi-volume studies, Donald Mitchell's Mahler study (London, v. I, 1958), Henry-Louis de la Grange's *Mahler* (New York, v. I, 1973), and Norman Del Mar's *Richard Strauss* (London, 1962; 1969). Romain Rolland's *Musicians of Today* (Paris, 1908; tr. New York 1915) has the status of a document; so do the Busoni *Sketch* (English translation reprinted in *Three Classics in the Aesthetic of Music*, New York, 1962) and the various writings of Schoenberg (see *Harmonielehre* [Vienna, 1911]; abridged translation as *Theory of Harmony* [New York, 1948]; see also essays in *Style and Idea* [New York, 1950]).

THREE

THE REVOLUTION: PARIS

In the late nineteenth century, Paris regained its old position as intellectual and artistic center of the West. Native musical tradition was not strong: the Opéra reigned supreme and the operatic tradition was that of Meyerbeer, Offenbach, and the Italians tempered by the genteel sentimentalities of Gounod; there was a revival of symphonic and chamber music, but it was dominated by a watered-down classicism. The answer to this "philistinism" and "academicism" was Wagnerism; Wagner had an overwhelming impact on French intellectual life not yet absorbed or overcome. But the Paris of the post-Prussian War period had an enormous intellectual and artistic vitality of its own, especially in the visual arts (academic and impressionist) and in literature; the line that descends from Baudelaire to Mallarmé and to the twentieth century also left deep traces on the history of music. *Fin-de-siècle* sensibility and a conscious search for new forms and new means combined with a rather special French refinement and subtle, abstracted sensuality. We recognize the kind of sensibility that we find in Mallarmé also in Fauré and, especially, in Debussy.

There was another aspect to the intellectual style of the times: a mordant, dry, ironic wit. In the visual arts, it appears in the work of an artist like Toulouse-Lautrec; in music, it turns up in Chabrier as a conscious antidote to Wagnerism. But its most important musical exponent was Erik Satie (1866–1925), a remarkable innovator with a great deal of

Erik Satie by Jean Cocteau. Meyer Collection, Paris. Reproduction forbidden.

genius if little talent. Satie came to music late and struggled to find the
form for his ideas; his remarkable inventions were almost off-hand:
casual, amusing discoveries which took form as literary–musical wit. Satie
constructed aphorisms and then turned them into simple musical expressions. As often as not, the point is in the idea, the title: "Cold Pieces,"
"Three Pieces in the Form of a Pear," "Truly Flabby Preludes," "Automatic Descriptions," "Disagreeable Impressions." However, the larger
works (the ballets *Parade* [1917] and *Relâche* [1924], and the remarkable
setting from Plato, *Socrate* [1918]) as well as a few of the shorter works
display a quality of simple invention that transcends many of the shortcomings and reflect the extraordinary originality of Satie's mind.

Satie was by no means the only example of a French composer at
the turn of the century who tried to break with the past in an attempt to
make music a vehicle for some kind of literary taste; the thing was in the
air. And, ultimately, although Satie had both an immediate and a long-
range influence, a great deal of his work was in fact produced in the
shade of composers better fitted than he to accomplish the break with

Left to right: Stravinsky, Diaghilev, Cocteau, and Satie (dated 1917). Sketch by
M. Larionov. Meyer Collection, Paris. Reproduction forbidden.

traditional formal techniques that he so clearly foreshadowed. But he continues to occupy a special place in the history of recent music not only as the godfather to a generation of composers but also as a spiritual grandfather of some latter-day avant-gardism. He was the first to *use* sound—disconnected, static, objectified sound—in an abstract way, essentially divorced from the organizational and structural principles of tonal form and development. The importance of this is as wide-ranging as the actual results in Satie's music are limited.

DEBUSSY

The problem of finding new modes of discourse, of replacing classical developmental-variational principles of tonality with new content and new expressive form, occupied the best musical minds in the decades around 1900. In Germany and Austria, the process had a strongly evolutionary aspect, growing out of the inner development of the tradition itself. In France, where classical tonality was much less firmly rooted or, in any event, more artificially cultivated, the break occurred earlier and with greater ease and thoroughness. We have discussed a number of people who helped to bring this about, but by far the most important was Claude Debussy. Debussy was, from the start, further removed from Bach and Beethoven than Schoenberg ever could be; *La Mer* has less to do with fugues and sonatas than even the most radical works of the Viennese.

Debussy (1862–1918), like most French composers, was intensively trained in the Central European classical tradition. The French Conservatoire, where he spent eleven years, has—since its directorship, 1821–1841, by an Italian, Luigi Cherubini—specialized in the very principles, techniques, and forms which have not been especially characteristic of French musical creativity.[1] To some extent, French music has been stifled by this, but for Debussy it was a source of strength. All the first great innovators of the twentieth century—Debussy, Stravinsky, the Viennese—met the challenge of the classical tradition and the classical disciplines in one way or another. But it is a curious fact that Debussy, in many ways the most independent of that tradition, was the only one to have had an intense classical conservatory training. For Schoenberg, the

---

[1] This is not so surprising as it might seem. In the history of art, theory generally *follows* practice and codification is most easily performed, not by a practitioner, but by someone on the outside—in space or time—looking in.

tradition provided an intellectual model and suggested underlying universal principles; for Debussy, it was a matter of *métier*, of fluency, and of complete, natural control.

Debussy's innovations, while expressed in great part in instrumental works, were based to some extent on the special and subtle inflections of French language and poetry; on the character and length of sound (as opposed to strong metrical and rhythmic accent); on the fluid and non-symmetrical organization of French meter, rhythm, accent, and phrase. Debussy extended this kind of rhythmical and phrase organization into every aspect of music; thus melodic, harmonic, rhythmic, and timbral ideas, blended and unified in essentially new ways, are organized around

Claude Debussy. Sketch by Henri Detouche. Meyer Collection, Paris. Reproduction forbidden.

qualities of sound patterns and relationships rather than around the significance of these in an overall rhythmic, phrase, and contrapuntal scheme. Melody, harmony, rhythm, and color become different aspects of a single basic conception; sounds and sound patterns are related to one another by arbitrary and sensual aural criteria rather than by the old necessities of motion and resolution governed by linear, tonal logic. Debussy was able—and this was his genius—to organize these new relationships into new forms which retain their psychological and even organic intellectual validity without depending on previously accepted conventions of tonal language and structure. In *Tristan,* even ultra-chromaticism and the most extended false resolutions are still governed by the laws of tonal motion and expectation; in *Pelléas et Mélisande,* no such criteria are operative. Debussy's vocabulary of sound is chosen for its empirical (i.e., "sensual" in both meanings) qualities, and the motion from one sound pattern to the next is built on intervallic relationships and on parallelisms of structure, using very clear, immediate, and localized aural and psychological insights. In Debussy's earlier work, the simple and classical patterns of contrast and return still govern the large forms; later even these vanish, to be replaced by ongoing associative forms which depart from one point and, without the necessity of substantive recapitulation, arrive at another. In a sense, this non-narrative, non-cyclical form—achieved by Debussy in a work like the ballet *Jeux* of 1912—represents the large intellectual tendency of the pre-World War I revolutions which we call "atonal." While our experience of complex chromatic forms over the last sixty or seventy years allows us to accept the new tonal relationships in Debussy as unexceptional and even traditional, there is no question that works like *La Mer* and *Jeux* mark as thorough and significant a break with the tonal tradition as any of the most complex works of Schoenberg or his colleagues.

Like many of his contemporaries, Debussy was influenced not only by the implications of the French language but also by the prevailing literary culture of France. Its esthetic, partly Wagnerian in origin, was allied with the late-Romantic ideal of expressive musical poetry, and until his last few works, Debussy was generally concerned with expressive subjects, programs, and texts closely associated with the work of the "symbolist" poets: the *Prélude à l'après-midi d'un faune* of 1892–1894 (after Mallarmé), *La Mer* of 1902–1905, *Images* for orchestra of 1909, the various sets of piano pieces written between the 1880's and 1910, and, of course, the songs and theatrical works. It is a mistake to ignore the importance of non-musical, poetic ideas on the development of Debussy's musical ideas and the forms of his musical thought, but it is equally important to realize that his expressive and poetic intent can be understood in strictly musical terms as well.

It is often suggested that the whole-tone scale forms the basis of Debussy's musical technique, with the implication that the old seven-note major-minor scale hierarchies were replaced by the ambiguities of the six-note whole-step scale. However, in point of fact, whole-tone relationships are used by Debussy in conjunction with, or as part of, much more complex melodic and harmonic usages—interlocking pentatonic forms, for example—based on a fundamental principle of symmetry. The whole-tone scale itself is, of course, symmetrical, as are most of the harmonies associated with it (e.g., the augmented triad). But there are many Debussyian patterns based on symmetrical structures which are not necessarily derived from whole-tone scales at all; some of these are individual events, others are combinations of events generally arranged in parallels. Characteristic are chains of triads, of seventh, ninth, or eleventh chords, or of related structures built on fourths or major seconds arranged in pentatonic, whole-tone, diatonic, or chromatic patterns, the last named including free, sliding chromatic shifts based on "secondary-function" chords but often arrived at through parallel or sequential motion. This parallel, symmetrical (rather than contrapuntal, contrary) motion has its counterpart in the rhythmic and phrase structure, also built on parallelism and symmetry. Thus the principle which obtains in the choice of chord and melodic line extends to the broad melodic and harmonic movement of Debussy's music and ultimately determines the larger motion and form of each piece. (See Appendix; Example 3-1.)

The fine, elegant tonal imagination of Debussy is thus given a much wider and profounder field of action and expression than its apparently limited character might initially seem to suggest. In traditional tonality, the musical motion, expression, and, ultimately, structure are all interrelated functions of the unequal and fundamentally asymmetrical character of the basic material—the major-minor scales and triads, with their unequal intervals and hierarchies of motion and value. Debussy was the first composer to substitute successfully another set of values, a kind of musical thought based on symmetrical patterns and structures with a highly weakened directional motion and thus a very ambiguous sense of tonal organization. Debussy consciously exploits this ambiguity, often setting it by contrast against clear, tonal, cadential statements and reinterpreting identical melodic or harmonic events in parallel, contrasting ways —somewhat in the manner of certain classical techniques but with a difference. Traditional tonal techniques, such as the sequence, function as delaying or extending devices which create secondary areas of tonal ambiguity to reinforce a bigger motion from one primary area to another; in Debussy's music, these ambiguities are built into the structure of the musical thought.

One result of this ambiguity of tonal relationships is that rhythm, phrase, dynamic, accent, and tone color are largely freed from direct dependence on tonal motion; they tend to gain an importance in the musical process almost equal to that of melody and harmony. This extremely significant development was as important in a positive sense as the breakdown of the old tonality was in a negative one. The rhythmic and phrase forms, the dynamics, the articulation, and the tone color are as basic in the music of Debussy as the actual choice of pitches, or very nearly so. In a sense, the qualities of the musical ideas are often so interdependent that the various components of the sound seem to shade off into one another; that is, under certain circumstances, pitch almost functions as color, color takes the place of line (there is often a clear "rhythm" of color changes), dynamics and articulation provide rhythmic and phrase impetus, and so forth. There are individual sound patterns and even isolated sounds which seem to create their own context. These formations are endowed in equal part with pitch, a dynamic, accent, rhythm, and color, all inseparable and interdependent and forming the sound structures, the basic ideas of each piece. These ideas are valid, so to speak, in their own terms—for their value as sound and perhaps for their psychological effect, not for their position in a directional development or ongoing variations. They build up in relatively static structures organized in the juxtaposition of linked and parallel ideas. Tonal centers are ultimately established, not by linear motion, but by the focusing and refocusing of shifting, fluctuating patterns which in themselves are fluid yet unified and full of specific, identifiable character, and which combine through analogy, juxtaposition, and symmetry. An analogy might be drawn from one of Debussy's own musical "subjects": the sea, whose waves form a powerful surge of undulating motion in varying crests and troughs without necessarily any real movement underneath.

The development of Debussy's style can be traced with a great deal of clarity from the derivative, even Wagnerian sound of his early music to the final, remarkable abstract pieces of the war years. The Baudelaire songs of 1890, the String Quartet of 1893, and the *Prélude à l'après-midi d'un faune* are the first mature works. The composer's style is completely established in the *Chansons de Bilitis* and in the Verlaine songs of the period 1898–1904, the *Estampes* and *Images* for piano of 1903, 1905, and 1907, and the orchestral *La Mer* and *Images*. A still greater broadening of techniques and resources can be found in works around 1910: the *Trois Ballades de François Villon*, the two sets of *Préludes* for piano, the music for d'Annunzio's *Le Martyre de St. Sébastien*, and the ballet *Jeux*. The last works of 1915–1917—the twelve *Etudes* for piano and the sonatas for cello and piano, for flute, viola, and harp, and for violin and piano—suggest striking new directions. For the first time since the String Quartet, Debussy abandoned literary associations.

In the *Etudes,* Debussy set himself quite literally a series of specifically technical-creative problems to solve, problems which lie at the very root of new musical organization and communication. In the sonatas, he similarly attacked questions of musical structure and of the organization of thought projected onto broader, simpler planes of large, neo-tonal form and intimate, precise communication.

AFTER DEBUSSY

The musical manner of Debussy has been widely imitated, and an attempt has been made to elevate this manner into a style or school which has, by analogy with the terminology of art history, been dubbed "impressionism." Musical impressionism seems to imply certain kinds of colorful "tone painting" based on Debussy's harmonic and melodic palette and, especially, on a range of shimmering, blended instrumental colors.[2] His originally rather subtle and esoteric manner quickly became adapted to the functions of background music, partly because of the easy identification of coloristic resources, partly because the fluidity and non-assertive character of the style made it an ideally unobtrusive and psychologically apt material for dramatic accompaniment, and partly because the static ambiguity of the tonal motion made it easy to create musical materials of flexible length without assertive beginning, middle, or end.

Nevertheless, in spite of the fact that there has been—and continues to be—a good deal of Debussyism in a superficial sense, there has never been any real Debussy school. If the minor imitators and movie-music pastiches are ruled out, the "impressionist" movement boils down to Debussy himself, a few early works of Maurice Ravel (1875–1937), and a handful of pages in the work of a few outlanders. Ravel's early style does derive from Debussy although, in a few cases, Ravel's development seems parallel to or even in advance of Debussy. It is in his piano music, especially, and in his music for the theater that Ravel's originality and independence from Debussy can be best understood. *Jeux d'eau* of 1901, *Miroirs* of 1905, and *Gaspard de la nuit* of 1908 (all for piano), the one-act comic opera *L'Heure espagnole* of 1907, and the ballet *Daphnis et Chloé* of 1909–1911 are the works in which Ravel remains closest to Debussy and the conventional notions of "impressionism"; but, already in these pieces, the far more classical orientation of Ravel is evident. Ravel is always fastidious as to detail and closely concerned with a recognizable

---

[2] A much better and more precise analogy could be drawn between the music of Debussy and the organic forms and sensual esthetic of Art Nouveau and related literary movements.

frame of external structure; he is involved with line, clarity of articulation, brilliant, idiomatic writing, and careful tonal organization. In the end, Ravel may be classified as a classicist; his particular contribution might be described as a unique ability to combine the rich harmonic and melodic vocabulary of ninths and elevenths with free motion of parallel chords and chromatic sidesteps, all animating simple forms which are themselves the result of a new and clear sense of tonal movement.

There is scarcely another composer of note who can be described as "impressionist." Paul Dukas (1865–1935), an elegant and fastidious composer of very limited output, was influenced by Debussy, and the very prolific Florent Schmitt (1870–1958) has sometimes been classified in this way. The English composer Frederick Delius (1862–1934), who lived a good part of his life in France, evolved something of an original version of the Debussy manner, and the style is represented in America by the talented Charles Griffes (1884–1920), who died just at a point when he was developing a personal idiom, free of Debussyism. The list is hardly longer than that; as we have seen, Debussy himself was hardly a "Debussyiste" by the end of his life.

Nevertheless, Debussy's influence on the music of this century was incalculable, and it has hardly ended. The techniques which he evolved are most obviously in evidence in the work of a number of non-Germanic composers—most notably Vaughan Williams but also De Falla, Bartók and Kodály, Ernest Bloch, Respighi and Puccini, one or two of the Russians—who were all in one way or another interested in establishing some kind of new tonal-modal style based on a particular local musical tradition or language that lay outside of or broke the bonds of classical tonality. For them, the new Debussyian vocabulary offered a set of expressive and formal resources within which a great variety of ideas and materials could be expanded, integrated, and made expressive in terms of a high artistic style. Also, the new free harmonic techniques could often be combined with modal melodic tradition—a fact which Debussy himself exploited and which suggested a natural way of using folk material without squeezing it into pre-cut tonal patterns.

The long-range influence of Debussy has, however, been even more profound. The disassociation of the individual sound event, the elevation of timbre and articulation to a point equal to harmony and melody, the use of constructions free from tonal patterns and based on symmetry, and the consequent building up of new static and associative forms are all important twentieth-century ideas which find a point of origin in the work of Debussy. In this broader sense, the French composer's influence is traceable in the developing ideas of Schoenberg, Berg, and Webern as well as of Stravinsky and Bartók; indeed, it can be found in most of the principal trends of the century and is still significant in the work of certain latter-day avant-gardists, notably Pierre Boulez.

THE RUSSIANS

The role of Paris as an international artistic and intellectual center in the years preceding World War I was enhanced by the presence in the French capital of a considerable number of foreign artists. Of the musicians resident in or closely associated with Paris, the Russians

Pablo Picasso and Igor Stravinsky by Jean Cocteau. Meyer Collection, Paris. Reproduction forbidden. "After the reprise of 'Sacre' and of 'Parade' [Satie ballet for which Picasso did the decor], Picasso comforts Stravinsky. He drank too much vodka."

were the most important. Russian musical thought had, through-out the nineteenth century, maintained some independence from that of Central Europe, and the continuing vitality of older folk and liturgical traditions was a continuous challenge to classical tonality. The Russianism of "The Five" provided non-Western elements that were occasionally more than decorative; in Mussorgsky's music the Russian materials are deeply felt and penetrate to the core of the style. Mussorgsky's so-called crudities were in reality departures from the accepted Western tonal norms; even Rimsky-Korsakov could not conventionalize Mussorgsky's forms.

At the beginning of this century, Russian art was in the vanguard of European development and it continued to be so well into the Soviet period. The Stalinization of Soviet music and the subsequent insistence on a national and popular symphonic style have served to obscure the work and the very existence of an important and original group of Russian composers active in the first quarter of the century, including the remarkable Nikolay Rosslavetz (1881–1944), who anticipated aspects of twelve-tone

Stravinsky playing *Le Sacre du Printemps*, 1913. Sketch by Jean Cocteau. Meyer Collection, Paris. Reproduction forbidden.

music, and Alexander Mossolov (b. 1900), a kind of Soviet Varèse who experimented with percussion materials.

The first Russian composer, however, to influence the course of western musical thought was Alexander Scriabin (1872–1915). A little younger than Debussy, two years older than Schoenberg and influenced by both, Scriabin was a profoundly original creative mind who never quite found new forms for his profoundly new ideas. He was an excellent pianist who started out as a Chopinist and used the piano all his life as the medium for his profoundest creations.[3] He was a declared visionary, and the gradual suspension of tonality in his music was associated with a kind of post-Wagnerian chromatic mysticism. Whatever its mainsprings, his style eventually evolved into a kind of exotic modality (based on a scale of three whole steps, minor third, and a minor second) and, finally, into a crystalline, motionless atonality built on harmonies compounded in fourths. Some of the early theorists of contemporary music (including Schoenberg) attempted to systematize the use of harmonic structures built in fourths by analogy with the old constructions in thirds. But the parallels are misleading and we can see today that the major "theoretical" significance of the fourth lies in the fact that, along with the minor second, it is the basic unit of a series which generates the complete tempered chromatic scale. In any case, Scriabin's use of fourths was based on symmetrical structures and clearly derived from an intensified, dissonant "impressionistic" chromaticism.

Scriabin toured a great deal as a pianist and lived for periods in Paris and other parts of Western Europe, but he died before the Revolution forced the fateful split between Russian expatriate and Soviet artist. Sergei Prokofiev (1891–1953), after producing a series of highly original works based on a kind of dissonant, rhythmical, sophisticated primitivism, left (Czarist) Russia for Paris, where he elaborated a symphonic and theatrical style of considerable scope. He later went back to (Soviet) Russia to develop a lyric-symphonic popular Soviet manner. On the other hand, Stravinsky (1882–1971), who derived from Rimsky-Korsakov and started out as a purveyor of stylized Russian and Eastern exoticisms in Paris, never went back but settled in the West, developing a mature style which was to become the dominant influence in Western music for more than a quarter-century. Stravinsky's first important works were written under the influence of his teacher, Rimsky-Korsakov, tempered by a little Debussy and a decidedly original and volatile imagination. Only the use of orches-

---

[3] Scriabin was influenced by Chopin and Liszt; he was, like them, a performing musician who linked Eastern European origins with a Central European style and (to a point) French taste, to produce a series of innovations and, in the end, a style of great originality. Scriabin's influence might seem greater if we knew more about chromatic music in the Soviet Union.

tral color and a few piquant harmonies and rhythms amid the genteel exoticism of *L'Oiseau de feu* of 1910 and the picturesque and wry, fantastic humor of *Petrouchka* of the following year suggest what was to follow: the violence of *Le Sacre du printemps* and the establishment of a new kind of tonality.

Le Sacre was completed in 1912,[4] the same year that Debussy composed his *Jeux* and Schoenberg his *Pierrot lunaire*. Just as *Jeux* suggests the crisis of form and *Pierrot* that of harmonic and melodic organization, *Le Sacre* marks a definitive break with the old rhythm-phrase-accent structures. In Stravinsky's pivotal ballet score, rhythm and accent are clearly divorced from their old dependence on melodic and harmonic tonal organization and motion; indeed, if anything, the harmonic sense of the music is actually closely dependent on the rhythmic and accentual organization. The way things happen in *Le Sacre* is determined by the almost kinesthetic impact of violent rhythmic articulation and accents organized in asymmetrical, shifting patterns. The harmonic structures and simple melodic patterns are virtually isolated; "chords" and melodic bits appear as individual static objects; they relate to each other often only by virtue of patterns of repetition and of shifting metrical accent. Ideas based on simple, insistent repetition gain long-range power and significance through the juxtaposition of contrasting patterns and planes and through their constant rhythmic and metrical reinterpretation. (See Appendix; Example 3-2.)

Everything in *Le Sacre* is asserted, everything is given by the piece itself; nothing falls into place naturally or by expectation. This is a piece of high artifice in the best sense: the idea that it is a "primitive" work is misleading; it is about primitivism, but is not itself primitive at all. The quality of disassociated insistence, combined with a striking use of chordal, non-contrapuntal dissonance, produces the effect of an arbitrary motionless, elemental power, but in actual fact every gesture is carefully calculated and the dynamic articulation of the whole is almost schematic. *Le Sacre* is less obviously "atonal" and seemingly more primitive than corresponding works of the Viennese school only because it is not linear-chromatic in the German tradition. But it presents and resolves some very complex psychological and music problems. Disassociated ideas appear as artifacts, set into block structures built up in layers. The piece unfolds in time, not through the old play of energy to produce motion but by the complete and explosive rhythmic release of confined and volatile musical energies. For Stravinsky, *Le Sacre* was in many ways a beginning, middle, and end; he quickly went on to other things. Nevertheless, many of his

---

[4] Stravinsky did not move to Paris until 1920, and *Le Sacre* was composed in French Switzerland, where the composer lived between 1910 and 1920. But it is with the Paris of the Russian Ballet that the work is inextricably associated.

characteristic and fundamental techniques first appeared in this work. Most important, *Le Sacre* is a work that takes shape, not through the extension of line and counterpoint, but through the juxtaposition of static levels of sound and statement, dividing up and punctuating psychological time with rhythm and accent, statement and articulation.

BIBLIOGRAPHICAL NOTES

For the intellectual climate in late nineteenth-century France, see A. G. Lehmann, *The Symbolist Aesthetic in France* (Oxford, 1950). There are books in English on Satie and Ravel as well as a survey of *Modern French Music From Fauré to Boulez* by Rollo W. Meyers (London, 1948, 1960; New York, 1971). The major study on Debussy in English is Edward Lockspeiser's two-volume work (London, 1962, 1964). The basic French sources are the writings of Léon Vallas; one work in English translation is *The Theories of Debussy* (London, 1929). See also Debussy's own "Monsieur Croche" articles translated and reprinted in the *Three Classics* volume cited in the bibliography for Chapter 2. For one view of the relationship between Debussy and Ravel, see Charles Rosen's "Where Ravel Ends and Debussy Begins" in the May, 1959 issue of *High Fidelity* magazine. For modern views of Debussy's importance, see *Debussy et l'évolution de la musique au 20e siècle*, ed. Edith Weber (Paris, 1965). A modern analysis of *Jeux*, by Herbert Eimert, appears in Vol. 5 of the journal *Die Reihe*.

For the early works of Stravinsky and the background of *Le Sacre du printemps*, see especially Stravinsky's own *Chronicles of My Life* (London, 1936) and the many references in the four volumes of conversations with Robert Craft; *Conversations With Igor Stravinsky, Memories and Commentaries, Expositions and Developments, Dialogues and a Diary* (Garden City, N.Y., 1959, 1960, 1962, 1963); additional Stravinsky bibliography appears at the end of Chapter 5. A modern view of *Le Sacre* by Pierre Boulez appears in his *Relevés d'apprenti* (Paris, 1966; English translation, New York, 1968).

FOUR

THE REVOLUTION: VIENNA

At the turn of the twentieth century, Paris had only one rival as the capital of Europe: Vienna, still the seat of the Austro-Hungarian Empire and still a cultural crossroads. Vienna had once been the meeting place of the musical North and South, where the contrapuntal and instrumental techniques of the Germans mingled with the operatic and instrumental styles of Italy; the child of that Viennese marriage was the classical symphony. At the opening of this century, Vienna—the city of Freud and Schnitzler, of the Secessionist movement and Gustav Mahler— was to become the center of the transformation of that very classical tonality which had produced some of her greatest musical achievements.

The author of that transformation, Arnold Schoenberg, was born in Vienna in 1874 (he was to die in Los Angeles in 1951). Schoenberg was essentially self-taught and always remained outside the powerful Vienna musical "establishment," but he entirely mastered traditional technique and he remained all his life involved in the study and teaching, not only of the classical disciplines but also of the profoundest and most universal aspects of the tradition. Schoenberg's starting point was, of course, Wagner—specifically the Wagner of *Tristan* and *Parsifal*—but his real intellectual antecedents were Bach, Beethoven, and Brahms. He began with the Wagnerian chromatic vocabulary, but from the start his basic concerns were with that intellectual integrity and totality of conception which—as he himself did so much to show—were basic to the classical tradition. Schoenberg's music is steeped in contrapuntal principles, in notions of the complex interrelationships between the vertical and the horizontal, and in concepts of total form, and it is through these ideas, older and more universal than classical tonality itself, that we can understand his development. He was also a thorough-going Hegelian; that is, he believed that music, like all aspects of human life, is part of a process of change and that there are universal and inevitable principles which control history and historical change. For Schoenberg the classical tradition of form—the concept of an all-pervasive intellectual organization—represented a universal principle, while the development of chromaticism represented a principle of change and evolution. The growth of equal temperament, chromaticism, and modulation had made possible the historical rise of functional tonality in the seventeenth and eighteenth centuries and destroyed it in the twentieth; thus tonality contained within itself from the start the seed of its own destruction.

Schoenberg's *Verklärte Nacht*—originally written for string sextet, later recast for string orchestra—and his massive *Gurrelieder* (orchestrated in 1910), for soloists, chorus, and large orchestra, are still, in spite of their great originality, within the Wagnerian orbit. The works of the years 1902–1907—including the symphonic poem *Pelleas und Melisande* (after Maeterlinck and written at about the time that Debussy completed his operatic version), the First String Quartet in D minor, and the *Kammersinfonie*—show a steady but marked expansion of chromatic and contrapuntal techniques with the effect of delaying tonal resolution over longer and longer periods. This is particularly true of the Chamber Symphony, in which whole-tone patterns and melodic and harmonic constructions in fourths appear. These techniques, related to those of Debussy, represent aspects of the total chromatic material: adjacent whole-tone scales as well as cycles of fourths will generate the complete chromatic gamut; also, half-step, whole-step, and fourth patterns have important characteristics of symmetry which distinguish them from the unbalanced, "hierarchical" structures of major-minor triads and scales. But Schoenberg was never primarily interested in working out the harmonic implications of these kinds of structures; his instinct (later formalized) was to seek out the meaning of harmonic structures in their relationship to line, and the technique of most of his later music (with some exceptions) is based on complex, chromatic, contrapuntal thinking with motivic and, increasingly, intervallic construction carried out within smaller and smaller revolutions of the total chromatic cycle. The Second String Quartet (completed 1908) shows the germ of the process within a single work; the composition begins well within the bounds of a contrapuntal, chromatic tonality, organized thematically, and then proceeds towards a linear chromaticism in which motives and intervals assume the structural force exerted formerly by tonal expectation and function. With a quotation of the popular Viennese tune "Ach, du lieber Augustin," Schoenberg bids an ironic farewell to tonality; the unexpected appearance of the human voice in the last two movements introduces a new conceptual universe with the words of Stefan Georg, "I feel a breath of air from other planets."

In the work which followed, the Three Piano Pieces, Op. 11 (completed 1909), the new non-tonal motivic chromaticism is completely dominant. The opening phrases still have a thematic function, but they also form fundamental sound matter which accounts for a good deal of what happens in the piece. There is, of course, simple thematic statement and development. But this must now function entirely without the aid of tonal motion, support, or superstructure. For the first time, every sound, every interval, every event has a unique and independent value, free of the hierarchies of tonal discourse—and equally free of the meanings formerly invested in them. Thematic development remains, but totally abstracted from its old contexts. But this was not enough for Schoenberg; it was necessary for him to transform all the musical materials so that the old balance and interaction between all aspects of the musical matter and discourse were restored in some new artistic synthesis. His solution, from the start, was to affirm a basic unity between linear and vertical events and to assert (not merely assume but aggressively assert, through the music itself) the fundamental identity of the individual elements of the tempered, chromatic scale (See Appendix; Example 4-1).

The piano pieces of Op. 11 were followed by a series of important works including the song cycle from Stefan Georg's "Book of the Hanging Gardens" (Op. 15, begun in 1907); the *Five Orchestral Pieces*, Op. 16, of 1909; the operas *Erwartung* and *Die Glückliche Hand* of 1909 and 1913; the *Six Little Piano Pieces*, Op. 19 (1911), *Herzgewächse* for soprano, celesta, harmonium, and harp, Op. 20 (also 1911); *Pierrot lunaire*, Op. 21, of 1912; and the *Four Orchestral Songs*, Op. 22, of 1913–1916. In all of these works, chromatic motion functions without tonal controls to indicate direction or to set up long-range relationships. There is a definite impulse towards the highest chromatic density and, as a result, a strong tendency towards the constant and repeated use of all twelve notes on an even and revolving basis. The pieces hold together not only through the extended use of motives in the thematic sense but also through the play of distinctive pitch combinations which give characteristic sound and shape to each work. The writing is contrapuntally conceived; but harmonic, articulative, timbral, and rhythmic statement may all be decisive in the character of the ideas and their organization. Thus, although we now see that the rhythmic and phrase structures of these works come out of their immediate late-tonal predecessors, these structures are not governed by a more basic (tonal) impulse but themselves give motion to the music.[1] Similarly, dynamics, accent, articulation, and coloration are indicated with unprecedented exactness and detail; nothing could be assumed any more from context; every event and every aspect of every event had a new and independent meaning. Each of the pieces sets forth its own musical, expressive, and formal premises; every event is unique; each piece becomes the particular development and realization of unique and independent events interrelating through a unique set of premises.

Each of these works represents some very particular discoveries and explorations of new and distinctive aspects of musical experience. Some of these experiences are timbral; there is an enormous expansion of instrumental and orchestral technique in these works (as in comparable works of Berg and Webern), parallel to the expansion of materials and resources in the other musical domains. Instrumental colors formerly considered exceptional (mutes, *sul ponticello,* harmonics, fluttertonguing, etc.) are normal here, and techniques formerly of great rarity (*col legno battuto* and *tratto,* harmonics on the piano, etc.) are common. Instruments are used in extreme and unusual registers and dynamic levels, while an enormous variety of instrumental combinations are employed The movement of the *Five Orchestral Pieces* entitled "Farben" is realized completely in terms of a series of subtle harmonic and timbral changes rung on a chordal structure. In the monodrama *Erwartung,* Schoenberg even abandons thematic-motivic structure in order to create a psychological-dramatic form based on ongoing chromatic line, on an articulation of changing intensities, and on an athematic intervallic structure; the kaleidoscopic orchestral treatment—in a consistent state of flux—is used to project a single, long psychological form and motion. Yet, at the same time, in the unfinished orchestral pieces of 1909, Schoenberg, like Webern, used an entirely different concept of the orchestra as an interweaving of solo sounds used to project miniature form. Conversely, the sound of a solo instrument is "scored" in timbral terms in a work like the *Six Little Piano Pieces,* Op. 19—studies in concise, aphoristic expression, each one of which articulates some brief, precise aspect of the chromatic experience.

---

[1] This is one reason why this aspect of this music, which today seems the most related to the past, appeared for a long time as the most difficult and impenetrable.

Nearly all of the techniques of Schoenberg's early period (including even brief reminiscences of tonality) are present in his *Pierrot lunaire,* twenty-one poems by Albert Giraud in a German translation, set for *Sprechstimme* and chamber ensemble. Characteristically, the work is severely patterned in a symmetrical and prophetically serialized arrangement: the poems, strict *rondeaux,* are grouped in three sets of seven each, and the chamber instrumentation is varied from song to song to obtain maximum differentiation. Motivic and intervallic constructions of every kind are used, incorporated into complex linear textures employing some of the classical canonic forms, sometimes closely organized, sometimes free. The vocal line, for the most part, is not actually sung but declaimed according to the *Sprechstimme* or "speech-song" technique first used by Schoenberg in his *Gurrelieder*: fixed pitches are indicated but the vocalist is directed only to approximate the curve of the notated line in a manner somewhere between song and speech. These songs—like many early works of Schoenberg—show an exceptional sensitivity to texture, and indeed the most basic and compelling formal aspect of the composition is its underlying organization in fluid, flashing, chromatic textures set into patterns of great severity and profundity.

It is not insignificant that the early pivotal works of Debussy, Stravinsky, and Schoenberg were involved with some kind of theatrical or literary statement; in Schoenberg's case, we can easily infer the importance of "expressive intent" in his chromatic revolution. But none of the great innovators of the twentieth century—least of all Schoenberg—was exclusively concerned with expressive detail, and the key problem was how to derive meaningful form out of the new materials generated by an expressive upheaval. Schoenberg was eventually to solve this problem in a characteristic and significant way, but in the meantime he devised a series of interim solutions which grew organically out of a remarkable series of new materials and new experiences. It is interesting to note, in the light of our latter-day new music—as it has emerged from a strict and intellectual serialism derived from the later work of Schoenberg and Webern—that their earlier explorations and approaches seem more remarkable and meaningful than ever.

BERG AND WEBERN

Schoenberg was the only one of the major composers of the early part of the century to have had important pupils and two of these, Alban Berg (1885–1935) and Anton Webern (1883–1945), have a major place in the development of modern creative ideas. Convenient historical niches have been found for both: Berg has been described as an instinctual lyricist whose music links with tradition, while Webern has been seen as the intellectual, numerical abstractionist and the prophet of the avant-garde. Like most such generalizations, these labels cover a rich reality with a thin tissue of truths. Over half of Webern's output is vocal, for example, and many aspects of his work are a deliberate re-casting of tra-

Alban Berg by Franz Rederer. Reproduced by permission of the Music Division of The New York Public Library.

ditional patterns in a new aphoristic style often conceived in terms of an underlying lyricism. In certain ways, Berg's music is actually more independent of tradition. It is true that Berg did not take up Schoenberg's twelve-tone idea with as much enthusiasm as Webern, but on the other hand, Berg was the most numerologically inclined of the three; his works are full of the most elaborate—often arbitrary—number sequences, precise and fearful symmetries carried out in every dimension and domain. Berg

Portrait of Anton Webern by Oskar Kokoschka. Reproduced by permission of Annie Knize.

was the kind of "instinctualist" who placed great faith in elaborate, mystical, and arbitrary systems.

Berg's early songs and his Piano Sonata, Op. 1 (1906–1908), come out of a post-Wagnerian tradition touched by Debussy and the contrapuntal genius of Schoenberg. The sonata, with its chromatic lines pulsing in a continual ebb and flow, is, by courtesy, tonal, but the shifting Scriabinesque harmonic impact of lines never articulates an organic tonal structure with any clarity. The piece resolves itself on its B–minor point of tonal departure, but the resolution is imposed. The real structure of the piece—like that of the related String Quartet, Op. 3—is a complex of unresolved motions deriving from an inner web of motives and motivic intervals which never seem to articulate or be articulated by the ongoing harmonic flux. In a sense, these were the problems and contradictions with which Berg was to wrestle all his life; in the end, he was able to deal with them by recognizing the contradictions and building his music on the very concept of conflict and opposition.

The Four Songs, Op. 2, written between 1907 and 1909, derive from the late-Romantic lied tradition and from Wagnerian harmony tinged with not a little Debussy; yet the mixture is personal, and in the end it brings Berg close to an expressive atonality. The *"Altenberg" Lieder*, Op. 4, for soprano and orchestra (1912), are the first fully mature works in consistency and quality of invention and expression; they have Berg's characteristically intense linear-melodic style combined with a remarkable sense of color as an organic part of his conception. Berg's pieces grow out of an interplay between line (the concept of line and phrase which comes out of the tradition) and the play of color and texture (the most original and far-reaching aspect of his work); it is in this sense that the forms are organic and original.

Both the Clarinet and Piano Pieces, Op. 5 (1913), and the Three Orchestral Pieces, Op. 6 (1913–1914), achieve expressive form through a complex interplay of line, register, color, and texture. Op. 5 is a set of miniatures, closely related to contemporaneous pieces by Schoenberg and Webern. The pieces of Op. 6 are at the opposite extreme in scope and specific gravity, although their enormous contrapuntal density ends up by communicating analogous structures made out of timbre and sonority as well as line. The first movement is an early and exceptional example of a piece framed in percussion sound (but see Webern's Op. 6, No. 4); and the long, contrapuntal pile-up of the march-like third movement is built up in accumulations of orchestral sound. All of these works depend in great part on the effect of a complex irresolution. The Piano Sonata is virtually the last word in chromatic tonality, built up in shifting, oscillating, ambiguous harmonic structures which, nevertheless, are still presumed to have tonal and directional functions. In the following works, tonal functions persist only obliquely, and, in the Op. 6 pieces, ideas are expressed in dense, insistent lines weighted down with a tremendous expressive baggage and are almost impossible to clarify in performance. At times, Berg seems actually to be composing in textures and densities whose inner detail is complex, very free and variable, and not at all clearly defined aurally. The music is formed through a process of accumulation; Berg replaces the directional movement of tonality with a new and simpler kind of directionality based on the accumulation of tension and texture.

In *Wozzeck,* written between 1914 and 1921, Berg used the whole range of techniques found in his early works but now enormously expanded by the simultaneous use of a complex of dramatic, literary, and classical musical forms. Berg arranged a remarkable series of fragments by Georg Büchner into a kaleidoscopic libretto about a wretched army orderly who kills his unfaithful mistress and drowns himself. *Wozzeck* is, from one point of view, a social document cast in the theatrical and musical idiom of the early part of the century known as "expressionism." But on a profounder level, *Wozzeck* is about the human condition. The seemingly brutalized Wozzeck is a character of a certain grandeur; a visionary who, in his essential uniqueness and humanity, has just what the other characters lack—some natural nobility. Similarly, the music has a range and grandeur even in the almost touching sordidness and literalness of certain details. The intentionally vulgarized stage music stands next to a whole series of chamber and symphonic patterns which are sketched out underneath. Berg has imposed a classical shape or procedure on each of the fifteen scenes, and the larger forms of the acts are arranged as a series of interconnected formal patterns and symmetries; even in small details, number and system play a surprisingly decisive role. Berg, whose musical style was complex, free, and fluid, set himself rigid frameworks as if to give his musical imagination something solid from which to push off. In a sense, these rigid patterns serve something of the same function (on a simpler level, to be sure) as the twelve-tone conception in Schoenberg's later work. *Wozzeck* is, of course, in no sense twelve-tone—it was completed before Schoenberg's first twelve-tone pieces—but it does contain a prominent theme made up of all twelve notes (as does, for that matter, Strauss's *Also sprach Zarathustra*) and there is often a striking tendency towards a total chromatic density. Indeed, the techniques run from simple triadic writing to the most intense "atonality," from *Sprechstimme* to lyric line, from diatonic melody to chromatic parlando, from chamber-ensemble counterpoint to broad orchestral strokes, from complex, busy motion to static intensity, from isolated, aphoristic punctuation to broad ongoing development. There are sonata and variation forms, *Leitmotiv* development, bits of popular song, small closed forms, and big, open psychological ones that ultimately determine the shape of the whole. The famous orchestral interlude that precedes the final scene takes on the function of summation; it universalizes the trivial and sordid tragedy. *Wozzeck* thus becomes more than a proletarian tragedy and more than the cumulative effect of a series of expressive and immediately comprehensible musical strokes. It remains the only post-Wagnerian, post-tonal work written in a heavily dissonant, chromatic style to have had a consistent theatrical success, and it remains the classic example of chromatic, "atonal" style combined with classical, closed forms applied, uniquely and with great psychological validity, to a modern, intense, dramatic expression.

Whereas Berg expanded Schoenberg's chromatic vision into large forms, dependent on tradition and psychological insight, Webern worked almost from the first in an opposite direction—towards the isolation of the single event, the disassociation of adjacent events within a context of the total interrelationship of the whole. Webern is at once the simplest and the most difficult of composers: the most and least intellectual, the easiest to take apart yet the hardest to follow, the most esoteric yet the most comprehensible, the most classical yet the most advanced, the most individual and personal yet the most influential and widely imitated. It is the simplicity of Webern's esthetic which explains the paradoxes. Webern's music consists of few notes set forth over a very short period of time; he reduced the problem of expressive form to the fact of the isolated, individual event and in so doing made every interpretation of the single event a possible one. It is from this point of view that Webern can be said to have re-invigorated a "classical" view of form while, at the same time, completing the destruction of tonal thinking.

Webern achieved his mature style very quickly, and his later development took place almost entirely within the narrow limits of his personal esthetic of clarity and concision. His principle is that of maximum variety within an extremely tight and condensed unity. Theme, development, and structural motion and relationship appear as a single sound or event. The unit is the interval between adjacent or simultaneous sounds—isolated, carefully defined, and packed with the maximum possible expressive and intellectual content. This concept of the interval had, even before the formulation of twelve-tone principles, the notion of succession as its fundamental principle. This linear-melodic basis to Webern's music (even its harmonic structure is a matter of the simultaneity of musical events whose origin can be found in linear succession) is reflected in the fact that over half of his works are vocal; among the early compositions, Op. 2, 3, 4, 8, 12, 13, 14, and 15 are for voices. All of these works employ traditional pitched singing—Webern never used *Sprechstimme*—and most of them use solo voices with piano and instruments in the tradition of the German lied.

Webern's detached, intense way of building up phrases by linking isolated tones and intervals and relating small groups of "melodic" tones also carries over into his early instrumental pieces as a way of unfolding very abstract and static formal conceptions in real time. These works are characterized by intense brevity, a pure, even lyric, quality, and a care- ful constructed unity. The pitch successions, whether isolated or grouped in small cells, form a series of points which tend to fill up a distinct and very carefully defined musical space. Thus a succession will be divided between various registers and between various instruments and instru- mental groupings. Colors and registers form a succession equally impor- tant to that of the pitches themselves, and all elements are closely grouped in clear and close relationships.

Already in the *Five Movements* for string quartet, Op. 5, of 1909, Webern applied elaborate principles of complex unity within a vastly restricted space. The *Six Pieces,* Op. 6, constitute a comparatively large work for a comparatively large orchestra, but the other works written in 1910 and after turn again towards miniaturization: *Four Pieces* for vio- lin and piano, Op. 7; *Six Bagatelles* for string quartet, Op. 9; *Five Pieces for Orchestra,* Op. 10; *Three Small Pieces* for cello and piano, Op. 11. There is, to be sure, more than a trace of late-Romantic statement still remaining—Mahler in an atonal nutshell! Some of the movements of Op. 5, 6, and 10 are comparatively large in scope and even the briefest ges- tures are full of intense, expressionist-Romantic *Angst;* indeed, the con- centration and the intensity of the concentration itself are a result of the enormous, unreleased energies inherent in the laconic ideas and terse forms.

Webern's principle is always "maximization of the minimum": an intentionally limited collection of pitches, registers, colors, rhythms, ac- cents, and articulations is revealed in its greatest possible variety. Portions of the complete chromatic gamut are filled in by half-steps (or, by the analogy of octave equivalence, by major sevenths and minor ninths) or, secondarily, by short figures arranged in whole-steps, thirds, and sixths; a good example of this is the first of the *Bagatelles,* Op. 9. The single event becomes striking and, most significantly, the single repetition, iden- tity, or association becomes crucial; perhaps the most extreme example here is Op. 11, three movements in a bare handful of measures, a few tiny gestures, mere seconds of isolated sound emerging briefly from the silence that becomes, for Webern, a basic condition of the musical experi- ence. The fourth piece of Op. 10 consists of six measures with only forty- eight separate note indications, about half of which are repeated notes (see Appendix; Example 4-2).

Webern did not pursue this line any further for a number of years; in the rest of his early period, up through his first twelve-tone works, he returned to vocal and polyphonic forms. Between 1915 and 1927—from his Op. 12 to Op. 19—he wrote exclusively for solo voices with instruments, recreating, often with considerable complexity, the forms of the polyphonic lied[2] in terms of expressive chromatic ideas and dense, carefully controlled dissonant counterpoint. Webern's "historical" contribution was certainly his elaboration—and eventually refinement and systemization—of techniques of construction through the isolation of the individual event and the tightly bound relationship of pitch, duration, intensity, and color, all expressed in terms of the maximum differentiation within the most minimal, economic sequence of events in the briefest, most compressed structural time span. But Webern, like Berg, had first to follow Schoenberg in the reconstruction of a complex counterpoint, based on the classical relationships but systematically chromatic and free of tonal implications. This symmetrical, chromatic, complex polyphony was, of course, to provide the basis for the twelve-tone consolidation to follow.

BIBLIOGRAPHICAL NOTES

For the background on this important period, see the Schoenberg writings already mentioned as well as the recently issued letters (New York, 1965). The new translation of Willi Reich's biography of Berg (New York, 1965) contains articles by Berg himself on Schoenberg and on "atonality" which are important documents of the period. Webern's *Path to the New Music* (tr. Bryn Mawr, Pa., 1963) consists of transcriptions of lectures given during the "twelve-tone period," but the historical transition from tonality to atonality in pre-World War I Vienna is also discussed. For specific treatment of an individual work, see George Perle's article on *Pierrot lunaire* in the Curt Sachs commemorative volume *The Commonwealth of Music* (New York, 1965). Perle's *Serial Composition and Atonality* (3rd ed.; Berkeley and Los Angeles, 1972) and the Webern issue of *Die Reihe* (No. 2) contain specific discussions of pre-twelve-tone works. Walter Kolneder's *Anton Webern* guide (Roden Kirchen, 1961) discusses all of the early works. For additional material on this period, see the list of other general works on Schoenberg, Berg, and Webern at the end of Chapter 10.

[2] It should be remembered that Webern was a trained musicologist whose doctoral dissertation, written under the guidance of Guido Adler, was on the music of the Renaissance composer Heinrich Isaac (ca. 1450–1517), one of the masters of polyphonic song.

part three

The New Tonalities

FIVE

STRAVINSKY AND NEO-CLASSICISM

The effective result of the new musical developments everywhere in the early years of the century was the weakening or the destruction of the accepted implications of traditional functional tonality. The cumulative effect, not only of the work of the "atonal" Viennese but also of Debussy, of Strauss's *Elektra* and *Salome,* of *Le Sacre du printemps,* of the early works of Bartók and the folklorists, and of a dozen lesser developments, has so permeated our musical consciousness that, except in certain very limited areas of folk and popular music, the old tonal way of thinking is no longer operative. Even in pop and traditional jazz pieces where triadic tonality is still a dominant feature, we accept the triad with added tones or even more complex structures as consonant. Contrapuntal voice-leading is generally replaced by parallel harmonic structures including chains of unresolved sevenths and ninths. Modal inflections outweigh the purely tonal impulses, and forms of the subdominant—rather than the dominant—often lead the cadences. The final cadence is replaced by the fade-out. Only the diatonic, four-measure melodic structures seem to reflect the strong functional hierarchies of the old tonal music; and even these often give way to more complex forms.

In the more complex and serious forms of pop music and jazz as well as in nearly every form of concert and operatic music—even the most conservative—the old tonal forms can no longer be taken for granted, and they have often been totally replaced by some kind of *new* tonal conception. Of the major figures who participated in the tonal revolutions before the First World War, only Strauss backed away, first into a kind of proto-neo-classicism and later into a quiet absorption with traditional techniques and forms. Debussy, at the time of his death, was on the verge of creating new tonal forms; in fact, such new forms and techniques came into existence within a few years of the end of World War I. All of these were synthetic: none depended on traditional tonal functions but instead synthesized anew—even from piece to piece—their tonal structures. To put it another way, the tonal works of the past had been specific instances of processes that can be generalized; the new tonal works established their general processes as part of their individual creative statement.

A large body of the new tonal music, centered on the work of Igor Stravinsky, has been known as "neo-classical"; a more logical and more inclusive term might be "neo-tonal." Much of this music has been concerned with forms and materials derived from the classical tradition, but a great part of it also derives from an earlier or a more recent past or no particular past at all. For Stravinsky himself, the uses of the past are very significant; but restrictive and essentially polemical terms like "neo-classicism" cannot serve to indicate the range of Stravinsky's "past"—from Dufay and Isaac to Tchaikovsky and Webern—or the essential interiorization of that past, radically transformed into something new and essentially Stravinskyian. The essence of Stravinskyian "neo-classicism" lies in the thorough renovation of classical form achieved through a new and creative rebuilding of tonal practice independent of the traditional functions which had first established those forms.[1]

After the first performance of *Le Sacre* in 1913 with its famous *succès de scandale*, Stravinsky returned to an unfinished theater work, his opera *Le Rossignol*, which he completed in a manner markedly at variance with the original Debussy-and-Rimsky-Korsakov conception. Stravinsky could not return to the colorful semi-tonal world of the beginning of the work after the experience of *Le Sacre*, but a generalized tonal sense still seems to linger in the much more spare and dissonant character of the later parts of the opera. More significantly, however, Stravinsky com-

---

[1] There are many parallels with Picasso and the two forms of cubism—analytic and synthetic—separated by a period of neo-classicism. The analogy to tonality (which can be pushed surprisingly far) would be "realistic" perspective.

posed a number of short instrumental and instrumental-vocal works between 1912 and 1920—two sets of pieces for piano four-hands, two works
for string quartet, three pieces for solo clarinet, sets of songs for voice and
instruments—which correspond roughly with the slightly earlier tendencies towards miniaturization in the music of Schoenberg and Webern.
These neglected pieces are interesting because they employ tiny bits of
the gigantesque, dissonant vocabulary of *Le Sacre* in brief, aphoristic
forms based on nearly motionless ostinatos. This tendency towards clear,
static, ostinato-based forms is also clearly evident in the last two works
based largely on Russian materials: the burlesque opera *Renard* of 1916–
1917 and the "choreographic scenes," *Les Noces,* written between 1914
and 1917 but given final and characteristic instrumental setting (for four
pianos and percussion) only in 1923. Both of these works use a high degree of static "color" dissonance combined with and set off from diatonic,
"neo-Russian" melodic ideas. Even a cursory glance at *Le Sacre* will reveal that these techniques are actually already present in that score, but
they are fully realized in *Les Noces. Les Noces* is the first of Stravinsky's
works to re-establish an ancient and thorough-going tonal principle—
tonality by assertion. These remarkable choral sketches of a Russian
peasant wedding employ a simple yet effective melodic technique which
juxtaposes brief melodic motives with ornamented figures and insistent
choral chants, all set in cyclical patterns of repetition turning around one
or two insistent pitches. The ritualistic quality of this writing, much
enhanced by the remarkable piano-and-percussion orchestration, is further
emphasized by a basic structural technique of juxtaposition of alternating
and contrasting static layers of sound patterns. This technique, already
present in *Le Sacre,* is the basis for the so-called "additive" construction
which Stravinsky was to use throughout his life—big building-blocks of
sounds and sound patterns, often based on static ostinatos, set against one
another in repetitive, alternating cycles which, although assertive and unyielding in nature, gain vitality and even a sense of motion by being constantly re-interpreted in shifting overlaps of accent, rhythm, meter, and
phrase.

    Les Noces is one of many Stravinsky works which proved a source
of inspiration to other composers but not—except in the basic ways suggested above—to Stravinsky himself. Stravinsky's next work, *L'Histoire du
soldat* (1918), uses Russian folklore, but it contains few musical Rus-
sianisms;[2] up-to-date popular, dance, and jazz materials are enclosed in
small forms. *L'Histoire* was conceived for a small travelling theater and it
employs a narrator, mimed or danced action, and an ensemble of seven

---

[2] The recurring three-note cadential phrase in the violin solo is very close to
one in the recently popular Russian song "Moscow Nights"; a common source would
be suggested.

instruments including an important percussion part.[3] It is, in effect, the first of Stravinsky's "neo-classic" pieces, although in fact it contains nothing more classical than a pair of off-key chorales, a few simple, closed dance forms, and a dependence on the triad (used as an articulative rather than classical tonal device). Nevertheless, *L'Histoire* is the prototype for later "neo-classical" works in its references to other music, its spare but vigorous lines and colors, its shifting rhythmic and accentual organization, its use of small closed forms, its ironic wit, and its method of achieving tonal centers of gravity through assertion and juxtaposition.

Stravinsky's "neo-classic" period is generally dated from 1919, the year of the ballet *Pulcinella,* after Pergolesi. To the extent that material by Pergolesi (or whoever really wrote the music Stravinsky used as source material) actually appears, the work might be said to be tonal in the old way. Heard in this way, *Pulcinella* becomes an eccentric set of arrangements of and intrusions on eighteenth-century style. But it is nothing of the sort, of course; Pergolesi has been transformed at every moment into something quite new. The Baroque progressions are no longer representatives of a musical direction and motion; they are literally sound objects or blocks of sound which gain new meanings from new contexts. A progression or melodic pattern may begin from the middle, so to speak, or stop at some point short of a satisfactory "resolution"; such patterns are set into the typical overlapping cycles of repetition with shifting accents and metrical values; and all of this is reinforced by a clear and brilliant if restrained orchestration in which color functions analogously to rhythm and phrase.

Almost simultaneously with this derivative and "neo-classical" work, Stravinsky composed the most original and independent of his instrumental compositions, the *Symphonies of Wind Instruments* of 1920. This important if neglected work, dedicated to the memory of Debussy, is as unclassical as it is un-Debussyesque (although perhaps it owes something both to the great tradition and to the work of the French master in its absolute clarity and its originality of form, which moves from one block sonority to another through the juxtaposition of static rhythm and texture). Again, this work—although it looks back and ahead —suggests a development and a direction which Stravinsky himself never followed directly; it is, like many Stravinsky works, typical only of itself.

Stravinsky's other instrumental compositions of this period show a marked tendency to develop the kind of rhythmic and harmonic vitality within closed, static forms already found in *L'Histoire:* the *Ragtime* for eleven instruments of 1918 and the *Piano Rag-Music* of 1920, the remarkable *Five-Fingers* piano pieces (whose melodies turn out to be simple

[3] The musicians are to be visible; they play roles equal to those of the other performers.

permutations of *Le Sacre*-like themes), the *Three Pieces* for solo clarinet of 1919 and the Concertino for string quartet of 1920, the Suite for chamber orchestra of 1921, the fine Piano Sonata of 1922, the important Octet for winds of 1923, the Concerto for piano and winds of 1924, and the *Sérénade en La* for piano of 1925 move almost step by step towards the re-establishment of tonal form without a single instance of traditional tonal structure.

Parody is a word that can be used in reference to these works if the term is understood in its original sense, not necessarily implying satire. Parody technique—that is, the use and transformation of pre-existing material—was a recognized way of writing music during the Renaissance, and much more recently, a similar procedure can be found in the other arts: the use of Homeric materials in James Joyce, the quotes and references in T. S. Eliot, Picasso's paintings after Delacroix. Stravinsky's esthetic is, to some extent, that of art removed to the second degree; that is, art about art or, more to the point, about the experience of art.[4] Stravinsky's own musical experience—never limited merely to the so-called "Classical" period—is the subject matter, taken in hand and transformed with the most careful and brilliant art and artifice; the entire range of musical experience, Renaissance to ragtime, is the material for a new and entirely contemporary commentary, sometimes witty, sometimes merely elegant and decorative, sometimes kinetic and "tangible" in its rhythmic pulse, sometimes concerned with formal patternings, often dealing at a deeper level with very real problems of expressive structure and communication.

Through it all, Stravinsky is never anything less than precise. This very precision and the clarity and dryness of his style, taken in conjunction with certain polemical remarks by the composer himself, have led to the facile conclusion that Stravinsky's music is "inexpressive" (apparently in contradistinction not only to the Romantic tradition but also to the contemporary Viennese "expressionists"); it is, supposedly, intended to "express" or communicate nothing at all. Stravinsky was largely responsible for the introduction of what we might call the "cabinet-maker" theory of the composer's role in society: the composer, like his colleague the joiner, creates beautiful things that have no more or less meaning than the beautiful curve on the leg of a fine chair. A chair, of course, has a function (and the curve may express something about that function); thus to some extent Stravinsky, and to a larger extent Hindemith and others, attempted to re-establish music as a "functional" art (just as they attempted to construct new tonalities with new musical hierarchies or "functions"). Nevertheless, Stravinsky's art is by no means exclusively

---

[4] In a very different context, the notion of "second degree" has returned in the recent vogue for quotation and transformation (see last chapter).

craftsmanship, and Stravinsky himself subsequently denied that he ever meant to say that his music is in no sense "expressive." That his music is the product of a refined craftsmanship there can be no doubt, but that it is no more than a simple flat statement which is the mere aggregate of its parts is never true. Nor is it merely decorative or merely constructivist— any more than is the cubism of Picasso. Just as cubism is a poetic state- ment about objects and forms, about the nature of vision and the way we perceive and know forms, and about the experience of art and the artistic transformation of objects and forms, so Stravinsky's music is a poetic statement about musical objects and aural forms, about the way we hear and the way we perceive and understand aural forms, about our ex- perience of musical art and the artistic transformation of musical ma- terials, always measured in that special domain of musical experience, time.

In 1922, Stravinsky wrote the one-act opera *Mavra,* dedicated to the memories of Glinka, Pushkin, and Tchaikovsky; six years later he wrote a ballet, *Le Baiser de la fée,* which so thoroughly absorbs and transforms music of Tchaikovsky that it is often virtually impossible to tell where Tchaikovsky leaves off and Stravinsky begins. These works shocked those followers of Stravinsky who understood classicism as a historic and esthetic principle. In actual fact, Stravinsky can be said to have derived his neo-classical taste directly from his nineteenth-century predecessors; Tchaikovsky himself, for example, wrote a prototype of a neo-classical work in a suite based on Mozart. The very close relationship between Stravinsky's music and the nineteenth century is often over- looked. Stravinsky's real musical inheritance from the immediate past has, after the early ballets, little to do with Romantic exoticism or lushness and nothing at all to do with Wagnerian music drama and a giant sym- phonic style; but it has a great deal to do with the *salon* and the fashion- able theater of the ballet and French-Italian opera. The *salon* and ballet traditions preserved certain classical ideas of closed form and a simple, closed melodic-harmonic style which are in fact to be found (suitably transformed, of course) in *Le Baiser de la fée,* in the Piano Sonata and *Sérénade en La,* in the *Duo Concertant* for violin and piano of 1922, in the *Four Etudes* for orchestra of 1928–1930, in the *Capriccio* for piano and orchestra of 1929, and, along with certain classical derivations, in the ballet *Apollon musagète* of 1928. To be sure, like any musical ideas used by Stravinsky, these elements are treated in typical Stravinskyian fashion. The essence of the technique always lies not in the source of the ideas but in the character and technique of the transformations.

Beginning with the Piano Concerto of 1923–1924, another element enters into many of Stravinsky's works: we might characterize it as a tendency (related to that of "synthetic cubism") to construct prototypical, abstracted materials and forms. This is particularly true of the whole series of symphonic and concerted works written in the 1930's and 1940's, but it is already fully developed in the big opera-oratorio based on Sophocles's *Oedipus Rex* (1927). The text, by Jean Cocteau, consists of a series of short and simple narrations in the vernacular which punctuate big arias, duets, and choruses written originally in French but translated into a solemn, dead, hierarchical and prototypical language: Latin. *Oedipus Rex* is not tragedy or even, in the ordinary sense, drama—nothing actually happens except what we are told about between the scenes—but it contains an abstracted idea of mythic-ritual musical drama refined almost down to the skeletal framework. The simplest possible diction is everywhere employed, and this laconic declamation is organized into blocked-out set–speeches and choruses. The narrator stands apart in modern clothes; the characters, although costumed and masked, have neither individuality nor the power to act—they are not even symbolic in the conventional sense but merely abstracted, particular manifestations of a human condition. There is no motion, because whatever transpires is pre–ordained; all that is necessary is to reveal it. The motion lacking on the stage is offered by the music in the form of rhetorical gesture, and almost every gesture—like the elements of the myth itself—is familiar. The music of *Oedipus* is neither really operatic nor dramatic but represents the "idea" of these things. The very conventionality of the musical figures (Creon's trombone triad tune, the Verdiana in Jocasta's aria and the following duet with Oedipus, the grand-opera music of the "Gloria," the suggestions of Handelian oratorio) suggests detachment, abstraction, and generalization; but these materials are also redefined through the musical and literary associations. Out of all this arises a kind of reconstruction of what is traditionally referred to as "style"—what Stravinsky calls "manner." The familiar and conventional gestures are thus redefined and given a certain new and powerful inevitability in their new environment. *Oedipus* is not Verdian or Handelian any more than it is Greek tragedy. It is not "about" the tragedy of a Greek hero or of anyone at all but about tragedy itself—the form and artistic experience of tragedy in its grandest operatic-oratorio guise.

In the same way, the subject matter of the Violin Concerto of 1931 is the conception of the concerto—the relationship between solo and tutti. The concerti grossi of 1938 and 1946, the important symphonies of 1940 and 1945, the minor *Danses concertantes* of 1942 and *Scènes de ballet* of 1944, and even the *Ebony Concerto* of 1945 are all in some sense archetypical. Only the theater works of the period—the ballet *Jeu de cartes* of 1936, *Perséphone* of 1933, with its mixture of narration (text by André Gide) and dance, and the ballet *Orpheus* of 1946 with its subtle neo-Baroque forms—show an independent line of thought. Stravinsky's

last major "neo-classical" works are, in widely differing ways, again prototypical: the *Mass* for men's and boys' voices and ten instruments
(1948), with its medieval evocations, and the opera *The Rake's Progress*
of 1951 (to an ironic "classical" libretto by W. H. Auden and Chester
Kallman), with its recreation of operatic gesture, convention, and pattern.
The Rake's Progress is a kind of meta-opera, a second-degree opera
whose subject matter is largely opera itself. It is also, among other things,
a compendium of Stravinskyian style and form and the last gasp of neo-
classicism; with the *Cantata* of 1952 Stravinsky began again to move in
new directions.

It is important to realize that these "second-order" forms stand
outside classical procedure, to which they are no more bound than
Stravinsky's melodic ideas—even when explicitly borrowed—are committed to classical continuations. Classical forms and types are based on
process; they evolve according to tonal principles and it is through this
process of evolution that they come to be. Stravinsky's types are not involved with process and tonal function; they come into being through
statement and assertion. Classical music defines its time span through a
chain of processes and developing relationships; Stravinsky organizes his
time spans by precise, given articulations and rhythmic divisions. As we
have said, classical form is the result of the ongoing process of functional
tonality; with Stravinsky, form is prior and itself creates the tonality.

Stravinsky himself has spoken of his technique of "composing by
interval" and of his use of "polarity" as a tonal organizing principle. In
classical usage there is a network of contrapuntal motion away from and
back towards goals which are partly defined culturally, partly by the
nature of this motion itself. In Stravinsky, tonality is represented by the
emphasis, the repetition, or the sustaining of chords or chordal patterns;
by a stated, fixed set of relationships between tones that remains constant for a movement or a piece. There is nothing inevitable about the
tonal centers in Stravinsky's music; they are present and effective because
they are stated and asserted to be so; and the means of assertion—repetition, ostinato, pedal point, juxtaposition of melodic and harmonic levels
on specific tones and intervals, accent and articulation, rhythmic and
metrical displacement—provide the basis for both the tonality and the
form (see Appendix; Example 5-1).

Stravinsky's music is nearly always art to the second degree, art
about art. In the absence of a wider social context (out of which traditional craftsmanship grew) Stravinsky chose Western culture itself—not in
the historical sense but as a contemporary phenomenon—as his subject
matter. In so doing he could not help expressing the crisis of traditional
culture even as he defined a musical sensibility that is still very much
part of our contemporary awareness.

BIBLIOGRAPHICAL NOTES

The development and change in Stravinsky's own views over the years would require a text unto itself; to the sources already given at the end of Chapter 3, the important *Poetics of Music* (Cambridge, Mass., 1947) should be added. Like all of Stravinsky's public statements, it was written with a collaborator (in the case of *Poetics*, the Russo-French esthetician Pierre Souvtchinsky) but is hardly less significant for that.

Out of the mass of Stravinskyiana, two works, both available in English translation, might be mentioned: Heinrich Strobel's *Stravinsky: Classic Humanist* (New York, 1955) and Roman Vlad's *Stravinsky* (New York, 1960). Several collections of essays honoring Stravinsky have appeared at different periods of his life: Merle Armitage, ed. (New York, 1936); Edwin Corle, ed. (New York, 1949), adopting material from the Armitage book; the 75th anniversary issue of *The Score* (London, May–June 1957); the 80th birthday issue of *The Musical Quarterly* (New York, 1962; also paperback, New York, 1963). Modern analytic views appear in Arthur Berger's "Problems of Pitch Organization in Stravinsky" (*Perspectives of New Music*, Fall–Winter, 1963, v. 2, No. 1) and in Pierre Boulez's *Notes of an Apprenticeship* (New York, 1968; a poor translation with many errors). A discussion of the "neo-classical" problem appears in Edward T. Cone's "The Uses of Convention: Stravinsky and His Models" (*Musical Quarterly*, July, 1962). See also the author's assessment in the November 1971 issue of *Stereo Review*. Eric Walter White's *Stravinsky* (University of California, 1966) is, in spite of some shortcomings, a substantial reference work.

SIX

NEO-CLASSICISM AND
NEO-TONALITY IN FRANCE

Classicism—defined historically as a return to certain periods of high accomplishment and style and esthetically as the use of certain strict intellectual standards of form and form-enclosed content—has always been an important element in French culture (a situation emphasized by the fact that French tradition itself lies somewhat outside the organic development of classical norms). The classical impulse which periodically recurs in French painting right up to Picasso has always been based on a rationalization of the external trappings of the antique as transmitted by the masters of the Italian Renaissance and early Baroque. Similarly, French musical classicism through the nineteenth and well into the twentieth century was not based on French music itself—French tradition is not strong on symphonic-tonal practice, and France produced little important "classical" instrumental music—but on an external, rational synthesis of the practice of the Central European masters. This kind of classicism was extensively taught at the Paris Conservatoire and constantly recurred in French music even through the crisis of Wagnerism that shook French music at the end of the nineteenth century. It was by no means very deeply concerned with the fundamental techniques of classical tonality but rather with its external manifestations. Thus, paradoxically, the classical system, never deeply rooted in French musical thought, was rather easily undermined and replaced by Debussy and Stravinsky; yet, on the other hand, non-classical and neo-classical tonal practice is an essential and strong part of modern French music up until recently.[1]

RAVEL

As pointed out earlier, the notion of an impressionist "school" in French music is of dubious validity. Even in his earlier and most characteristically Debussyesque works, Ravel maintains a certain independence from the complex, shifting sonorities and ambiguous tonal relationships of the older composer. Ravel was always more of a classicist than Debussy, yet paradoxically his musical thinking was always far less abstract. He was, in his way, a far more brilliant orchestrator than Debussy, yet his orchestration was imposed from the outside and was never as organic as that of Debussy. Ravel produced no independent, abstract orchestral music except for two piano concertos; virtually everything else stems from the theater or the dance, or is orchestrated from piano works. Nevertheless, the strong strain of classicism in Ravel's work is present from his earliest period; in his later years it became a dominant factor in his music. The early *Menuet* and the famous *Pavane,* the String Quartet of 1902–1903 and, to a lesser extent, the song cycles *Shéhérazade* (1902) and *Histoires naturelles* (1906), with their refined elegance, all show not only classical forms but also a notable tendency to enrich the traditional harmonic and color vocabulary while remaining close to the constraints and conditions of classical practice. The one-act comic opera, *L'Heure espagnole,* uses the shifting ninth and eleventh chords, parallel structures, tonal ambiguities, and color phrases of impressionism, but even where obvious classical form is not used, the clarity of texture and line, the directionality of the musical motion, as well as the dry, detached wit (and even the use of popular, Spanish elements) suggest the strong influence of certain aspects of classical tradition.

---

[1] This is equally true of another country in which the classical tradition was even weaker—the United States. On the one hand, this country could produce Ives and a strong avant-garde position outside the European tradition; on the other, the United States also produced a late-blooming "neo-tonal" style in the works of Copland and others whose commitment and influence remained strong over a period of years.

Maurice Ravel at the seashore, Saint-Jean-de-Luz, near his native Village of Ciboure on the Basque coast of France. Sketch by Alexandre Benoit. Meyer Collection, Paris. Reproduction forbidden.

Most of Ravel's other pre-war works, culminating in the ballet *Daphnis et Chloé,* are much more clearly related to Debussy; indeed they have served as better prototypes of "impressionism" than any works of Debussy. However, even before the war (and hence even before Stravinsky), Ravel began to simplify his style in the direction of greater clarity of means and economy of expression. The *Trois Poèmes de Mallarmé* of 1913 uses voice, piano, string quartet, two flutes, and two clarinets, and the Piano Trio of 1914 shows a careful and deliberate attempt to revive old or create new "classical" forms. *Le Tombeau de Couperin,* first written for piano and later orchestrated, also dates from this period; its relationship to eighteenth-century practice is explicit.

Ravel's post-war music, beginning with *La Valse* in 1920, shows an enormous expansion of technique within the clearly formed stylistic lines of his earlier music; works like the Sonata for violin and cello of 1920–1922 and the *Chansons madécasses* for voice, piano, flute, and cello (1926) use freely dissonant harmonic and linear combinations in ways that go far beyond the old tonal and even "impressionist" techniques. The popular *Boléro* of 1928 is exceptional in Ravel's works for its intentionally primitive style, but its primitivism conceals a great deal of art; the obsession with a single idea and the assertive, unrelenting C-major tonality which breaks just before the end serve to highlight the distinctive instrumentation. Following the charming *L'Enfant et les sortilèges* (1924; text by Colette)—virtually a "number opera" with its succession of picturesque arias and ensembles—Ravel's important late works are two piano concertos written in 1930–1931, one in D for the left hand alone, the other in G for two hands. These works, worlds away from "impressionism," represent new directions for Ravel. Both show elements of jazz and create tonal feeling by the use of added tones and appoggiatura chords; the effect of these new values that have been attached to the concepts of consonance and dissonance is somewhat analogous to that of Debussy's last sonatas, and it is exactly that achieved by certain modern jazz musicians who violate functional tonality at every chord yet in some sense also recreate it out of a new set of conventions. It is perhaps significant that although, of all the major masters of the century, Ravel had the least influence on the development of contemporary ideas, he had possibly the greatest influence on the popular musical imagination.

"LES SIX"

Ravel's neo-classicism was essentially a refinement of and a growth out of his Debussyism, modified by a refined original temperament, a taste for jazz and for Spanish music, and an ability to assimilate new ideas. The composers of "Les Six" on the other hand were strongly anti-Debussy from the start (not to mention anti-Wagner, anti-Fauré, and anti-D'Indy as well), and they cultivated light popular, music-hall, and café style as well as jazz. There was actually never any consistent or coherent esthetic position taken by the six young composers, who were named as a group almost accidentally, through an obvious analogy with the Russian nationalist "Five." Satie was their sponsor, however, and they were strongly influenced by his formidable musico-literary irreverence and irrelevance. To some extent, the literary and artistic movements of Dada and surrealism are also reflected in their music; but it is curious that the nihilist, anti-art of the Dadaists and the intense, associative and disassociative psychological techniques of the surrealists found little echo in their music beyond a mild if witty use of quotation and parody.

Two of "Les Six," Louis Durey (b. 1888) and Germaine Tailleferre (b. 1892), wrote little of importance; a third, Georges Auric (b.1899), composed one notable ballet score and a good deal of latter-day film music. Arthur Honegger (1892–1955), a Swiss, had little relation stylistically to the rest of the group and must be considered separately. The music of "Les Six" today is represented almost entirely by the work of Darius Milhaud (b. 1892) and Francis Poulenc (1899–1963).

The creative output of Milhaud is immense, and it is almost impossible to make any effective generalizations about it. Milhaud had the most rigorous classical training at the Conservatoire; this, added to his natural proficiency, produced a composing technique of the utmost facility. In general he uses a rich harmonic vocabulary, derived from pile-ups of thirds and triads, combined with a very simple, flexible, melodic sense. Milhaud developed a kind of free counterpoint of triads and triad-like formations which in turn suggested a counterpoint of tonal areas. The idea of the manipulation of simultaneous tonalities—"polytonality"—already employed before World War I by Bartók (the *Bagatelles* for piano) and Charles Ives (the choral *67th Psalm*) achieved a certain importance in the 1920's. This expansion of tonal thought seemed to offer new possibilities for known materials and structures: Milhaud made a conscious attempt to create polytonal movement and form in early works such as *Les Choéphores* and *Saudades do Brasil* (1921). The notion of "polytonality" as such, however, had little further development; in a sense, the concept of different yet simultaneous tonalities is self-contradictory. The derivation and perceptibility of harmonic structures made out of interlocking or juxtaposed triads may be unquestionable, but long strings of these "polychords"—no matter how separated in space and timbre—cannot meaningfully establish simultaneous, contradictory tonal centers. Indeed, the significance of "polytonality" in Milhaud's music is neither formal nor systematic but is to be found rather in the use of separate bands or layers of sound which, in works like the ballet *L'Homme et son désir,* actually form a polyphony made up of densities of sound. Often the use of diatonic ideas which clash with and contradict each other has a specifically witty intent. The forms are generally small, derived from vocal and dance patterns, and full of quotes and parodies of popular, dance, folk, jazz, café, and music-hall music. A great number of these pieces are "occasional" in nature, written with some specific purpose in mind; others seem like mere idle amusement for composer or performer. There is an offhand quality about much of Milhaud's music that goes beyond the inevitable unevenness of a prolific composer and takes on the character of an esthetic position.

Milhaud has also written a great quantity of extended and serious instrumental work, mainly for chamber combinations, but his most important contributions have undoubtedly been in the theater, where he has collaborated with writers of the stature of Paul Claudel, Cocteau, and Franz Werfel. Milhaud has always responded imaginatively to the theatrical situation. His "Orestes" trilogy, written with Claudel and including most notably *Les Choéphores* (1915–1916), makes striking use of a number of new and combined techniques including narration and rhythmic speaking-chorus with percussion. The ballet *L'Homme et son désir* (1918) employs instrumental forces disposed in particular spatial arrangements, a prophetic idea. The famous *Le Boeuf sur le toit* of 1919 is a compendium of popular tunes, mostly South American in origin (Milhaud had been an attaché in the French embassy at Rio de Janeiro during World War I) and treated in a noisy, rattling, racy manner. *La Création du monde,* a ballet of 1923, often considered Milhaud's masterpiece, is the first major composition to make extensive, serious, and subtle use of jazz. Milhaud did not actually "write" jazz, but the music is imbued with the sound and style of the jazz of that day.

The list could be extended. *Le Pauvre matelot* of 1916 is a curiously grim but effective piece of verismo opera with a text by Cocteau. At another extreme are the infinitesimal *"opéras minutes"* of the following year with their absurdly condensed bits of classical tragedy. And the *Christophe Colomb* of 1929–1930 presents still another huge contrast; it is a very grand symbolic opera with an allegorical text by Claudel and a musical and dramatic apparatus of considerable weight and power.

The pairing of Milhaud with his contemporary Francis Poulenc has obvious historical and even some esthetic justification, but they are in fact two vastly different musical personalities. Milhaud, the intensely trained "natural" musician, was brought up in the classical tradition and rejected it or used it to his own ends with the utter ease of a fluent and prolific master. Poulenc, virtually self-taught, slowly and painstakingly re-created tradition in a series of small, witty, elegant, and fastidious pieces, carefully worked out almost from note to note. This, of course, is not the Poulenc of wide popularity, composer of *buffa* works like *Le Bal masqué* (1932), the Concerto for two pianos (1932), and *Les Mamelles de Tirésias* (1944) where wrong notes, movie music, barroom ballads, and sentimental chansons jostle each other in racy profusion. It is rather the Poulenc who was a direct heir to the nineteenth-century neo-classical and salon tradition—a durable factor in French musical life. A work like the Organ Concerto (1938), although superficially derived from Bach, is really a direct descendant of the lyric, popular classicism of composers like Viotti and Saint-Saëns. Traces of this lyric gift are actually present even in the most outrageous of the parody-and-quote pieces, and a simple, *cantabile* expression can be found in much of the piano and a good deal of the chamber music. It was present already in early works like the ballet *Les Biches* (1923); it is the dominant musical speech in the simple, effective *Dialogues des Carmélites* (1957), which crosses Duparc with Mussorgsky, and in choral works like *Stabat Mater* (1951), *Gloria* (1960), and the *Sept Répons des Ténèbres* (1962). Poulenc's gift for lyric line is most evident in his songs, among which are his most attractive and successful works, and which, apart from the very different case of Strauss, represent a clearer continuation or reinstatement of the tradition than any other music we shall be discussing in this book.

The third important member of "Les Six" scarcely belongs with the others at all. Honegger's connection with the group really came about through his association with his fellow-pupil Milhaud and through the intellectual and moral patronage of Satie. Honegger's starting point was the Central European tradition up to and including even early Schoenberg but tempered considerably by Debussy and the Russians. His first reputation was based on a semi-dramatic biblical oratorio, *Le Roi David* (1921), and on several picturesque orchestral works: *Pastorale d'été* (1921), *Pacific 231* (the famous musical railroad train of 1924), and *Rugby* (1928). His early reputation as a composer of picturesque, noisy, avant-garde tone poems was, however, to prove misleading. *Le Roi David* —originally conceived, like *L'Histoire du soldat*, as a stage work with spoken narration and dialogue, mime, and dance—is scored for a chamber ensemble and intentionally built around a simple, almost popular melodic style. Even in the later concert version for large orchestra, the essentially simple closed forms remain unaltered, and the modified, unsystematic modal tonality remains fundamental to the effect; only the big contrapuntal choruses that close the main sections of the piece have extended classical form. Honegger returned to this genre in 1938 with the popular *Jeanne d'Arc au bûcher;* and *Le Roi David* itself is the prototype for a widespread popular choral style built on simple modal tonality, modest choral counterpoint, local color, and small, easily apprehended forms. Honegger himself was concerned with the expansion of these techniques (minus the pseudo-Orientalisms of *Le Roi David*) into a more complex contrapuntal symphonic and chamber style: in the list of his later works, large-scale symphonic and chamber works predominate. Long lines, moving across large, free diatonic and modal areas, with harmonic structures built on accumulations of thirds and added diatonic tones, and a highly accented but basically regular, even motoric rhythm are the hallmarks of his style; it accommodated the classical tradition to a modified, conservative, and accessible modern idiom with a good deal of expressive effect. Like the much more consistent and highly organized tonal style developed by Hindemith in his later years, the idiom had considerable influence over a period of about a quarter of a century. Honegger's work represented a strong and serious recasting of tradition in a style that had, in spite of serious formal defects (structures far too extended for the light tonal supports), a certain amount of scope and purpose; as such it remained one of the starting points for twentieth-century tonal symphonic tradition.

BIBLIOGRAPHICAL NOTES

In addition to the Ravel book noted at the end of Chapter 3, mention might be made of a view from the avant-garde: Pierre Boulez's "Trajectories: Ravel, Stravinsky, Schoenberg," an essay of 1949 reprinted in English translation in *Notes of an Apprenticeship* (New York, 1968). Material on "Les Six" may be found in Henri Hell's *Poulenc* (New York, 1959), Darius Milhaud's autobiographical *Notes Without Music* (New York, 1953), and, in French, Honegger's *Je suis compositeur* (Paris, 1951).

SEVEN

NEO-CLASSICISM AND
NEO-TONALITY OUTSIDE OF FRANCE

HINDEMITH AND GEBRAUCHSMUSIK

The most highly developed of the new tonal styles was that of
Paul Hindemith (1895–1963). Hindemith was the youngest of the first
group of major twentieth-century pioneers, and his artistic development
follows the general pattern of the early decades but at a distance of some
years. Thus his early work, written at about the time of World War I and
shortly thereafter, comes out of the Central European line—the tradition
of Brahms and Reger, however, rather than that of Wagner. Like Reger,
Hindemith extended the chromatic range with great mastery, always in
terms of the great contrapuntal tradition; to the end of his life, he remained a contrapuntist. With the early string sonatas of 1920–1923 (Opus
11), we are already in the composer's first mature phase. A long series of
important works followed: the one-act operas of 1921, *Cardillac* of 1926,

Paul Hindemith by Rémusat. Meyer Collection, Paris. Reproduction forbidden.

Hin und Zurück and *Neues vom Tage* of 1927 and 1929, the song cycles
Die junge Magd and *Das Marienleben* of 1922 and 1924, more sonatas
for strings, a series of string quartets, a number of works for piano, the
famous *Kleine Kammermusik* for winds (Op. 24, No. 2) of 1922, and a
group of concerted works with chamber orchestra. All of this music has
a contrapuntal aggressiveness and a free use of dissonance that led to its
being described initially as "atonal"; it now seems neither systematically
tonal nor really atonal. The harmonic sense and the big construction of
the lines, though often extremely chromatic, nearly always suggest a
clear but undefined sense of underlying tonal shape and direction; a
rather intense, expressive invention dominates the surface. Works like
Das Marienleben (in its original version) come very close in many ways
to the Viennese expressionists; on the other hand, pieces like the *Suite
1922* for piano and some of the *Kammermusik* compositions show a wit
and an irreverent boisterousness that approach and even—in matters of
satire and irony—outdo "Les Six."

About 1927, Hindemith began to change his musical style and outlook in the direction of simplicity and clarity, and towards a careful new
tonal style which was to characterize his music until his death. In the
end, his style was conditioned by a number of factors, nearly all of which
derived from his extraordinary musicality. Hindemith was an exceptional
type of "natural" musician; he composed with extraordinary facility and
he was active as a violist and conductor. Almost all of his works of the
1920's (including the operas) were conceived for chamber performance,
often with the composer himself playing the violin, viola, or viola
d'amore; and he was one of the first modern musicians to explore—
through performance as well as research—the vast areas of early music.
He was a well-known teacher and an influential theorist. In 1927, Hindemith formulated a definitive statement of his conception of the role of the
composer in society; like Stravinsky, he placed great emphasis on the
composer as craftsman, but he also stressed the importance of the relationship between the composer and the performer. In the late 1920's and
early 1930's he wrote a series of ensemble and solo works for amateur
and student performance, including a musical play for children and a
whole day's worth of music written for young students at a school. On a
more advanced level came a long series of sonatas for virtually every
important instrument and a further series of concerted works for solo
instruments with small and large orchestras. This so-called *Gebrauchsmusik* or "music for use" represents in part a return—or at least an
idealization—of the relationships that had existed between composers,
performers, patrons, and audiences before the nineteenth century. The
Romantic composer was presumably inspired by an inner compulsion, by
a need to communicate something; Hindemith was inspired by a com-

mission, by the presence of a performer (himself perhaps), and by the reality of an actual performing situation. It is probable that the re-establishment of the composer-performer relationship, and of the significance of the realities of performance and the performance situation, was Hindemith's most enduring theoretical contribution.

As a theorist, however, Hindemith wanted to accomplish a great deal more than that. Coincident with the establishment of the *Gebrauchs-musik* ideal came the simplification of his style and the definitive return to tonal ways of thinking. This is clear not only in the solo and chamber works but also in the major compositions of the 1930's and 1940's, beginning with the *Konzertmusik* for strings and brass of 1930 and continuing with the opera *Mathis der Maler* (1934), the symphony extracted from it, a pair of concertos for orchestra, and several ballet scores. During this period Hindemith also began to systematize his ideas; this ultimately resulted in a series of theoretical works (never wholly completed) and in the big, didactic cycle of fugues and interludes for piano published in 1943 as *Ludus Tonalis*. Hindemith consciously attempted to formulate a new tonal system which, growing out of certain acoustical principles and some fundamental notions of linear counterpoint, was to include a complete range of chromatic expression. The basic conception was that of the weight and tension of individual intervals, determined by an acoustic and psychological classification and revealed through a system of harmonic and melodic necessity (derived in part from the overtone series). Hindemith's music after the late 1920's was increasingly based on such ideas. Tonal centers are established by a kind of gravitational melodic movement and a harmonic motion based on chords of greater and lesser tension; the triad remains primary, the focal point of cadence and rest.[1] This remarkable parallel to the old tonal system—based, not on tradition and usage, but on presumed acoustical and psychological validities—was adopted by the composer in such a thorough-going manner that he even returned to some of his important older works and revised them in order to make them conform more closely to his later thinking, e.g., *Das Marienleben*, settings of texts on the life of the Virgin by Rainer Maria Rilke, revised in 1948 and its outlines softened, its harmonic and melodic movement more rationalized, more goal-directed (see Appendix; Example 7-1).

Although Hindemith thought of his theoretical ideas and method of teaching as a synthesis, they have in fact proved to be relevant only to certain kinds of music—principally Hindemith's own. For Hindemith himself, however (less so perhaps for his pupils and imitators), they provided

---

[1] Hindemith's classification of chordal structures, of intervals, and of triadic relationships has been described as a tonal system without the notion of "key." The classical system would then be, presumably, a special case of this wider theoretical principle.

a way of achieving a coherent kind of musical speech which could sustain invention and produce consistent and large-scale forms in an individual and contemporary tonal language. Hindemith's later works fit the patterns thus established—his opera based on the life of Kepler, *Die Harmonie der Welt* (1956); his opera based on Thornton Wilder's *The Long Christmas Dinner* (1960); his setting of Whitman's *When Lilacs Last in the Dooryard Bloom'd* (1946); the *Octet* (1956); and the later choral works. Hindemith tried to synthesize the great linear tradition with a kind of chromatically accented tonality; in doing so he created an individual style with its unmistakable sound of major and minor seconds, fourths and fifths. Everything works, everything is under perfect control. The music lies well for the instruments; within a narrow rhythmic compass, energy, impulse, and forward motion generate larger periods which are woven into large-scale forms through a carefully controlled use of intervallic tension and succession. Hindemith's music can be expressive; it is always idiomatic, if sometimes routine. He himself considered his later work as a logical and maturing development, but his major creative powers seem better expressed in the freer earlier work; certainly the early versions of the revised works are preferable.

There is unquestionably a logic and—up to a point at least—an inner development in Hindemith's work. Unlike other prolific composers, Hindemith was never uncritical about his own work; his standards of craftsmanship never flagged, only his inspiration. When his imagination was equal to his craft—as it tended to be especially in his dramatic works— he was able to turn his personal synthesis of theory and practice into the highest artistic communication.

THE DIFFUSION OF NEO-CLASSICISM

Neo-classicism or neo-tonality in one form or another became the dominant international idea in the 1930's and 1940's. Neo-classicism as such hardly constituted a "style" or a "school," and the broadest impact of the new tonal techniques was on the development of the national styles to be discussed in the next chapter. There remain, however, a number of composers and works to be mentioned here whose outlook, essentially international in character, was strongly conditioned by classic ideals as re-expressed through new tonal forms.

In France, there are several lesser figures who, while officially outside of "Les Six," were related to them in style and temperament. The most important of these are Jacques Ibert (1890–1962) and Jean Françaix (b. 1912), two witty, minor talents whose esthetic ranges from a kind of neo-impressionism (Ibert's *Escales* of 1922) to a musical jollity that is very close to Poulenc and Milhaud (Ibert's wind quintet; Françaix's Concertino for piano and orchestra). Mention should also be made of the later work of Vincent d'Indy (1851–1931). D'Indy, who derived from Franck, was an important pedagogue, and the Schola Cantorum, of which he was director from its inception in 1900 to his death, was an important center of new ideas as well as of the revival of old ones. Under d'Indy's direction, the Schola pioneered in the authentic performance of old music; it also evolved new techniques of teaching composition. D'Indy's own work is a curious mixture of a rich Franck-Wagner late-nineteenth-century symphonic style, a sense of classical technique and form, an expanded modern chromatic palette somewhat cautiously used, and a love of folk song and folk-song-like simplicity. Some of these ideas were carried further by d'Indy's pupil Albert Roussel (1869–1937) who, starting with a kind of amalgamation of d'Indy and Debussy, achieved an individual neo-classical style whose development seems parallel to rather than directly influenced by the work of a composer like Stravinsky.

Outside of France, certain composers in Italy, Germany, Russia, England, and the United States contributed to an essentially international movement.

The classical tradition was, in great part, Italian, but neo-classicism as an intellectual or expressive idea has had a relatively minor role in modern Italian musical life, with one major exception. Alfredo Casella (1883–1947), a once influential but now neglected composer, developed a tonal style based on a free use of the seven diatonic steps combined with traditional forms derived from the Monteverdi-Scarlatti tradition. Casella was an important figure in Italian musical life, and he played a major role in the revival of Italian instrumental music; he also helped to create a modern Italian tonal idiom and to insure that ultra-chromatic, atonal, and twelve-tone ideas would not penetrate Italian musical life—as, indeed, they did not until after his death. The most important younger Italian neo-classicist was Goffredo Petrassi (b. 1904) who, until his involvement in serialism, wrote a number of works in a serious, colorful, abstract, limber tonal style.[2]

In most of Europe "neo-classicism" was long considered by many as a form of musical intellectualizing and even ultra-modernity. In Germany, however, a number of composers picked up some of the simpler aspects and techniques of Stravinsky, Hindemith, and the French to synthesize an accessible, popular, neo-tonal style. The most important of these is Carl Orff (b. 1895), whose blocky, triadic theater music is built on obsessively repeated harmonic structures, semi-chanted, repetitious

---

[2] The work of other "neo-tonal" Italians—Respighi, Pizzetti, Malipiero—is considered in Chapter 8.

melodic figurations, and a simple, colorful orchestration based on percussion sounds, most of it quite clearly derived from Stravinsky, especially from *Les Noces*. Orff has applied some of these materials to a kind of creative-play teaching method for children which has had a great deal of success in Germany and elsewhere. Werner Egk (b. 1901), whose name and music are often linked with those of Orff, writes a more elaborate kind of piece, based on popular types and influenced by French style. Egk's music has simple direction and development; Orff's intentionally has none. Orff's music stands as virtually the last and simplest representative of an esthetic of simplicity which had considerable influence in European and American music between the wars.[3]

In his "Classical" Symphony and in many of his later works as well, Prokofiev achieved something of a tonal synthesis which constitutes an authentic and—by and large—convincing "neo-classicism"; the same is true (but to a much lesser degree) of the work of Dmitri Shostakovich (b. 1906). In England, a work like William Walton's *Façade* is very close in wit and intent to the French style of the period, especially in its original form with Edith Sitwell's poetry recited to a chamber accompaniment. All of Benjamin Britten's highly original tonal music could be placed here; and important American works like the early music of Roger Sessions, the *Short Symphony* and other pieces of Aaron Copland, the Gertrude Stein settings of Virgil Thomson, earlier works of Elliott Carter, Lukas Foss, and Arthur Berger, most of the music of Irving Fine, many compositions by Walter Piston and Roy Harris, as well as a large group of works by younger composers show a strong neo-classical or neo-tonal bent of one kind or another.

"Neo-classicism" petered out in a series of modest styles, eclectic in nature and severely limited in scope. Composers like Stravinsky and Hindemith could re-create tonal forms out of which big pieces could be made, works which were at once clever, craftsmanlike, clear and even accessible, idiomatic and full of vitality, allied with tradition but essentially new and capable of assimilating with ease such divergent elements as quotes from the classics, folk music, and jazz; parody, wit, and elegance; and a great deal of serious intellectual thought and communication about the nature of musical form, craft, art, and experience. The experience was, after a certain point, too limiting, too restricted for another generation—indeed, even for Stravinsky himself. If tonality were to retain vitality, it was clear that it had to find new forms.

---

[3] Although it has completely different origins, the comparatively recent phenomenon of minimalism (see Chapter 17) is also a return to simplicity. There are links between the work of Orff and Krzysztof Penderecki, the "do-it-yourself" ideas of Harry Partch and Henry Brant, and of certain younger composers.

BIBLIOGRAPHICAL NOTES

There is little or no general literature on "neo-classicism," a fact which may be partly due to the inadequacy of that useful but misleading and catch-all term. For Hindemith, the composer's own *Craft of Musical Composition* (New York, 1941, 1942) and *A Composer's World* (Cambridge, 1952) are fundamental. A good general book in German is Heinrich Strobel's *Paul Hindemith* (Mainz, Germany, 1948). Allen Forte's *Contemporary Tone Structures* (New York, 1955) is a rare and serious attempt to discuss new tonal ideas.

EIGHT

NATIONAL STYLES

The development of national styles outside of Central Europe and the general international evolution of twentieth-century music are closely related. The discovery of folk music, particularly that of Eastern Europe, was one of the factors that broadened the horizons of Western music. At the same time, no extensive independent developments of great significance could take place until the dominance of the central, "common practice" tonal system was ended. In general, some new kind of tonal framework was needed within which distinctly national idioms—derived from the small forms of folk and dance music—could be expanded into larger means of creative communication. Thus, outside of Germany and France, a whole series of local styles developed, adapting to local modes of musical speech influences first from Debussy and Ravel, later from Stravinsky, Hindemith, and others. In spite of the fact that the principal ideological opposition in the first part of the twentieth century was between Stravinskyian "neo-classicism" and Schoenbergian chromatic and twelve-tone ideas, it was rather the strong local and national styles which proved the principal bulwark against atonal and twelve-tone ideas. This was by no means merely a question of conservatism or of local pride. Amid the economic, political, and social crises of the late 1920's and 1930's, a dominant strain of social and esthetic thought appeared which rejected the atonal and experimental avant-gardism of the earlier part of the century in favor of a kind of musical populism, of simplicity and accessibility expressed through the use of tonal forms and popular and folk materials.

EASTERN EUROPE: BARTÓK

The most important figure to come out of Eastern Europe was Béla Bartók (1881–1945). Hungary, although an intensely musical country, had long been under the political and artistic hegemony of Vienna and Central Europe; Bartók was thoroughly trained in the traditional manner, and his early works are strongly resonant of Brahms and Richard Strauss. The liberating influences were Debussy and Magyar folk song. With Zoltán Kodály, Bartók went out into the Hungarian countryside and made the first definitive collections of Eastern European folk music. He transcribed this music in a manner virtually free of the nineteenth-century prejudices which had squeezed the highly distinctive character of folk art into the Procrustean bed of traditional tonality and which had confused genuine Hungarian folk expression with the popularized "Gypsy" music of the cafés. Bartók was not only able to establish the distinctive character of the true Magyar style; he was also able to record and distinguish other Eastern folk music of differing and equally distinct character. None of this music adheres to the conventions of Central European tonal thinking. Much of it is heterophonic in nature; a drone or rhythmic accompaniment underlays a single-line melody which often appears in different versions, sometimes simultaneous and often highly embellished.

In Bartók's earliest published works, his *Rhapsody*, Op. 1 (1904) and his *Suites* for orchestra, Op. 3 and 4 (1905, 1907), the setting of the Hungarian material already seems to owe something to Debussy; a certain special kind of impressionist color and form can be found in works like *Bluebeard's Castle* (1911) and the many characteristic "Night Music" movements of the later instrumental works. In his *Two Portraits* of 1907–1908 and, especially, in his *Bagatelles* for piano of 1908, Bartók moved quickly and with assurance into a mature and original phase—a phase quite equal and parallel to other developments elsewhere. The *Bagatelles*, besides being technical studies in new rhythmic, melodic, and harmonic devices, also suggest the way in which Bartók stylized melodic and rhyth-

Béla Bartók, drawn in 1944, one year before his death, by Alexander Dolbin. Meyer
Collection, Paris. Reproduction forbidden.

mic ideas and extracted from them their characteristic sound qualities, now transformed into harmonies, counterlines, and colors. In his String Quartet No. 1, of 1908–1909, Bartók reverts to a big contrapuntal, Central European style with a wandering kind of tonal chromaticism that is not always persuasive. But in the piano music of 1909–1911 (especially the well-known *Allegro barbaro*), in the *Two Pictures* for orchestra of 1910, in the two big theater works of 1911 and 1915–1916 (*Bluebeard's Castle* and the ballet *The Wooden Prince*), and in the Piano Suite, Op. 14, of 1916, Bartók develops a broad and colorful speech of great force and vitality. There is little if any actual folk material in the music, but the Hungarian character is omnipresent. The harmonic structure is still basically triadic; or, at least, the triad represents the main point of departure and return. The basic structures are tonal, although of course not in the old sense. Bartók's tonal writing and his structural sense are not completely consistent; rather he proceeds from point to point with the modal character of the melodic invention sustained by rhythmic vitality, changing meters, Debussyian color, and parallel harmonic motion. Softer ninth- and eleventh-chord sounds, punctuated by sharp harmonic dissonance, open out at key points of articulation into triads.

At about this time Bartók must have become acquainted with recent developments in Vienna and Paris: his String Quartet No. 2 of 1917 and *The Miraculous Mandarin,* a ballet of 1919, show, respectively, strong influences from Schoenberg and Stravinsky. These two impressive works present a remarkable contrast: the former contrapuntal, highly developed, and intensely expressive in an introspective way; the latter big and violent in the manner of the sophisticated primitivism of *Le Sacre du printemps.* It is almost as if Bartók had to recapitulate for himself the revolutionary experiences of a few years earlier in order to gain mastery of the rhythmic freedom, harmonic dissonance, color range, block-form, and additive structures of a Stravinsky and the intense, crowded, contrapuntal, expressive chromaticism and organizational control of a Schoenberg. Afterwards, Bartók was able to create his own imaginative world in which all these techniques and materials—folk song, tonal harmonies built in thirds, ultra-chromaticism and dissonant "atonality," contrapuntal, serial construction, percussive color-rhythm—could function (often side by side) as expressive and structural ideas compatible with the special qualities of his own invention.

The 1920's were a decade of chamber composition for Bartók: the "difficult" violin and piano sonatas of 1921–1922, the Piano Sonata and *Out of Doors* suite of 1926 and the Third and Fourth String Quartets of 1927–1928 are works of great intensity in which Bartók for the first time extended his own personal style into utterances of considerable size and shape. (The construction of the theater works, although extended, had been essentially an accumulation of localized events.) The String Quartets No. 3, with its extended one-movement construction, and No. 4, with its tightly organized transformations and returns, sustain unified lines of thought over long expressive periods through a rather subtle manipulation of material that is imaginative in shape (if limited in content) and of broad and striking implications (see Appendix; Example 8-1).

These chamber works are built on a rhythmic and phrase character that is often strongly suggestive of folk ideas and dependent on a kind of assertive tonality-in-the-small, but they are organized in their large structure according to other principles. The typical method is one in which entire movements are permeated with a particular kind of sound (characteristic harmonic, melodic and rhythmic shapes, timbres, and/or articulations), a method that is about halfway between certain Stravinskyian tonal techniques and the more highly ordered serial construction of Schoenberg.

By contrast, Bartók's relatively few orchestral works of this period —orchestrations of folk song sets originally written for piano, the *Dance Suite* of 1923, the Piano Concerto No. 1 of 1926, and the two *Rhapsodies* for violin and orchestra of 1928—are written in a more accessible tonal vein, and the use of Hungarian material is broader and somewhat more popular in nature. Beginning with the *Cantata Profana* of 1930 and the Piano Concerto No. 2 of the following year, Bartók showed a strong tendency to synthesize these aspects of his work. The Fifth String Quartet of 1934 is a piece of dissonant, lean and rhythmic, hard-driving Bartókiana; but its tonal construction is clearer than that of the Third or Fourth. The Sixth String Quartet of 1939 is built on a clear triadic tonality derived from contrapuntal movement and intervallic structures based principally on thirds and fifths. In sound, the Sixth Quartet seems to be a reversion to an earlier, clearer tonal idiom. But the triadic construction, although clearly tonal in nature, is an extension of the intervallic principle which, in the earlier quartets, had been worked out of intervals like minor seconds and major sevenths but are replaced in the Sixth Quartet by thirds and fifths. Similarly, Bartók's earlier cyclical treatment of form is extended here, in that an introduction to the first movement expands, as it recurs before the others, until it constitutes the whole of the last movement. A transition between chromatic and diatonic, triadic-tonal styles is actually accomplished within certain individual compositions, notably the *Music for Strings, Percussion, and Celesta* of 1936. (See Appendix; Example 8-2). The range of Bartókian techniques can also be studied in the remarkable series of studies which constitute the *Mikrokomos* (1926–1937), a "Gradus ad Parnassum" not only for the piano student but also for the student of compositional ideas. Many later works of Bartók show some kind of creative synthesis: The Sonata for Two Pianos and Percussion (1937), the Violin Concerto (1938), *Contrasts* for clarinet, violin and piano (1938), the *Divertimento for Strings* (1939), the Concerto for Orchestra (1944), the Third Piano Concerto (1945), and the Viola Concerto (1945; completed by Tibor Serly). A variety of clear, open, expressive elements, synthesized in large, tonal forms, has made these works some of Bartók's most popular—one of the few examples of a twentieth-century composer's later output achieving wider currency than his earlier and, artistically, more influential work. Bartók's style, which for a brief time was extremely influential among younger composers, was ultimately too personal to maintain a direct and continuous impact on the course of creative development, but the nature of his synthesis and the inclusive character of his composing techniques are perhaps of greater importance than has yet been recognized. There are universal qualities in Bartók's work which transcend the appealing and personal but surface character of his music; as time passes, they will emerge with greater clarity.

EASTERN EUROPE: HUNGARY AND CZECHOSLOVAKIA

The most important Hungarian composer besides Bartók was Zoltán Kodály (1882–1967), Bartók's close colleague and collaborator in collecting East European folk music. Kodály's best known music is the suite derived from the musical play *Háry János*, but its amusing if somewhat trivial adaptations of popular and folk styles are not necessarily representative of his serious work. Kodály's music is, in any case, more tonally and triadically oriented than Bartók's. There is a considerable body of chamber music; especially notable are a sonata for solo cello (1915), a *Serenade* for two violins and viola (1919–1920), and two string quartets (1908, 1916–1917) which, while without Bartók's special qualities of intensity, originality, and reflective thought, are strong, lyric essays of convincing shape. Kodály's style, with its open, triadic sound and its derivation from a lyric, Hungarian melos, is eminently suited to—even derived from—the human voice. Kodály established in Hungary the principle that singing should be the basis of music education and he introduced a series of reforms and innovations in the organization and teaching of sight singing which have had a wide influence. He wanted every child to participate in choral singing, and a great many of his own choral works are intended for performance by children, amateurs, and students. The core of Kodály's art is to be found in his songs, his choruses, and in big chorus-and-orchestra compositions like his *Psalmus Hungaricus* (1923).

A striking example of the liberation of the creative imagination of an Eastern European composer through the assimilation of new ideas is provided by the Czech composer, Leoš Janáček (1854–1928), ten years older than Strauss and hardly more than a decade younger than Dvořák. For years Janáček was a provincial music teacher in a little-known corner of what was to become Czechoslovakia, and his music was that of a provincial Dvořák. Suddenly, just at the turn of the century, his style and his creative powers broadened with the remarkable opera *Jenufa* (1904). Even so, it was more than ten years before *Jenufa* was produced in Prague and Vienna (in 1916), and it was only in the last years of his life that Janáček produced the remarkable series of original and powerful works on which his reputation now rests: *The Diary of One Who Vanished* (1916), *Katya Kabanová* (from Ostrovsky; 1919–1921), *The Cunning Little Vixen* (1921–1923), *The Makropulos Affair* (text by Capek; 1923–1924), *From the House of the Dead* (after Dostoyevsky; 1928); the *Slavonic Mass,* the *Sinfonietta* of 1926, and several chamber works. Like Kodály, Janáček combined a folk melos with a basically triadic style, but the character of Janáček's music is utterly unlike that of his younger contemporaries in Hungary—and not only because of the differences between Czech and Hungarian folk music. Janáček never quoted actual folk material, but he derived his melodic speech from the prose-poetry character of Slavic folk music with its typical intervals and scales, its close identification with language, and the insistent, repeated character of its melodic lines. An almost obsessive concern with repetition is very characteristic, with small figures of an insistent, prosaic character repeated over and over in block-like sections; the larger sections are built up through the juxtaposition and contrast of these very grand and simple building-blocks arranged in strong and persistent rhythmic layers. The technique is at work in the single successful large symphonic piece—the *Sinfonietta*—but it is most basic to Janáček's dramatic works; he was, above all, a man of the theater with an intense, intuitive understanding of the role of simplicity and the impact of repetition and striking contrast in dramatic construction. The ironic pessimism of these works—strongly in the Slavic tradition—is expressed through the rather affirmative and sophisticated naïveté of the music, and this itself produces some of the great dramatic tensions. Janáček's mature style was almost certainly achieved through his contact with the main currents of Western musical thought after World War I—Stravinsky may have been an influence—but these currents (not easily recognizable at all except in the character of lean, even angular, poetic simplicity on the surface and the "additive" construction underneath) are transformed into a style of expressive precision and dramatic originality.

Dvořák's principal pupil and successor, Josef Suk (1874–1935), began as a kind of polyphonic Dvořák whose harmonic horizons later expanded to include a range of modern techniques. In turn, Suk's best-known pupil was Bohuslav Martinu (1890–1959) who studied also with Roussel in Paris and mixed the Czech tradition with strong doses of French style (Ravel, d'Indy, Roussel), eventually turning to a rather international manner with a strong tonal and neo-classic bent.

EASTERN EUROPE: RUSSIA

Strong currents both of ultra-traditional conservatism and radical innovation co-existed in Russia from the late nineteenth century until the Stalinist anti-modern campaigns of the 1930's. The older Romantic tradition can be represented by Sergei Rachmaninoff (1873–1943) who, although he left Russia permanently in 1917 and lived for twenty-six more years, had already composed all but two or three of his best-known works before World War I. On the other hand, the strong personality of Scriabin attracted the attention of mystically inclined younger Russian musicians, who also began to show remarkable tendencies to strike out on their own. It is difficult to say what exactly are the sources of Prokofiev's early music—partly Scriabin, perhaps, but in any event not Stravinsky. Prokofiev composed his First Piano Concerto in 1911, his early piano works between 1908 and 1913, and his First Violin Concerto in 1915–1917, before he could have known much about Stravinsky's development; and even the *Scythian Suite* of 1914, for all its obvious Stravinskyisms, is really a parallel to *Le Sacre* rather than clearly derived from it. The *Scythian Suite* marks the beginning of a distinct period in Prokofiev's life, a development only briefly interrupted by the composer's lively re-interpretation of tradition in his "Classical" Symphony. Such works as *Sarcasms* and *Visions fugitives* for piano, the Third and Fourth Piano Sonatas, the ballet *Chout,* and the opera *The Gambler* (1915–1917; after Dostoyevsky), *Sept, ils sont sept* for tenor, chorus, and orchestra—all dating from before 1920—are built on highly dissonant textures often coupled with great motoric drive. Prokofiev's music at this period had the widest range of means, and within a few years between 1919 and 1923 he produced the masterpieces of his early period, *The Love for Three Oranges* and *The Flaming Angel,* utterly contrasting works, the former satirical and ironic, written with great wit and flair, the latter intensely dramatic, expressionistic, a curious and effective combination of the ironic and the visionary.

Prokofiev left Russia in 1918 and went to the United States and later to Paris, where he worked throughout the 1920's, composing two ballets for Diaghilev (*Le Pas d'acier* and *L'Enfant prodigue*), his symphonies Nos. 2, 3, and 4, and his piano concertos Nos. 3, 4, and 5. After *The Flaming Angel* and the remarkable Symphony derived from it (No. 3), the music of Prokofiev's Paris period is brilliant, hard-driving, and powerful but, with one or two exceptions, not on a level with his earlier works. It is possible that he found it difficult to work in Paris and away from Russia; at any rate, in 1934 he went back and almost immediately plunged into a whole series of "practical" projects which included the scores for the films *Lieutenant Kije* and Eisenstein's *Alexander Nevsky*, the ballets *Romeo and Juliet* and *Cinderella*, the propagandistic operas *Simeon Kotko* and *A Tale of a Real Man*, an operatic setting of Tolstoy's *War and Peace*, the admirable children's tale *Peter and the Wolf*, and cantatas and other vocal works with patriotic or propagandistic texts. Several chamber works, his Sixth, Seventh, and Eighth Piano Sonatas, his Violin Concerto No. 2, and his last three symphonies (including the popular Fifth) are also products of his Soviet period. Most of this music is characterized by a drastic simplification of style; in line with the political pressures of Soviet life and some of the prevailing esthetic ideas of the period, there is a strong revival of tonal procedures. This stylistic evolution took the form, not so much of any kind of conscious Russian nationalism or populism, as of a very distinctive, accessible neo-classicism. Eighteenth-century ideals are invoked in the use of "sonata form"—at least its external shell—in triadic harmonic structure, in the use of simple accompaniment figures of the "Alberti bass" type, in simple rhythmic and phrase structures, and in the character of the cadences. The classical cadence is very important Prokofiev's style; he uses it as a point of reference, as a local articulation, to clarify a constant series of sideslips into distant keys. These cycles of keys, often very loosely related and only briefly touched upon, give Prokofiev's music its characteristic sound—diatonic but constantly "modulating."

In spite of the composer's modification of his style in the direction of clarity and simplicity, his music remained under frequent attack in the Soviet Union for reasons which remain obscure to Western observers; perhaps its lack of overtly nationalist character was a factor. Nevertheless, there are many points of correspondence between Prokofiev's development and that of Stravinsky—not to mention younger Russian emigré composers like Alexander Tcherepnin (b. 1899) and Nicolas Nabokov (b. 1903)—and it seems reasonable to speak of a Russian tradition of "neoclassicism" of which Prokofiev's music forms a distinctive part. As with Stravinsky, Prokofiev's artistic choices were careful and conscious; unlike Stravinsky, he never succeeded in finding new and organic forms for either his new or his neo-classical ideas and ideals; the attraction of his work ultimately lies in qualities like the lyrical character of the invention and, in his earlier compositions, the strong, motoric character of the musical motion.

Prokofiev's musical personality was largely formed before the Revolution of 1917. Of the younger composers whose careers coincide with the advent of the Communist regime, only three have more than a local significance: the Armenian, Aram Khatchaturian (b. 1903), Dmitri Kabalevsky (b. 1904), and Dmitri Shostakovich (b. 1906). The first two have upheld the ideals of a musical populism superficially based on folk materials but amplified in a big, colorful, late-Romantic, bourgeois, symphonic manner. Shostakovich is, however, a far more original and distinctive musical personality whose career and development have been closely identified with the political and esthetic vicissitudes of Soviet life in the last forty years; Shostakovich himself has declared on several occasions that his art has a "political basis" and he has consistently accepted political and social criticism of his work, even to the point of repudiating publicly many of his compositions.

Shostakovich's orientation was, from the first, "neo-classic" and tonal, with a primary bias towards a simple, symphonic idiom. As with many of the later works of Prokofiev, the classical starting point for Shostakovich is Beethoven (from the viewpoint of Soviet Marxist criticism, Beethoven was the first "socialist realist" composer). But Shostakovich's individuality grows out of the contrast between an extended, almost sentimental lyricism and a vigorous, grotesque, dissonant wit—stylistic characteristics which have apparently not always resulted in music consonant with the dictates of official taste. (To the extent that Shostakovich's genius runs to parody and grotesquerie, the conflict is clearer from a Western point of view than the similar controversy over Prokofiev's music.) Shostakovich's First Symphony, the work that first brought him to world-wide attention and still possibly his most remarkable composition, is a lean, hard piece of music full of mordant wit; it is like a caricature of the classical symphony (unlike Prokofiev's similar early work, which is executed with respect and affection for the traditional form). At this time, the Russian modernists were closely in touch with developments in Western music, and there is no doubt that Shostakovich was acquainted with and influenced by German and French art. His opera, *The Nose,* based on Gogol (1927–1928), *The Golden Age* ballet of 1929–1930, and the famous *Lady Macbeth of the Mtsensk District* of 1930–1932 are brilliant works of the most intense, satiric sort. Even in the composer's Second Symphony of 1927, dedicated to the October Revolution, there are the strong, intense, biting chromaticism, hard rhythmic edges, and lean, brittle orchestral sound with which Shostakovich made his mark and which brought him so many difficulties.

A visit by Stalin to *Lady Macbeth* marked the beginning of trouble. Shostakovich was bitterly attacked in the press; both the opera and the Fourth Symphony, then in rehearsal, were withdrawn. A ballet about a collectivist farm was not good enough; the manner was still too lean, too stylized. Only with the Fifth Symphony of 1937 did Shostakovich redeem himself; and thereafter he devoted himself in his major works largely to a new synthetic, heroic style. The influence of Mahler, already present in compositions like the withdrawn Fourth Symphony, is basic in a whole series of long, long symphonic works of enormous size and pretension: the Seventh ("Leningrad"); the ambitious Eighth; the Twelfth, also dedicated to the Revolution; and others.

In addition to the usual patriotic cantatas, Shostakovich has composed a great deal of incidental music for the theater and the films. He has also written concertos for piano and for two pianos—clattering, breezy, ironic, jaunty works—and a quantity of solo piano and chamber music of simple, almost elementary musical qualities. The classicism and directness of the eight or nine string quartets have commanded admiration in some quarters, but Shostakovich remains primarily a symphonist, secondarily a dramatist. (*Lady Macbeth* has been produced again under the title *Katerina Ismailova*, and *The Nose* has had much success recently in Europe.) His large structures, built on long, simple tonal planes, endless repetition, rhythmic and harmonic insistence, and big dramatic contrasts spaced out on a Mahlerian time scale, are not profound though they generally affect the appearance of profundity. Nevertheless, they do achieve, almost by sheer force of will, a certain scope and grandeur.

NORTHERN EUROPE: SCANDINAVIA

Leaving aside the late-Romantic Danish composer, Carl Nielsen (1865–1931), who was touched by neo-classicism in his later work, the only important Scandinavian composer who will be considered here is Jean Sibelius (1865–1957). Sibelius's position in twentieth-century music is an odd one; he is a rare example of a composer of this century who evolved a notably original style out of nineteenth-century methods and conceptions. He began at the end of the 1800's as a composer of salon music, fashionable tone poems, and a First Symphony of a strongly Tchaikovskyian cast. In a large number of songs, solo piano and solo string works, Sibelius remained essentially—like Tchaikovsky in his smaller works—a salon composer of trivial taste. Only in a few of these compositions and particularly in choruses, where something of a folk character predominates, does the music take on a little more profile—even if the profile sometimes resembles Grieg.[1] The tone poems too, in spite of their dark and impressive color and unmistakably personal style, are works of limited means, full of the grand gestures of the German and Slavic Romantic masters made to do service for Finnish mythology.

Aside from a string quartet (*Voces Intimae* of 1909), and the Violin Concerto (1903), Sibelius's significant development must be traced in his seven symphonies, written over a period of twenty-five years, between 1899 and 1924. The Second Symphony of 1901 and, to a lesser extent, the Third of a few years later show a strong handling of traditional materials; but the most original of the series is the Fourth, written in 1911—the period of the great musical upheavals on the continent. The personal crisis in Sibelius's music was also, in part, a tonal crisis. The Fourth Symphony centers on the ambiguous interval of the augmented fourth, and from its opening measures until some point near its conclusion the tonal resolution of the piece is in doubt. The remarkable thing about this work, aside from its moody and dissonant character, is its strong conception of form generated organically out of the musical ideas. The ideas come in fragments, and the formal process—almost the reverse of traditional developmental concepts—is one of gradual cohesion; the fragments merge and develop into coherent tonal structures of considerable power. None of Sibelius's later symphonies—the Fifth of 1914–1915 and the last two dating from the 1920's—shows anything like the harmonic, melodic, and orchestral originality of the Fourth; Sibelius even returned to firmer tonal ground in these later works. But they share his typical halting, expressive, tortured kind of musical speech; and they retain—and even expand—this remarkable "synthetic" technique, preserving a sense of organic, tonal symphonic form which, in the traditional sense, had otherwise vanished.

NORTHERN EUROPE: ENGLAND

England, like the countries of Eastern and Northern Europe, was long a cultural dependency of Central Europe which finally established a measure of musical independence and national idiom partly through folk style. Sir Edward Elgar (1857–1934) was a late and somewhat provincial representative of the great symphonic tradition, and both Gustav Holst (1874–1934) and Delius—two of the most important creative musi-

---

[1] There are, however, among the songs a few works of a spare and striking character in a class with the best of Sibelius's symphonic music.

cians in the development of English musical life in the early part of the century—had Central European parental and musical antecedents. Delius, as previously noted, was attracted by the new French style with its floating, suspended sense of tonality and its exaltation of timbre as a basic expressive and formal means of musical expression. Delius's "impressionism" has individuality, but the first composer to use these techniques in a distinctly English manner was Ralph Vaughan Williams (1872–1958).[2] Like Delius, Vaughan Williams was brought up in the Classical-Romantic Central European tradition, both in England where it was dominant and in Germany where he studied with Max Bruch. Later, like Bartók, he began to collect folk songs; still later, he studied with Maurice Ravel. These facts are not unconnected. Vaughan Williams was never an "impressionist" in any meaningful sense, but impulses from old English music—including Tudor art music, also pre-tonal in its basis—combined with "impressionist" harmonic and coloristic techniques to form a personal and indisputably English style. After the early vocal works and fantasias on folk and Tudor themes, actual quotation of old English music is not prominent in Vaughan Williams's music, but as in the case of Bartók the double experience of pre- and post-tonal music made possible the formation of a distinctive style, anchored in some kind of modal-tonality but free of the traditional tonal way of thinking. Vaughan Williams's later work is characterized by an expansion and consolidation of technique and style in an attempt to create a large-scale English symphonic manner, with new tonal techniques enclosed in adaptations of traditional forms. This big symphonic style, characteristic of English twentieth-century music, particularly in the 1930's—see Arnold Bax (1883–1953), Arthur Bliss (b. 1891), and William Walton (b. 1902)—is not unrelated to parallel Russian and Scandinavian developments, and it is significant that composers like Shostakovich, Sibelius, and Nielsen have always been notably well received in England.

The development of the big modern English symphonic (and vocal) style—even in the strongest and most original works of Vaughan Williams—moved steadily towards an evocation of a full Romantic style; at the same time, however, England developed a strong classical strain of considerable originality. The initial impulses came from France—from the Paris of Stravinsky and "Les Six"; indeed, the piano music and ballet scores of Lord Berners (1883–1950) were written for and produced in the

---

[2] The combination of folk-song and early-music revival, with or without some kind of "impressionist" treatment, characterizes a number of highly individualistic English composers in the early part of the century. Cyril Scott (1879–1970), Philip Heseltine (Peter Warlock; 1894–1930), Percy Grainger (Australian-born, active in England and America; 1882–1961) are not very highly regarded any more but time may well reverse some of those judgments.

French capital. The most important English production of this period was Walton's *Façade,* a setting of Edith Sitwell poems declaimed (originally by Miss Sitwell herself) to the witty, agile commentary of a chamber orchestra. Walton later abandoned the free, lean, dissonant, chamber style of the work to turn towards a more neutral, accessible, "English" symphonic style. (Significantly, he later romanticized *Façade* in a ballet version scored for large orchestra.)

The most important and original English neo-tonal music has been that of Benjamin Britten. Britten, who was born in 1913, developed under the influence of the art of Stravinsky and the French, but he has been able to strike a distinctive and original note. His fundamental idiom is based on a synthetic tonal technique elucidated with great simplicity, naturalness, and skillful clarity growing out of a kind of melodic thinking which is often vocal in origin. He has also responded to English tradition—the tradition of Purcell and of English choral music, rather than that of the folk song or Elizabethan madrigal, but any specifically English quality which can be ascribed to his music is the result of its force of character rather than of any easily isolated musical features. Britten has never hesitated to use—and often with conspicuous success—a wide range of musical techniques integrated by means of simple, artful, new tonal forms. His forms are nearly always, in spite of appearances, highly constructed; a problem is that they are not always organic. The music is typically put together in freely diatonic melodic-vocal phrases, often set into a simple contrapuntal web and punctuated by clipped, highly colored, triadic harmonies. The basic long-range motion, the big structure, and even ultimately the sense of convincing tonal organization depend, however, on a careful inner manipulation of relationships functioning at another and far less simple level than the attractive and easily apprehended exterior. This odd, double construction is not difficult to detect in works like the opera *The Turn of the Screw* (1953–1954)—based on a twelve-tone "row" which is simply a cycle of fourths—or the *War Requiem* (1963), where the opposition of levels and the transformation of intellectual and musical materials actually operate as a kind of intellectual drama beneath the more obvious Stravinsky-Verdi dramatic surface.

Any list of Britten's major compositions will serve to indicate the importance of the human voice in his work. Big choral-orchestral works like the *Spring Symphony* (1949) and the *War Requiem* and smaller conceptions like *Les Illuminations* (1939; Rimbaud settings for tenor and strings), the *Serenade* for tenor, horn, and strings (1943), *Rejoice in the Lamb* (1943; to a text by Christopher Smart), and *A Ceremony of Carols* (1942) are among his most successful pieces. Finally, his stage works, referred to later, are strongly oriented towards lyric-intellectual as well as purely dramatic expressions. Except for an "occasional" work like

Noye's Fludde (1959), with its children's orchestra of carillonneurs and recorder players, and the more recent *Curlew River* (1964), they are within the framework of conventional operatic gesture and plan; nevertheless, they represent the first important English operas since Purcell's, and containing as they do some of Britten's best music they serve to confirm the vocal basis of his art.

The special form of English classicism found in Britten's music has another representative in Michael Tippett (b. 1905), regarded by some as Britten's equal at the very least but less well-known outside of England. Classicism continues to have a hold on the conservative English public but, as nearly everywhere else, classicism and neo-tonality have been turned aside by or absorbed into chromatic style. Even Britten has cautiously expanded his own techniques to utilize ideas from serial and even post-serial music.

SOUTHERN EUROPE: ITALY AND SPAIN

In spite of the great role that Italy played in the early establishment of the classical tradition, there was a complete break in the tradition in every field except opera. After 1900, Italian instrumental and even vocal music had to renew itself in a manner not so different from that of East Europe, Scandinavia, and England. The difference—and it is an important one—is that the Italians did not strike out anew from folk music but rather from their Renaissance and Baroque backgrounds.

Two Italians with strong musical roots in the nineteenth century were touched by new ideas. One, Ferruccio Busoni, actually anticipated many important contemporary ideas in his remarkable writings about music, although as a composer he participated in the century's revolutions only to a limited degree; in any case, his work belongs largely to Central European musical life and had only small influence in his native country. The other, Giacomo Puccini (1858–1924), is an extraordinary case of a brilliant and successful composer in a conservative tradition who consciously enriched his own means of expression with new ideas: from the parallel fifths in *La Bohème* (1896) to the Debussyisms of *Il Tabarro* (1918) and the striking dissonances of *Turandot* (1924; completed by Franco Alfano), his operatic style continually assimilated techniques which had originated outside the conventional operatic apparatus. Puccini's tonal-vocal style is contemporary in this essential respect, and its influence is still great in the theater and in popular music.

A definitive break with the operatic tradition and the establishment of a new Italian symphonic-tonal—and, later, also vocal-operatic—

style were accomplished by a younger group of composers including Casella (already discussed above in connection with neo-classicism), Ottorino Respighi (1879–1936), Ildebrando Pizzetti (1880–1968), and Gian Francesco Malipiero (1882–1973). Respighi, a kind of modern Italian Rimsky-Korsakov (with whom he actually studied), was a sensualist who synthesized a variety of sure-fire ingredients from Gregorian chant to Debussy, all in a brilliant, popular manner. Respighi's popularity rests on a small group of orchestral works, although the bulk of his output is to be found in more than a dozen operatic compositions, all failures. With the exception of Casella, these composers made extensive attempts to revive and renovate Italian opera with a new and modern tonal technique based on free and wide-ranging diatonic elements, essentially unrelated to prior Italian operatic tradition but nonetheless distinctively Italian in its particular adaptation of contemporary ideas. The bulk of Pizzetti's work, outside of his songs, belongs in this category; the results, whatever their intrinsic musical merit, have not been notably successful.

Of this group of composers, undoubtedly the most important is Malipiero, whose long list of compositions includes a number of stage pieces (including an attractive and occasionally performed Goldoni triptych written in 1919–1921) and an even more extensive catalogue of instrumental and orchestral works. Malipiero's free diatonic technique, strongly imbued with a kind of vocally derived counterpoint, a mild use of dissonance, and rather improvisatory lyric-dramatic forms, contains scarcely a trace of anything that could be described as local color; the basic wandering modal character of the "tonal" writing has nothing to do with folk music. However, Malipiero strikes a distinctively Italian note due in part to his derivations from pre-tonal Italian music, particularly the great vocal tradition up through Monteverdi.

In contrast to the rather reserved, simple, but almost aristocratic ideals of the new Italian art music (of the group after Puccini which attempted to renovate vocal ideals and synthesize them with a new instrumental music, only Respighi developed a really popular idiom), the revival of Spanish music, in large part the creation of the composer Felipe Pedrell (1841–1922), was consciously and thoroughly based on traditional music. The familiar elements of this tradition, derived largely from an aural performance style,[3] consist principally of some fairly complex rhythmic patterns within a steady and obsessive metrical frame, and a rich and highly ornamented melos based on a few characteristic modal patterns—of obviously Eastern origin—to which have been added or adapted a few simple Western harmonies. The extensive transformation of this material into "art" music is almost entirely due to the harmonic

[3] Partly Gypsy and partly Spanish-Arabic in origin.

developments in French music at the end of the nineteenth and the beginning of the twentieth centuries. Some of the most important use of
Spanish material occurs in the work of Debussy and Ravel, and composers like Isaac Albéniz (1860–1909) and Enrique Granados (1867–1916)
were closely influenced by the "impressionists" (also by d'Indy, Fauré,
and Dukas). Debussy, Ravel, and later, Stravinskyian "neo-classicism"
were also starting points for Manuel de Falla (1876–1946), not merely because Falla had no native precedents on which to base a new, Spanish
style but also because the new materials of French music could give form
to other characteristic ideas without wrenching them into the conventions
of the old tonal system. Two of Falla's best-known pieces are concerted
works: *Nights in the Gardens of Spain* for piano and orchestra (1909–
1915) and the Concerto for harpsichord and chamber ensemble (1923–
1926), the latter the most obviously "neo-classical" of his works. There
are also piano pieces and vocal works including the *Seven Spanish Popular Songs,* one of the surprisingly rare examples of the actual use of
Spanish folk material in Falla's music. Falla's most important work, however, was for the theater; it ranges from the colorful, florid Spanish style
of the opera *La Vida breve* (1904–1905) and the ballet *El Amor brujo*
(1915) to the drier, wittier neo-classicism of *El Retablo de Maese Pedro*
(1919), a scenic play with puppets, adapted from an episode in *Don
Quixote,* and the attempted synthesis of the large *Atlántida* (unfinished;
completed and orchestrated in 1962 by Ernesto Halffter).

The range of Falla's activity framed nearly all of the work produced in Spain for many years, from Halffter (b. 1905), the most Stravinskyian of the Spaniards, to local-color composers like Joaquín Turina
(1882–1949), Joaquín Nin (1879–1949), Joaquín Rodrigo (b. 1902), and
others. Only recently and with great reluctance have Spanish composers
begun to abandon Spanish tradition as a primary source of musical ideas
and forms, and although the younger composers in Spain—as everywhere
else—are now committed to chromaticism, serialism, and beyond, and one
can still find attempts to synthesize new with traditional materials *à la*
Bartók or even shotgun marriages of *cante hondo* and serialism *à la* Boulez.

LATIN AMERICA

The impulse which produced the remarkable Mexican pictorial
school in the 1920's also generated a new Mexican music of significance.
Like the painting, this music was liberated by the new techniques and
new freedoms produced in Europe at the beginning of the century but it
developed—only up to a point, to be sure—in a distinctive way. A com-

poser like Carlos Chávez (b. 1899) benefited, like many of his colleagues in the United States at the time, from the opportunity to develop an intense original musicality at a long distance from the old tradition. Chávez's early works are his radical ones; in his free use of percussion, in the intense, linear, chromatic, expressive angularity and dissonance of a work like the ballet *Antígona* (1932; 1940) in the remarkable use of percussion in works like the *Sinfonía India* (1935) and the *Toccata* for percussion (1947), in the driving power of works like the ballet *HP* (i.e., horsepower) (1932), Chávez established a musical line of expression which was both contemporary and national without being narrowly folkloristic. Nevertheless, in spite of the composer's awareness of the limitations of mere folklorism, Chávez was inevitably involved—as were his painter contemporaries—in social consciousness and social expression. For Diego Rivera and José Orozco, this meant a focus on subject matter and interpretation of the social situation; for Chávez it meant clarified tonal techniques and direct communicativeness without or (preferably) with folklore. From this point, Chávez later turned to big symphonic and Classical-Romantic tonal form.

The most curious figure of the Mexican musical renaissance was Silvestre Revueltas (1899–1940), who, in the brief span of forty-one years, produced an *oeuvre* in which an actual or imagined Indian-Mexican music of primitive intensity was put together with a kind of obsessive, *Sacre du printemps* technique. Revueltas's music is like much other experimental music of the period—not quite fully realized. The Cuban composer Amadeo Roldán (1900–1939) is a similar case; like Revueltas he was a talented extremist and his *Rítmicas* V and VI (1930) are possibly the first works written for an all-percussion ensemble (they precede Varèse's *Ionisation* by a year or two). Like Revueltas, Roldán died young, before his talents were fully realized. In any case, the output of these composers, very much part of an important New World creative flowering, ought to be better known.

The North American tradition of experimentalism did not extend to South America, although the southern continent's one really important composer, Heitor Villa-Lobos (1887–1959), remained a considerable distance from European tradition in temperament and style. A Brazilian, Villa-Lobos had a natural affinity with modern French music. Milhaud's stay in Brazil in 1917–1919 as French cultural attaché had an important influence in introducing him to Debussy and other modern French music. Any rough description of Villa-Lobos's music would have to contend with "Les Six," Brazilian-Portuguese-African folk and popular style, "impressionism" (especially in the instrumental usage), a bit of Indian music, and a touch of jazz. Villa-Lobos began his musical career playing in café orchestras; essentially self-taught as a composer, he was one of the most

prolific—and uncritical—musicians who ever lived. The result is an enormous mass of music, tossed off with great ease and freedom, often utterly
charming, very often trivial, sometimes utterly confused and inconsistent,
sometimes impressive. Tonality was as natural a technique to Villa-Lobos
as it was to the street musicians who provided the model for the ditties he
loved so well; but his tonality is often clouded by huge masses of rich
sound-color applied liberally with the palette knife and without much
care. Perhaps the best—or at least the most characteristic—of Villa-Lobos's
music is to be found in the various works titled *Chôros* and *Bachianas
Brasileiras* written over a period of more than twenty-five years.

Among other South Americans, only the Argentinian Alberto
Ginastera (b. 1916) has produced important work in a national-tonal
tradition. His ballets, *Panambí* (1940) and *Estancia* (1941), have the now-
classical Indian-Latin-*Rite-of-Spring* mixture, but his later music is atonal-
serial in the post-war mode.

THE UNITED STATES

In another volume of this series,[4] twentieth-century music in the
United States is discussed in the context of the American past and of
American tradition. Here—and elsewhere in this volume—we shall only
discuss the position of music in the United States vis-à-vis the international development of contemporary style. Certainly the first attempts to
establish a new tonal, "national" style completely outside the tradition of
functional tonality must be ascribed—along with so many other things—to
Charles Ives (1874–1954), but Ives is perhaps more fruitfully considered
along with the great American experimental and avant-garde movements
discussed below. In several important and individual ways, the vast
changes in European music during the first part of the century were
paralleled—sometimes anticipated, sometimes followed—in the United
States. Similarly, the development of new tonal styles and the new musical nationalisms in the 1920's, 1930's, and 1940's were paralleled—and,
because of the war, often developed and continued—in this country. The
new preoccupations with the relationship of the composer to the musical
community, the public, and society; the brave attempt to re-integrate the
creative artist into his society through musical populism, music for use,
school music, worker's music, and songs for the masses; the preoccupation
with the use of recordings, radio, theater, and films as a means for reach-

---

[4] H. Wiley Hitchcock, *Music in the United States: A Historical Introduction*,
2nd ed. (Englewood Cliffs, N.J.; Prentice-Hall, Inc., 1974).

ing a mass audience; the phenomenal success of Kurt Weill (1900–1950) and the interest in music as a vehicle for social commentary; the mystique of purposefulness and utilitarianism; the search for a national music combined with the revived interest in national, popular, and folk expression —all had a profound effect on this side of the Atlantic. Ironically, at the very moment when the United States had to assume most of the burden of international contemporary musical life, its composers were looking inward and backward trying to find a specifically American musical identity.

The initial impulses for this new American tonal music came from Stravinsky and the French, to a lesser extent from Hindemith, and in the theater, from Kurt Weill. Stravinsky's neo-classic "idea" appeared as a stylistic vessel which could carry many different kinds of contents: jazz as well as Bach, a folk tune as well as a neo-Mozartian melody. Roger Sessions's First Symphony (1927), Aaron Copland's "Jazz" Concerto for piano and orchestra (1926), and a whole host of works by lesser composers—nearly all of whom studied how to make first-class neo-tonality with Nadia Boulanger in Paris—Americanized these techniques with skill and ease. A composer like Virgil Thomson (b. 1896), with his attitudes of elegance and artful simplicity, reduced such ideas to their absolute essentials: disassociated scales and triads treated exactly like the dissociated words and phrases in the texts of Gertrude Stein which he employed.

The center of this activity in the 1930's and early 1940's was the theater and related media. After a period of working with chromatic and even serial techniques, Copland (b. 1900) developed his popular style in a well-known series of ballets. George Gershwin (1898–1937; the first actual arrival from the world of popular music); Marc Blitzstein (1905–1964; an intellectual convert from highbrow music); Thomson; the quickly Americanized Kurt Weill; and others scored real theatrical successes. Copland, George Antheil (1900–1959), Louis Gruenberg (1884–1964), and Paul Bowles (b. 1910) wrote movie music; and there was considerable activity on the four radio networks, which sponsored a great deal of new music of the more popular sort. This was also the period of innumerable symphonic "Hoedowns" and "Square Dances" as well as of the growth of a broad, serious, symphonic style, strongly tonal (generally in a Stravinskyian or modal sort of way), based on traditional patterns often rather awkwardly arranged to fit the new local-color material; influenced by Stravinsky, Hindemith, and the Soviet composers but—in one way or another—definably American. The idea was, more or less, to adapt the great tradition to a New World style for the large, new American public—in short, to write "The Great American Symphony." Copland himself produced important music in this vein, notably his Third Symphony (1946) and his more ascetic Piano Sonata (1939–1941), but the best and most consistent representative of the style was perhaps Roy Harris (b. 1898).

Harris's works even his notable Third Symphony (1938) and Piano Quintet (1936)—seem to have lost ground in recent years, but in their day they were considered models of serious style and form combined with clear, handsome, and accessible ideas that were identifiably American. The "American" character of these works—and many others on the same model—is only partly due to the actual use of folk or folk-popular material. Certain types of stylized, expressive melody, popular in origin but much transformed—a simple, halting motion, in scale steps within a small diatonic compass or in wide leaps of fourths and fifths, with metrical changes based on alternating threes and twos, and with a certain amount of syncopation—became hallmarks. So did wide, open harmonies built on major seconds, fourths, and fifths and a flat, colorful, open orchestration. The three- and four-movement forms were—except in the dance and theater pieces—almost invariably and rather uncomfortably borrowed from traditional patterns.

By no means all of the American symphonic music of this type was restricted to this model; it was just that the model was the most typical, distinctive, and obviously American. Conservative composers like Howard Hanson (b. 1896) and Samuel Barber (b. 1910) remained closer or returned to European prototypes, particularly those derived from Romantic symphonic literature. On the other hand, William Schuman (b. 1910) was involved in a much wider range of materials in his development of a big symphonic style based on chromatic ideas, a rich, dissonant harmonic material, high-powered rhythmic impulse and orchestration, and structures which come out of these materials. The music of Walter Piston (b. 1894) belongs somewhere in between; highly polished, basically diatonic in its orientation, and strongly dependent on classical models, it remains poised between ideals of serious, classical workmanship and high degrees of tension and articulation.

The generation of composers whose work became known in the 1930's and 1940's can be divided—a little too neatly perhaps—between those who attempted to carry forward some kind of development of the "American School" popular-symphonic idea—like David Diamond (b. 1915), Peter Mennin (b. 1923), William Flanagan (1923–1969)—and those who were working towards a lively American "neo-classical" style full of elegance, wit, and resonance—Arthur Berger (b. 1912), Irving Fine (1914–1962), Elliott Carter (b. 1908), and Lukas Foss (b. 1922). The former style has remained rather constant in the new works of older composers (occasionally showing twelve-tone influence) and it is essentially without influence on the younger generation; the latter has evolved into or been completely superseded by serial or other avant-garde developments.

There remains one composer, Ernest Bloch (1880–1959), who must be considered here—partly for want of a better place and partly because he spent most of his creative life in the United States. In spite of the fact that Bloch wrote a large symphonic work, *America* (1926), employing American folk songs, hymns, and even jazz, he can hardly be considered an American composer, and indeed, in spite of his well-known works on Hebrew motifs, he cannot be accurately or meaningfully classified as a Jewish composer. Bloch was born in Switzerland, studied in Belgium, lived in Paris and—after 1916—in the United States. He was a composer rooted in the Central European late-Romantic tradition; in spite of some important vocal works, he was oriented towards a symphonic style covered with literary and poetic trappings. His early style is an amalgam of Debussy, Richard Strauss, and Mahler, to which he later adapted the expanded vocabulary of early twentieth-century modernism and even—in the mode of Honegger or Kodály—a certain amount of neo-classicism. Bloch was certainly not without influence on the development of American music, but he was a strong eclectic with an extremely various and uneven production that remains difficult to pigeon-hole.

BIBLIOGRAPHICAL NOTES

The literature on local style is enormous and spread out in a multitude of languages. The standard study of Bartók in English is that of Halsey Stevens (New York, 1953; 2nd edition, 1965); there is a major Hungarian study by Bence Szabolcsi published in Budapest in French (*Bartók: Sa Vie et son oeuvre,* 1952). See also the studies of the Bartók string quartets by Milton Babbitt (*Musical Quarterly,* July, 1949) and Matyas Seiber (London, 1945); Allan Forte's analysis of part of the Fourth Quartet appears in the *Problems of Modern Music* issue of *The Musical Quarterly* (April, 1960). For Russian and Soviet composers, see Gerald Abraham's *Eight Soviet Composers* (London, 1948), Stanley B. Krebs's *Soviet Composers and the Development of Soviet Music* (New York, 1970), and Boris Schwarz's *Music and Musical Life in Soviet Russia, 1917–1970* (New York, 1972). Israel Nestyev's *Prokofiev* (Eng. tr., New York, 1946) is distorted by its "Soviet"—not to say Stalinist—point of view; Pierre Souvtchinsky's *Musique russe,* already mentioned, is a useful corrective. For Sibelius, see the symposium edited by Gerald Abraham (*Music of Sibelius,* New York, 1947). There is an excellent book on Benjamin Britten's earlier works by Hans Keller and Donald Mitchell (London, 1953); see also Eric Walter White's *Benjamin Britten* (Berkeley, rev. 1970). For Chávez, see the composer's own *Musical Thought* (Norton Poetry Lectures of 1958–1959; published by Harvard, 1960). For comments on the development of neo-classic and neo-tonal styles in American music, see the author's own article "Modern Music in Retrospect" in the Spring–Summer, 1964, issue of *Perspectives of New Music,* as well as Arthur Berger's article "Stravinsky and the

Younger American Composers" in the June, 1955, issue of *The Score and I.M.A. Magazine;* see also Henry Cowell's *American Composers on American Music* (New York, 1960, but containing articles dating from 1926 on), Wilfrid Mellers's English view in *Music in a New Found Land* (London, 1964), Virgil Thomson's various writings, and H. Wiley Hitchcock's *Music in the United States: A Historical Introduction* in the Prentice-Hall History of Music Series.

NINE

MUSICAL THEATER

Musical theater ought not to be considered apart from the general development of musical creativity, but unfortunately it must be so treated in any discussion of the music of the first two-thirds of this century. For the first time since the origins of opera, about 1600, the theater ceased to be a primary generating or creative force in musical evolution. Opera, long at the leading edge of musical development, has become an ultra-conservative institution, resistant to change and highly dependent on routine. By contrast, the dance has been closely identified with new musical developments; however, this success has been achieved in part by weaning dance away from theater in the direction of lyric or intellectual—in short, abstract—forms.

It is only in the last few years that this situation has changed; the new electronic media and non-operatic theater have become central in the evolution of new music, and music has become an important creative force in new theater. These important developments are discussed in the final section of the book; this chapter will attempt to survey the state of opera and musical theater in the earlier part of the century.

PUCCINI AND VERISMO

The operas of Giacomo Puccini might seem scarcely to fall within the scope of this study at all, but *Turandot*—completed by Franco Alfano after the composer's death in 1924—is the last opera to enter the international repertory and one of the few in that repertory to employ definitively twentieth-century melodic, harmonic, and orchestral techniques. French "impressionism" produced comparatively little for the stage, although assuredly three masterpieces in Debussy's *Pelléas et Mélisande* and Ravel's charming one-act operas *L'Heure espagnole* and *L'Enfant et les sortilèges*. But as early as *La Bohème* Puccini began to come under the influence of Debussyian harmonic ideas. In spite of its origins in the Italian tradition, Puccini's melodic technique, with its "modal" turns of phrase, is essentially twentieth-century in conception, and his harmonic-melodic ideas are often quite surprisingly free—in implication at least—of traditional functional-tonal prejudices. Thus the series of unrelated triads at the beginning of *Tosca*, the parallel fifths that open the third act of *La Bohème*, the tonal irresolution of the end of *Madama Butterfly*, the dabs of detached harmonic and orchestral color at the beginning of *Il Tabarro*, and the sequences of parallel seventh and ninth chords that appear in the later works are by no means isolated usages. Puccini's rather flexible diatonic melodic style (often curiously modal or pentatonic, even in the non-oriental operas) combines with a rich and free harmonic style based on piled-up thirds, parallel motion, and dramatic harmonic and tonal shifts to form a consistent musical style distinct from traditional practice, closely interwoven with the dramatic conceptions, and distinctly twentieth-century in character. Puccini's greatest influence was on the development of popular musical theater, film music, and—to a lesser degree—on certain related, lighter forms of pop music. Parallel sequences of ninth and eleventh chords, first extensively employed by Puccini as a way of enriching the support of a simple modal or diatonic melodic line, have become clichés of popular-song harmonization. In theatrical idea and form, Puccini was not an innovator although his type of musical theater—as well as his musical style—has been much imitated. In general, the late operas of Verdi provide the models: set numbers of the classical type alternate with narrative or dialogue scenes, the whole framed in a continuous and prominent orchestral texture; indeed the orchestra often carries the entire musical motion and significance, with the vocal parts reduced to a simple, word-conveying *parlando*, sometimes the mere repetition of one or two tones. Puccini's contemporaries, Leoncavallo and Mascagni, introduced a popular or local subject-matter in their operas, which thus pass under the name of "verismo." Puccini's material, however, is far more wide-ranging—often exotic in a kind of *fin-de-siècle* way and always reflecting the theatrical taste of his period: *Tosca* (1900), *Madama Butterfly* (1904), and *The Girl of the Golden West* (1910) were based on popular plays of the time; *La Bohème* and *Il Tabarro* derive from scenes of contemporary life. Only in *Turandot*, a curious fantasy-comedy by the eighteenth-century Italian, Gozzi, did Puccini venture to treat a dramatic concept essentially removed from the missing-fourth-wall realistic theater concept. *Turandot* is a mythic, symbolic theater of masks, and its music—highly colored, full of dissonant accent, often tonally ambiguous—is equally far from tonal "realism."

Nearly all of Puccini's contemporaries—Umberto Giordano (1867–1948), Pietro Mascagni (1863–1945), Ruggiero Leoncavallo (1858–1919)—bogged down in the almost impossible task of creating a significant operatic parallel to the literary realism of Sardou or Verga. The remarkable success of *Cavalleria rusticana* and *I Pagliacci* and the exceptional ability of Puccini to overcome the inherent contradictions in the so-called realistic opera (which even Puccini deserted at the end of his life) misled a great many composers into thinking that a popular post-Puccini style was possible; it was not. Outside of the world of musical comedy, Puccini's operatic style has had dozens of imitators but few consequents of note. George Gershwin's *Porgy and Bess* (1935) stands apart; it remains, in spite of its ambitions, a masterpiece of musical comedy—not necessarily an inferior or less significant category but one which demands consideration under a different heading. The Puccini-ism of Gian-Carlo Menotti (b. 1911) is not merely musical: Menotti thinks of musical theater in terms of function, space, dramatic incident, and structure in much the same way that Puccini did, even when his subjects are most divergent. Menotti's theater is not always "realistic," but it is contemporary in its subject matter and its concerns; his particular musical talent enables him to create orchestral and vocal parts which heighten the dramatic context.

THE WAGNERIAN TRADITION AND EXPRESSIONIST OPERA

For all the significance of "The Music of the Future" at the end of the nineteenth and the beginning of the twentieth century, the essentials of the Wagnerian theatrical concept remained more or less the exclusive property of Wagner. A great many "Wagnerian" operas were written in Wagner's day and afterwards; none of them need concern us here. The possibilities of a development in the operatic theater out of the direct inheritance of Wagnerian style are represented—indeed exhausted—in the work of a single composer, Richard Strauss. As we have seen, Strauss extended Wagnerian contrapuntal chromaticism to the edge of atonality in *Salome* and *Elektra* and then backed away. The rich orchestral and vocal web of *Der Rosenkavalier* is Wagnerian in technique but classical and tonal in subject matter and style. From a certain point of view, *Ariadne auf Naxos* is actually a long dialogue—a conjunction of oppositions—concerning expressive freedom and classical form. Strauss's later operas are often concerned with this kind of opposition, an aspect which enhances their contemporary intellectual interest but which weakens them in the theater. His later musical style coalesces around an expanded contrapuntal tonality, diatonic and even functional in the old way, but freely moving with shifting triads and seventh chords sliding through the entire chromatic range; it is a kind of super-enharmonic diatonicism in which all the implications of chromaticism are present, not necessarily in detail at all, but on a grand scale.

The later operas of Strauss, whatever their final value may be, stand apart from the mainstreams of twentieth-century development; *Salome* and *Elektra,* on the other hand, are key works. Aside from the huge apparatus of post-Wagnerian technique, these dramas are remarkable for their concentration of means and materials and their penetrating psychological subject matter. The two aspects—which are not unrelated—mark a fundamental departure from the Wagnerian esthetic, which is slow, developmental, and narrative in plan, schematic and mythic in subject matter. Where Wagner may use 136 measures to unfold and explicate an idea as simple as a tonic triad (in the prelude to *Das Rheingold*), Strauss concentrates a whole mass of conflicting motives, a dense, contrasting harmonic motion, and elaborate rhythmic and orchestral textures into a relatively few minutes; what happens in Wagner as a sequence of events occurs in Strauss as simultaneities or as a quick dialogue of opposites. From this point of view, *Salome* and, especially, *Elektra* are difficult works to hear; they seem to be full of unsorted detail, of half-phrases without consequents, of tensions and energies never fully released. In a sense, the big shape of these works is neither a musical form nor, in the conventional sense, a dramatic one; the structure of both (excluding the irrelevant and banal insertion of "The Dance of the Seven Veils" in *Salome*) is psychological. Such a concentrated psychological form with its word-for-word setting, its constant opposition of conflicting elements, and its rapid, intense pulse does not really exist in Wagner although its

Richard Strauss as John the Baptist. Caricature by George Villa. Meyer Collection, Paris. Reproduction forbidden.

strictly musical techniques may seem at first to be superficially Wagnerian; Wagner approached it perhaps only in isolated sections such as Tristan's monologue at the beginning of the last act of *Tristan und Isolde*. It
exists in a limited way in late Verdi, and the clearest nineteenth-century
prototypes are to be found in Mussorgsky. But with Strauss the form is
essentially new and, one would be tempted to say, as valid in twentieth-
century—one would almost say Freudian—terms as the psychological
novel. Yet Strauss quickly abandoned the genre and, in the theater at
least, the idea seems to have had only one direct and significant consequent: Schoenberg's *Erwartung*, with its single character and its intense,
free, associative, atonal form.

All musical form is, of course, in some sense psychological, but
music resists literal verbal-psychological interpretations; the very specific
psychological, asymmetrical "free-association" form of *Erwartung* made
it impossible to duplicate or use as a model. Nevertheless, the experience
of this kind of form and expression—musical structure whose impulses
and tensions reflect, parallel, or suggest by analogy psychological states
and conflicts—had a profound effect on the music of Schoenberg and, particularly, of Alban Berg. These elements are apparent in Schoenberg's
later operas *Die Glückliche Hand* (1913), *Von Heute auf Morgen* (1928),
and even *Moses und Aron* (2 acts completed 1932; unfinished); they play
essential roles in Berg's *Wozzeck* (1914–1921) and *Lulu* (1928–1934), both
of which are thus transformed from mere social and symbolic documents
to intense studies of the human condition. The classical forms of *Wozzeck*
—the sonatas, variations, and passacaglias into which the individual
scenes are molded—are not at all arbitrary but form the tight, tense
frames which push against and hold in place the inner developing form
of the detail. In the same way, the massive, cyclical structure of *Lulu*
(poorly represented, unfortunately, by the incomplete published version)
parallels the mythic and symbolic content of the work and surrounds—in
a sense, realizes on another plane—the intense, personal, gruesome, scab-
rous, or comic detail of the work.

A post-Wagnerian, post-Bergian style has more or less followed
the diffusion of twelve-tone music (discussed in Chapter 11). This line of
operatic development generally employs subjects of contemporary interest, a non-tonal or freely tonal style with chromatic or twelve-tone techniques, and long chromatic vocal lines alternating with angular lines and
Sprechstimme. The musical motion is generally continuous, in the tradition of Wagnerian "endless melody," but more condensed, more "expressionist," more psychologically oriented; in the manner of Berg, symphonic
or other traditional forms underlie the structure. Many of these works are
highly symbolic and, in one way or another, comment on modern life or
the human condition.

Ernst Krenek's (b. 1900) *Karl V* was the first major twelve-tone opera to be produced outside of the original Schoenberg circle. *II Prigioniero* of Luigi Dallapiccola (b. 1904) was one of the earliest outside of the German-speaking world. But the most important younger theater composer in this vein is Hans Werner Henze (b. 1926). *König Hirsch, Boulevard Solitude, Der Prinz von Hamburg, Elegy for Young Lovers, The Young Lords,* and *The Bassarids*—the last three to texts by W. H. Auden and Chester Kallmann—tend to merge the twelve-tone inheritance of Schoenberg and Berg with Stravinskyian formal and rhythmic structure as well as Stravinskyian-Audenesque detachment. More recently, Henze has combined radical politics and a somewhat more varied musical palette with some theatrical and musical experimentation in music-theater forms (*The Raft of the Medusa, the Tedious Way to the Flat of Natasha Frightful*).

There is a fair body of Central European works in this tradition, including operas by Wolfgang Fortner (b. 1907; *Blood Wedding*); Rolf Liebermann (b. 1910; *School for Wives*), and Gottfried von Einem (b. 1918; *The Trial, Dantons Tod*). Boris Blacher (b. 1903; *Abstract Opera No. 1; Romeo und Julia*), Werner Egk (b. 1901; *Der Revisor* and *The Inspector General*), and Nicolas Nabokov (*The Holy Devil*) are more distantly related. Two important American composers whose work ranks with European efforts in this are Roger Sessions (b. 1896; *The Trial of Lucullus, Montezuma*) and Hugo Weisgall (b. 1912; *The Stronger, The Tenor, Six Characters in Search of an Author, Athaliah*). The Argentinian Alberto Ginastera has developed an operatic style of considerable effectiveness by combining a post-Bergian twelve-tone and serial style with highly melodramatic stage material in the Verdian tradition: *Don Rodrigo, Bomarzo, Beatrix Cenci*.

In addition to the works that are directly heir to the Central European tradition, there were a number of important theater pieces composed between the wars that fall under an extended definition of the term "expressionism." In these pieces, intense, internal psychological conflicts are represented externally by certain violent, striking, artistic materials whose shape grows out of conflict, paradox, contradiction, and psychological conflict. Bartók's opera *Bluebeard's Castle* and his ballet-pantomime *The Miraculous Mandarin* belong here, as does Busoni's *Doktor Faust* (1916–1924), in subject matter if not musical technique, which is Wagnerian. By an extension of the term one might also include a number of works which relate to expressionist theater—Prokofiev's *The Gambler* and *The Flaming Angel,* Shostakovich's *Lady Macbeth of Mtsensk,* Hindemith's *Cardillac* and *Mathis der Maler,* Krenek's *Jonny spielt auf* (1925–1926), Milhaud's *Le Pauvre matelot* (first produced in 1927), *La Création du monde* and *Christophe Colomb,* even Louis Gruenberg's *The Emperor Jones* (1932). All these share, at the very least, the use of anti-realistic, "expressionist" techniques to represent and communicate some kind of symbolic, social, moral, or philosophical meaning. None of these works is psychologically oriented in a profound way, just as none of them is atonal or involved in the psychological significance of new materials and new forms. They are all operatic in the usual sense and they all deal with essentially contemporary problems with means that —however tonal—are certainly of the twentieth century; nevertheless, they have all remained essentially isolated expressions.

THE MIXED GENRE AND CHAMBER OPERA

The history of opera has often been described as a continuous struggle between the dominance of language and the dominance of music. Even more significantly, the problem of musical theater has always been the problem of form. Every composer who writes for the theater faces the problem of resolving his ideas in dramatic forms or self-contained musical ones. The solutions need not be mutually exclusive: Verdi's and Mozart's forms are musical but they are hardly undramatic. Nevertheless, the tendency of post-Wagnerian opera—well into the twentieth century—was towards dramatic, "expressive" structures, and this seemed, even for a composer like Schoenberg, an open road leading to the development of new forms for new ideas. Stravinsky, on the other hand, closed his forms, eliminated psychological development, and created the prototype of the one really new and successful music-theater form of the first part of the century.

The fact that so many of Stravinsky's major works were written for the theater is often overlooked. The ballet, of course, occupies the first place: the famous Diaghilev ballets—including *Pulcinella*—and later the "classical" ballets and the collaboration with Balanchine culminating in the remarkable *Agon* of 1957. The Stravinskyian ballet—or, one should say, the Stravinsky-Balanchine ballet—is characterized by the development of equal, abstract closed forms of movement and sound which in no way intersect or "express" each other but remain completely independent if parallel.

In addition to his ballets, however, Stravinsky also created a unique and important music theater built on closed forms and on abstraction—one would almost say ritualization—of content. Interestingly enough, while the forms remain closed, the materials are open and various. Thus, *Renard* uses an on-stage chamber orchestra, motionless singers, and actor-mimes; *L'Histoire du soldat* replaces the singing with narration and dialogue and adds dance. *Les Noces* uses an orchestra of percussion and pianos with solo and choral singing and dance-mime. *Oedipus Rex*—designated an "opera-oratorio" and often staged today—uses a narrator, orchestra, chorus, and soloists and is realized scenically in a series of masked marmoreal stage tableaux. *Perséphone* and *The Flood* (1962), originally created for television but also staged, similarly combine a variety of techniques. Stravinsky has also written three operas that use scene, singing, and stage action in the more-or-less usual way: *Le Rossignol,* an early work in the Russian-French manner (begun in 1909 but finished only after *Le Sacre*), *Mavra,* a one-act burlesque not far removed in manner from *L'Histoire* and *Renard,* and *The Rake's Progress* (1951), Stravinsky's farewell to opera and his final and most complete homage to classical form. In all of these works—after *Le Rossignol,* at least—Stravinsky abstracted the essence of an experience and the essence of a form, and in this process of abstraction he created perhaps the only new and workable musico-dramatic form of the first half-century. The importance of the Stravinskyian mixed-genre theater has perhaps been underestimated; the mixing of means in the context of schematic, prototypical, neo-classical forms; the abstraction of classical themes—musical and literary-dramatic; and the treatment of theatrical experience as a kind of ritual embody conceptions of modern musical theater which remain vital.

Some of the more superficial aspects of Stravinsky's theatrical conceptions had an immediate and important effect: simplification of treatment and reprise of tonal techniques; use of limited and practical means; stylized treatment of popular subject matter; clear, closed forms. Exactly like *L'Histoire,* Honegger's *Le Roi David* was written in small, closed forms on a "popular" or folkish text originally for a small Swiss travelling theatrical company; only later was it amplified to its full orchestral form. Milhaud's *Les Chóephores,* based on Aeschylus, and his tiny *opéras minutes* are highly stylized treatments of classical subjects. Poulenc's operas—the farce *Les Mamelles de Tirésias,* Cocteau's monodrama *La Voix humaine,* and the rather grand and impressive *Dialogues des Carmélites*—use clear, fastidious tonal techniques in contexts of great simplicity and directness. The clearest representative of Stravinskyian techniques on the modern stage, however, is Carl Orff, whose musico-theatrical style is based on tonal simplicity and directness carried to an extreme point. Works like *Carmina Burana* (a Stravinskyian type of scenic-dance oratorio) and its companions *Catulli Carmina* and *Il Trionfo di Afrodite* are vast expansions of one small part of the Stravinskyian esthetic—stylistic abstractions from *Les Noces* expanded to fill up an entire musical *Weltanschauung.* The later operatic works, such as *Der Mond, Die Kluge,* and *Antigonae,* are conceived more completely in terms of dramatic planes and juxtapositions. In *Antigonae* a huge percussion apparatus punctuates music of chant and intonation. Ostinato and rhythmic outburst are set against simple melodic curves, the whole structured in immobile blocks and layers.

The sheer size of the physical apparatus of nineteenth-century opera inevitably provoked a reaction in the twentieth century; the new

simplicity and concision of form and expression were accompanied
by an enormous reduction of means and scope. Strauss, surprisingly, was an important pioneer here, although his *Ariadne auf Naxos,*
scored for an orchestra of twenty-three musicians, now generally appears
in the context of "grand opera." Works like *L'Histoire, Mavra,* and
Renard actually established a new genre of short chamber opera that was
both practical and appealing. Hindemith (who, in *Wir bauen eine Stadt*
of 1930, wrote a tiny "opera" for performance by young children) composed several chamber operas in the 1920's—notably *Neues vom Tage* and
Hin und Zurück—with brief, lively, contemporary subjects and musical
matter. Kurt Weill's early operas are similar—short, bustling, concise and
small-scaled, freely diatonic and tonal in a serious, lively, contrapuntal
way. Later, under the influence of Brecht, Weill definitively turned to
popular forms. Like Stravinsky, Weill wanted to re-create the "number"
opera concept, but in the context of a meaningful musical play filled with
the popular music of the cabaret. With Weill, the divergent streams of
popular musical theater and opera merge in a musical theater of social
consciousness.

The Brecht-Weill theater, like the Stravinskyian, is anti-Wagnerian and anti-expressionist. Whereas Stravinsky generalizes and arche-
typifies to the point of abstraction, Brecht and Weill are specific and
engagé. The form is that of the moralistic entertainment; social commitment is expressed, paradoxically, through irony and detachment, qualities
that Weill caught perfectly in his neo-cabaret style. Expressionism is
cathartic in an Aristotelian sense, but Brecht and Weill were not interested in catharsis; their aim was to stir people, not so much to "move"
them in the theater as to send them out of the theater ready to act. Thus
Weill's use of popular style—his brilliant, bitter, deadpan, low-life melodic
style and his intentionally brutal and awkward rhythmic and instrumental
settings—represents neither commercial populism or Stravinskyian transformation but is the musical counterpart of the Brechtian theater of
alienation.

The Three-Penny Opera and, to a lesser degree, *Mahagonny* were
enormously successful and continue to hold the stage; some of the other
Brecht-Weill pieces are revived now and then. However, this kind of
theater has not had as great an influence as might have been expected.
Both Brecht and Weill had to flee Germany when the Nazis came to
power, and their collaboration came to an end. After the war, Brecht
went back to East Germany where he worked with the composers Hanns
Eisler (1898–1962) and Paul Dessau (b. 1894). Weill became active in
American musical theater, and works like *Street Scene, Knickerbocker
Holiday* and *Lady in the Dark* had a major influence on the course of
American lyric drama. The concept of a serious popular theater built on

contemporary themes of social significance, using popular, accessible musical and theatrical means, was much discussed in America beginning in the 1930's, and there is a direct line between Weill, Marc Blitzstein (*The Cradle Will Rock, No for an Answer, Regina*), and Leonard Bernstein (b. 1918; *Wonderful Town, Candide, West Side Story*). (The prototype of *West Side Story* is, recognizably, *Street Scene*.) From time to time there have been attempts to revive or renew the concept of Brechtian musical theater in works like the William Bolcom-Arnold Weinstein *Dynamite Tonight* or recent efforts by some of the younger English composers. It may well be that the future of music theater will involve some kind of reconciliation of latter-day multi-media and music-theater ideas (see Chapter 17) with Brechtian theater.

OPERA IN ENGLISH

The lack of success of opera in English is a complex phenomenon having nothing to do with the supposed lack of suitability of the language. Opera as a social institution has always been an exotic in both England and America; the native forms are ballad opera, operetta, and the musical. The only English-language composers to achieve any extended success in the opera house are Benjamin Britten and Gian-Carlo Menotti. Britten's *Peter Grimes, A Midsummer Night's Dream, The Rape of Lucretia,* and *The Turn of the Screw* (the last two chamber operas often adapted to larger operatic stages) renovate tradition in contemporary English-language terms. The starting point is the ongoing music drama, but Britten—like Berg but with a more tonal, neo-classical orientation—has imposed on it forms of classical severity. In addition to works of the grand and chamber opera type, Britten has also experimented with medieval and Eastern forms, in *Noye's Fludde,* based on a miracle play, and *Curlew River,* based on a Japanese Noh play.

Verismo opera, which had no important continuation in Europe, was kept alive in America by Menotti and a few American followers of him. Most of these works are suffocated by the past and by their dominant themes of nostalgia and regret. A few, like Carlisle Floyd's *Susannah,* have had some success in integrating *verismo* with American themes and musical matter, but there has been no long-range development in this direction. More in the vein is the "folk opera" tradition—really derived from Broadway and pop music—apparently inaugurated by Gershwin and continued by Kurt Weill in his American works. Douglas Moore's (1893–1969) *The Ballad of Baby Doe* is a successful latter-day example. The Virgil Thomson and Gertrude Stein collaborations—*Four Saints in*

Three Acts and *The Mother of Us All*—mix folk and popular ideas, a syntactical treatment of verbal and musical elements, a kind of popular surrealism, and what can only be described as an anticipation of minimalism (see Chapter 17) to produce unique results.

The Broadway musical itself seems to have come through a kind of golden age—Rodgers and Hart, Rodgers and Hammerstein, Cole Porter, Weill, Lerner and Loewe—and has perhaps passed its prime. Its more recent successes have drawn on the past (*Cabaret*, in which the influence of Weill's pre-Broadway works looms large) or the vitality of pop (*Hair, Jesus Christ Superstar*). There has been much discussion about the so-called "rock opera" or "rock musical"; whether this is a new form which will rescue opera and the musical can be doubted. It would seem that the time for new music theater forms, incorporating some really new kinds of synthesis, is ripe.

BIBLIOGRAPHICAL NOTES

Probably the best book in English on Puccini is Mosco Carner's (London, 1958). Norman Del Mar's Strauss project has already been mentioned as has the Mitchell-Keller book on Britten. The October-November, 1952, issue of *Musical Opinion* (London) was devoted to "Britten, Strauss, and the Future of Opera." Joseph Kerman's *Opera as Drama* (New York, 1956) is a general essay which includes contemporary problems; but there is surprisingly little material of note anywhere on opera and musical theater as popular forms—Menotti and neo-verismo, Weill, Blitzstein and Bernstein, the Broadway musical and the off-Broadway Brechtian show. The only musical publication to cover musical theater in all of its aspects over a period of years was the American magazine *Modern Music* in the years of its existence, 1926–1946 (see the author's article in *Perspectives of New Music* already cited; also the magazine itself, *passim*). There is a collection of essays on *Stravinsky in the Theatre* (ed. Minna Lederman, New York, 1949). The program of the 1964 Maggio Musicale Fiorentino, which was devoted to "expressionism," contains a number of studies (in Italian) concerning "expressionist theater." George Perle has published several articles on Alban Berg's *Wozzeck* and *Lulu* (see the Columbia University *Music Forum*, v. 1, 1966; *Journal of the American Musicological Society*, Summer, 1964; *Music Review*, November, 1965; etc.) and is working on a major study of these operas.

Brecht's still pertinent ideas on music and theater along with pertinent discussions of "epic theater," "alienations," and the notion of "gest" appear in *Brecht on Theater*, a collection of essays and notes edited and translated by John Willett (New York, 1964). Brecht's collaborations with Hindemith, Weill, Eisler, and Dessau are referred to in this volume.

part four

Atonality and Twelve-tone Music

TEN

THE VIENNESE SCHOOL

SCHOENBERG AND THE TWELVE-TONE IDEA

After *Pierrot lunaire*, Op. 21, and the *Four Orchestral Songs*, Op. 22, both written on the eve of World War I, no new work of Schoenberg appeared for almost ten years, although for part of that time he worked on a large oratorio, *Die Jacobsleiter*. All of the composers who participated in the revolutions of the first twelve or fifteen years of the century moved afterwards toward some kind of artistic, expressive, and/or intellectual synthesis of the new materials in new but clear and comprehensive forms. Schoenberg, whose atonal works of 1910–1915 represent the most thorough-going renovation and extension of the musical material, proposed the most radical and thorough consolidation. In *Die Jacobsleiter* he worked his way towards a systematic exploitation of the complete gamut of tempered chromatic sounds. The oratorio was never completed

—perhaps because Schoenberg discovered the basic conception only through the art of composition and each step forward seemed to imply a recasting of what had come before. But the Piano Pieces, Op. 23, and the *Serenade,* Op. 24 (both completed in 1923, contain twelve-tone music; and the Piano Suite, Op. 25 (1921–1923), and Wind Quintet, Op. 26 (1924), are complete twelve-tone conceptions.[1]

Schoenberg's twelve-tone procedure is a synthesis of two formal ideas which are actually separable and which have in fact been used independently; both ideas appear in embryo—not necessarily connected, and more or less informally—in the "atonal" music of Schoenberg himself, and of Berg and Webern. The first is the continuous use of patterns which contain all of the twelve pitches; the second is the organization of pitch materials according to a consistent order principle. Thus in Schoenberg's "classical" formulation of the technique, each piece is based on a given ordering of the twelve tempered pitches—abstracted (without regard for octave or register) as the twelve-tone series or row[2]—and the work itself is an exposition or realization of this order structure. Schoenberg thought of musical space as multi-dimensional and as having essential unity. Thus any given pattern of notes—and, specifically, a series of twelve different pitches—can appear unbroken and without internal change (like a physical object being rotated in space) in four forms: forward, backward, upside-down, and upside-down backward (see Appendix; Example 10-1).

The question of the repetition of tones in twelve-tone music is much misunderstood. Clearly, in the underlying ordering, each class of pitches (regardless of octave) can appear once and only once if all twelve pitches are to be always "rotated." In the actual compositional realization, however, small repetitions of notes or groups of notes often appear without disrupting the larger cycles of twelve notes. Furthermore, since the twelve-note groupings may appear as purely melodic voices in counterpoint (each line made up of constantly revolving cycles of the basic row), or as blocks of chords (e.g., three chords of four notes each or four chords of three notes), or as some combination of the above, certain duplications may appear between parts; this, however, can also be avoided by distributing the twelve notes between the melodic and harmonic parts or by conceiving the music in aggregates of sound in such a way that the complete twelve-note groupings constantly succeed each other in small time segments. All of these questions are, in the end, compositional mat-

---

[1] Apparently Schoenberg first formulated his twelve-tone ideas in precise form in 1921. It is not clear whether the last piece of Op. 23 or the first of Op. 25 was the first actual twelve-tone composition.

[2] The terms "series" and "row" (hence "serial" and "row" music) are used interchangeably. Milton Babbitt has proposed the mathematical term "set." Twelve-tone (or "twelve-note") music is sometimes called dodecaphony, the adjectival form of which is "dodecaphonic".

Portrait of Arnold Schoenberg by Oskar Kokoschka. Reproduced by permission of Annie Knize.

ters; they do not necessarily disturb the basic "twelve-toneness" of the conception.

Schoenberg's first tendency was to use the row melodically and contrapuntally, a technique which produces a kind of ongoing variational form. The variation principle, perhaps the oldest and most basic formal device in music, is not particularly associated with functional tonality (it was used long before tonality), and it remains a basic technique in many forms of popular and non-Western music. Oddly enough, it did not play an important role in early twentieth-century music but reappears in various forms in the new syntheses of the 1920's and 1930's; it is not without significance that some important works or movements of Stravinsky, Schoenberg, Berg, and Webern are explicit variations, and the technique appears in other guises throughout the period (see Appendix; Example 10-2).

Schoenberg also attempted to integrate the harmonic elements of his music through chordal groups fashioned from the row; and this, in turn, helped produce new melodic elements derived from but not restricted to the exact sequence of the original row (see Appendix; Example 10-3).

The mere counting of the notes of the row in a twelve-tone work is in itself meaningless without a clear understanding of the way in which the sound of the resulting harmonic and melodic combinations penetrates the entire piece; the way in which the parts intersect and relate forward (motion, energy) and backward (recall, association); the role of repetition, of changing register, of accent, and of dynamic in defining the phrase-structure, which itself is intimately related to the twelve-tone process; the way in which the piece moves from one type of structure and organization to another, e.g., from a static idea to a developmental one and then back again. The twelve-tone technique is not a form imposed from the outside, it *is* the piece; that is, it is the way the ideas of the piece take shape in time—at once, the content and the form.

A great deal of discussion has centered on the precise definition of the role that the twelve-tone idea should and does play in musical composition. Schoenberg himself rejected the term "system"; he preferred the word "method," in the sense of procedure, although in his actual composition it probably functioned more as a mode of musical thinking analogous in certain ways to tonality. The twelve-tone principle was, for him, a way of organizing musical thought that is coherent, that controls every aspect of every piece but is uniquely established anew by each piece, and that can generate appropriate and organic forms by relating every aspect of a piece to an overall and underlying conception. The mere arrangements of the row in a piece do not constitute the whole piece anymore than the E♭ tonality of Beethoven's Third Symphony equals the whole "Eroica"; but the twelve-tone conception in a Schoenberg piece—like the tonal conception in Beethoven—pervades the whole, gives it its characteristic sonorous and intellectual qualities, and permits the composer to express his ideas through a big, coherent, and organic form. To say that is to say a great deal. Schoenberg was perhaps the true classicist among contemporary composers because he understood the underlying principles of classical form and discovered a viable equivalent in modern terms.

Schoenberg set about establishing the universality and scope of his new art immediately. With the exception of the choruses of Op. 27 and 28, all of the early twelve-tone compositions are pieces of considerable size which evoke their classical equivalents not simply by references or parallels in texture, rhythm, or form but because they also embody a unity of thought and expression in terms of large-scale statement, process, and resolution. Thus in a multi-movement work like the Piano Suite, Op. 25, or the Septet, Op. 29 (1926), the basic material is realized in a series of different guises, each revealing aspects of the underlying idea, each with its own possibilities of discovery, elucidation, and expression. In the Wind Quintet, Op. 26, and the Third String Quartet, Op. 30 (1927), the twelve-tone ideas become subjects for development. The row—or significant segments from it—generates very specific shapes which, in turn, develop and interrelate over wide time-spans to make long and expressive structures formed, for the most part, at the very outer limits of performer and listener capabilities. The row itself does not really function as a theme nor, certainly, as a scale or mode (as it does sometimes in Berg's music), but as a set of materials, a complex of relationships, offering enormous possibilities to the ordered imagination that can master them. Schoenberg was able to rediscover organic large form—classical by analogy only, and not necessarily "neo-classical" at all; in Schoenberg's mature, large-scaled works, the big form is an essential and inevitable result of the working-out of the implications of a rich basic material.

At the end of the 1920's and specifically with the *Variations for Orchestra,* Op. 31, of 1928, Schoenberg centered his concern on the direct derivation of a form out of the implications of the basic material. Although the general plan of the *Variations* is traditional (introduction, theme, variations, coda), the conception of these variations is both universal and yet specific and unique to the work. The variations themselves grow out of the conflict between the generality of the basic material (the intervals and relationships which appear in the introduction in fragmented, unordered form) and its very specific realization as a row-based theme. The two very different conceptions of the row—on the one hand, as generative material far beneath the surface (functioning, as Schoenberg believed, in a manner somewhat analogous to tonality and not necessarily consciously perceived) and on the other, as thematic material—are here very deliberately juxtaposed; this is, so to speak, the dialectic of the piece. With each new variation-transformation, the thematic character of the row becomes again more and more generalized until, in the long and remarkable finale, virtually a new formal level is reached; in this finale, the idea of transformation has been taken up into an ongoing twelve-tone structure. The theme, as it were, is absorbed into the row idea which generated it in the first place. Thus the work moves from the specific towards the universal, from musical idea towards structure, from "inspiration" towards intellectual resolution.

In *Von Heute auf Morgen*, Schoenberg's Op. 32, and in the opera *Moses und Aron*, the completed portion of which was written in the early 1930's, the twelve-tone method was applied, apparently for the first time, to music for the theater. *Von Heute auf Morgen* treats a light, contemporary subject. *Moses und Aron* has a rather lofty philosophical text by Schoenberg himself, full of intellectual oppositions and dualisms which are reflected in the music itself. One curious thing about *Moses und Aron* is that although only two acts were set—the brief third act remains only in text—the existing music is complete in thought and structure; the work is a unity which generates a richness and diversity of ideas and means: huge divided singing-and-*Sprechstimme* choruses; the solo voice of Aron and the spoken part of Moses; a large and masterfully handled orchestra with a wide range of colors. The opposition between rich, even sensual variety and color on the one hand and a complex intellectual unity on the other[3] is a direct image of the philosophical issues which animate the text.

The forms of the *Accompaniment to a Film Scene*, Op. 34 (1929–1930), are also presumably dramatic, but this *Begleitungsmusik* was written for an imaginary cinema; the events of the scene are purely internal musical events, and the "dramatic" form is nothing but an expressive function of the ideas and the material.

In 1933, after the advent of Hitler, Schoenberg was forced to leave Germany. In the same year, he came to the United States, where he remained for the rest of his life—principally in California, where he taught at the University of California at Los Angeles. A number of his American works show a marked or partial return to a tonal idiom: a Suite for string orchestra (1934), a *Theme and Variations* for band, Op. 43, (1943), and the *Variations on a Recitative* for organ, Op. 40, (1941) are practical pieces, almost *Gebrauchsmusik;* and works like the *Ode to Napoleon* of 1942 and *A Survivor from Warsaw* of 1947 use tonal references in tension with twelve-tone techniques. On the other hand, the Fourth String Quartet (1936) and the Violin and Piano Concertos (1934–1936 and 1942) are large-scale, thematic, wholly twelve-tone structures in which the technique becomes fluent and pliable, focused in a way that parallels the role played by tonality in similar classical forms.

Schoenberg's attitude towards this material in no way implies a return from or a renunciation of his early ideas; quite the contrary, it

---

[3] Musically resolved in the existing two acts; hence the impossibility of music for the third, which was to demonstrate the triumph of the latter over the former.

suggests rather a widening of the possibilities of the technique. In certain early works of Schoenberg and other twelve-tone composers there is a conscious attempt to avoid any combination of tones which might suggest a tonal reference or center. Later on, this rather arbitrary rule of thumb was superseded or bypassed. (The reasons for banning, say, a major triad in a twelve-tone piece are, presumably, psychological rather than musical, and, in fact, there are some very successful twelve-tone pieces built largely on triads, e.g., the Webern String Quartet.) Schoenberg expanded his conception of the possibilities of twelve-tone technique enormously in the later part of his life, and very late works like the String Trio, Op. 45 (1946), and the *Phantasy* for violin and piano, Op. 47 (1949), evolve distinctive forms out of new material. Schoenberg came to think of the row material not as a specifically linear ordering but as a series of groupings of pitches and intervals whose potentialities would be revealed by the process of the piece (see Appendix, Example 10-4). These techniques, which bind harmonic and linear ideas closely together with timbre, dynamic, rhythmic, and phrase provide a sense of continuity and even inevitability within a musical material which is constantly changing, constantly in motion, yet always basically the same. This linking technique—a kind of continuous development—suggests the possibilities of strict forms which are nevertheless open at the far end, forms in which everything is intertwined and in which the motion from one sound to another, from one end of the piece to the other, seems inevitable yet remains, until it is actually realized, unforeseen.

Schoenberg's music, unlike that of his pupils Berg and Webern, has never been popular and it probably never will be. All his life Schoenberg faced obstinate incomprehension on the part of musicians and the public, but probably the deepest and most ironic challenge has come from the avant-gardists who have posthumously charged him with having failed to realize the consequences of his own revolution, with having remained a classicist all his life, faithful to the traditional notions of what constitutes a piece of music, and with having failed to extend the concept of serial technique beyond the organization of the twelve tempered chromatic pitches. There is more than a grain of truth in the charge; Schoenberg was, in deep sense, a classicist, and of all the early twentieth-century masters, the one most involved in re-discovering the deep and universal significance of the great tradition. But the charge that he was not sensitive to the implications of what he was doing is not just. It is true that Schoenberg's music was composed out of the traditional ideals of music-making and that it proposed no new context for musical communication; but that is equally true of most twentieth-century music. It is also true that Schoenberg wrote cause-and-effect music and that John

Cage and even Karlheinz Stockhausen do not. But Einstein's physics is hardly that of Newton, and cause and effect in Schoenberg is scarcely what it was in Rameau or Brahms.

Just as Schoenberg was the first to discover and explore a rich and complex new sonorous universe, he was the first to discover valid laws which operate in that universe. The parallel with scientific inquiry would have pleased Schoenberg, although he himself came out of the rather more dubiously scientific tradition of Hegel and historical determinism: he thought of himself as having, like Hegel or Marx, discovered immutable laws about the process of history which made his conquest of total chromaticism and his twelve-tone procedure a historical necessity. But it is not necessary to accept the analogy between the process of inquiry and discovery on the one hand and that of creation on the other (although the analogy has, interestingly enough, been recognized in many recent studies of the philosophy and psychology of scientific inquiry). Schoenberg's early music is the fruit of what we might call analytic inquiry: the refusal to accept traditional hypotheses; the discovery of a whole new set of realities; the creative exploration of the artistic, intellectual, and psychological significance of these new realities, "tested" in creative terms in a series of works of art. His later music is, in the best sense, synthetic—the statement of new unifying hypotheses which relate these realities in terms of a creative synthesis to underlying artistic, psychological, and intellectual truths. As we shall see, these processes have been recapitulated in avant-garde thought since World War II.

BERG AND WEBERN

Schoenberg's influence on Berg was, in one sense, decisive, yet Berg never took from Schoenberg any more than he needed to realize his own ideas. Thus, although Berg's later work is impossible to imagine without the influence of the twelve-tone idea, he never wrote a really thorough-going twelve-tone work. His *Chamber Concerto* for violin and piano with thirteen instruments (1923–1925) is not twelve-tone at all; it is, to be sure, full of complicated numerical patterns, but these are of a type characteristic of Berg, not of Schoenberg. The influence of Schoenberg is discernible in the complex and rich web of structural relationships derived from the initial statement of the material—not a twelve-tone row but a three-part subject based on those letters in the names "Schoenberg," "Berg," and "Webern" which have musical equivalents. Out of this unpromising and arbitrary material, Berg creates a big three-movement structure: a concerto movement with piano solo, one for violin solo, and a finale for both soloists. Like many of Berg's works, the *Concerto* tries to be inclusive; it is long and full of a great variety of ideas, materials, and techniques. The big shape of the piece emerges—not without problems which present formidable obstacles to the performers—from the free, disassociated character of Berg's imagination and the conscious restraints of form and technique that he imposed on himself with an almost mystical fervor.

The *Lyric Suite* for string quartet (1925–1926) is, in its individual movements at least, less ambitious, but by turning his imaginative enterprise to a series of shorter, characteristic movements Berg was able to create expressive structures that grow naturally out of the ideas themselves. These ideas are not only themes in the traditional sense but also colors and expressive shapes, an aspect which Berg emphasizes by qualifying the tempo indications with strong, associative "color" words: *Allegretto gioviale, Largo desolato, Presto delirando, Trio estatico,* and so forth. Two of the movements are twelve-tone; however, Berg uses the technique not so much as a structural principle but as a way to "color" the music from the inside. Thus the famous *Allegro misterioso* is the most elaborately twelve-tone movement Berg ever wrote, but all the careful, precise manipulations on the printed page are no more (and, to be sure, no less) than a great whispering, rustling, rushing murmur.

The concert aria *Der Wein,* after poetry by Baudelaire (1929), is Berg's first and only attempt at writing a large concert work completely unified in row technique, but even here the function of the row is special and peculiarly Bergian. The series, which begins with an ascending D-minor scale, works not so much as a theme nor, on the other hand, as underpinning but much more simply: as a kind of mode in the old, original meaning of that term. The ancient modes—or, for example, the Indian *raga*—are not "scales" or "tonalities" in the modern sense but repertoires of melodic formulas, often associated with specific kinds of rhythmic ideas, embellishments, and tone colors. Thus an Indian *raga* is not a theme, and there may be no definitive, meaningful way of writing it down as a "scale"; but a piece is instantly recognizable as being "in" a certain *raga* by its characteristic turns of phrase. Berg used the twelve-tone row in just this way (so did Schoenberg, but secondarily). In the opera *Lulu* this becomes the basis of a rich and complex technique of dramatic and psychological identification.

The text of *Lulu* was drawn by Berg himself from two plays of Franz Wedekind; the opera was finished in short-score form, but part of the orchestration of the last act was left incomplete by the composer and the work is known today in a makeshift form consisting of the first two acts and the final scene of the third. This is exceptionally unfortunate because, as George Perle has pointed out, *Lulu* was planned as a symmetrical form, with the third act providing a dramatic climax, psychological realization, a good deal of the intellectual meaning, and a musical recapitulation and resolution. Lulu is a kind of archetypical character, part whore, part Earth-mother; as an incarnation of female sexuality she moves with the sublime inevitability and indifference of Nature through a series of love adventures that are in turn macabre, tragic, comic, grotesque, and sublime. Berg's music is at once specific (it defines the characters by their rows, by the way they sing, even by the orchestral sounds that dog their footsteps) and general (in the way it universalizes an ironic, expressionist theater bordering on the grotesque into a grand tragicomedy).

Berg's last completed work was his Violin Concerto (1935), commissioned by the American violinist Louis Krasner; the work, dedicated to memory of Manon Gropius (the daughter of the architect and Alma Mahler, who was also Berg's patron), became Berg's own monument. The row consists of major and minor triads with a bit of whole-tone scale at the end; thus within the framework of this basic material Berg can make use of the open-string "tuning-up" sound of the violin, some tonal progressions, Viennese waltz motifs, an Austrian folk song, and a Bach chorale (see Appendix; Example 10-5). The intensity and diversity of Berg's ideas come close to shattering their structure; it is almost as if he wanted to charge his music with more expressive weight than it could bear. But the very range of expression, combined with the carefully defined freedom of technique, makes Berg much less of a traditionalist than he has sometimes been made out to be. Berg's obvious references to the past are no more a good model for a new music today than his specific musical personality is a good subject for imitation; but his work remains meaningful because he was able to communicate precise, predetermined, expressive forms that somehow seem to grow out of the wide scope of his creative imagination.

During and after World War I, Webern was occupied with a series of eight consecutive vocal sets, mostly for solo voice and instruments; among these are the songs of Op. 17 (1924), Webern's first twelve-tone works. Webern accepted Schoenberg's ideas neither casually nor quickly; but with the String Trio, Op. 20, of 1927, the Symphony, Op. 21, of the following year, the Quartet for violin, clarinet, tenor saxophone, and piano, Op. 22, of 1930, and the Concerto, Op. 24 (1934) he embraced the strictest kind of twelve-tone procedure and fully incorporated this into his own esthetic (see Appendix; Example 10-6).

From one point of view, Webern's solutions are classical; classical tonal music also had a one-to-one relationship between all aspects of the musical material—or, at any rate, between pitch, rhythm, and the dynamic shape of the phrase—and Webern's musical periods are of the traditional type. The first movement of the Symphony is a rather closely worked (and somewhat arbitrary) sonata form with a repeated exposition, "development," and a careful recapitulation. Many of Webern's later works are sets of variations based on a kind of "song-form" phrase-structure with real antecedent and consequent phrases. A classical sense of balance, symmetry, and stability is present throughout his work.

Webern's tendency to transform and re-create certain aspects of classical tradition is particularly evident in his twelve-tone instrumental works, which are in many ways much less far-reaching and more classically abstract than his earlier "atonal" pieces. To the works mentioned above can be added the Variations for piano, Op. 27 (1936), the String Quartet, Op. 28 (1938), and the Variations for orchestra, Op. 30 (1940). On the other hand, in the later vocal works, and most particularly in *Das Augenlicht,* Op. 26 (1935), and the two cantatas, Op. 29 and 31 (1939, 1941–43), the verbal material and the relationships between solo, choral, and instrumental sound at once seem to suggest a whole new set of problems and solutions. The conceptions of line and of the relationships between line and harmonic structure are new and generate new ideas of organizing expressive musical thoughts; indeed, the very obliteration of the classical distinction between line and harmony (and, to some extent, between pitch, duration, timbre, and intensity), characteristic of the early works of Webern and Schoenberg and later schematized by Webern in his earlier twelve-tone works, is taken up again in these later vocal compositions.

Webern extended serial principles into many musical domains and in such a way as to make his miniature forms a function of the ideas themselves. One superficial influence of Webern on later music was an esthetic of silence and brevity; more profound ones grew out of the organic qualities of his thinking, the sense of a delicately balanced web rather than a linear or dramatic process, and the totality of a work implied from the start yet unforeseen in its unfolding. In spite of the complex implications of Webern's music, its most immediate qualities are clarity and transparency of idea realized within tiny, schematic, and crystalline forms. These qualities are also, in spite of appearances, personal and inimitable. The long-range significance of Webern's work may turn out to be not so much the isolation of the single musical event—the bit of glowing sound set in a starry void—or the consistency and purity of the ideas as the richness of the reconstruction of form. Webern reduced the experience of sound to its essentials; he also demonstrated the possibility of an organic reintegration which evolved from universal prototypes into new and meaningful expressive structures.

BIBLIOGRAPHICAL NOTES

The founding fathers produced surprisingly little in the way of written formulations of the twelve-tone idea. The most important are Schoenberg's lecture "Composition with Twelve Tones" printed in *Style and Idea* (New York, 1950) and transcriptions of some of Webern's lectures published in translation as *The Path to the New Music* (Bryn Mawr, 1963). There has been, however, no shortage of texts from the later generations: Josef Rufer, *Composition with Twelve Notes* (New York, 1954); Ernst Krenek, *Studies in Counterpoint* (New York, 1940); Leopold Spinner, *A Short Introduction to the Technique of Twelve-Tone Composition;* Herbert Eimert, *Lehrbuch der Zwölftontechnik* (Wiesbaden, 1950; also translated into Italian). Most of these are prescriptive teaching abstractions which seldom reflect the reality (and sometimes actually violate the substance) of the music of the Viennese.

There is no generally adequate history of twelve-tone ideas or of the "school." It is now generally agreed that Josef Matthias Hauer's *Zwölftontechnik* (published Vienna, 1926, but developed earlier) and certain early compositions of Nicolay Rosslavetz preceded Schoenberg in arriving at a twelve-tone formulation. The origins of twelve-tone ideas have been discussed by Eimert; by Willi Reich, *Alte und neue Musik* (Zurich, 1952); and by Egon Wellesz, *The Origins of Schoenberg's Twelve-Tone System* (Washington, 1958). The best general discussion of the techniques can be found in Perle's *Serial Composition and Atonality* (3rd ed.; Berkeley and Los Angeles, 1972). Schoenberg's writings have been mentioned earlier; they can be supplemented by Rufer's catalogue of Schoenberg's works (London, 1962, from the German original of 1959), which contains many excerpts from unpublished writings of the composer. There seems to be no generally satisfactory critical assessment of Schoenberg presently in print, although the Schoenberg literature is large and growing. Willi Reich's book on Berg, now available in English (see Chapter 4), supplants the often-cited Redlich biography. An entire issue of *Die Reihe* (No. 2, 1955; tr., Bryn Mawr, 1958) is devoted to articles on and analyses of Webern; the volume of *Kontrapunkte* mentioned in Chapter 4 (No. 5, Walter Kolneder) contains general information as well as discussions of Opp. 1–31. Articles on and analyses of all three of the Viennese can be found in many issues of *Perspectives,* the *Journal of Music Theory, The Score,* and *Melos.*

ELEVEN

THE DIFFUSION
OF TWELVE-TONE MUSIC

Between the two World Wars modern music was often considered to be divided into two major opposing camps: the "neo-classicists" and the "dodecaphonists," Stravinskyians and Schoenberg followers. But after World War II and Schoenberg's death, even Stravinsky became a twelve-tone composer, and an immense number of other, younger composers adopted the method.

The reasons for this shift—which marked the end of an old era as much as the beginning of a new one—are complex. It is not necessary to accept any mystical superiority of twelve-tone music or even any particular notion of historical necessity to recognize that certain ideas have enough innate power and richness to gain, sooner or later, widespread acceptance. One important point is that the twelve-tone idea—in contrast to "neo-classicism"—does not presuppose any particular style. "Neo-classicism," in spite of its superficial ability to absorb many different kinds of contents, appeared as a dead end because it was a style or a specific set of styles located in a particular moment of history. So, indeed, were the "styles" of Schoenberg, Berg, and Webern; but the twelve-tone *con-*

ception by no means required the manner or even the forms employed by its originators.[1] Total chromaticism and the whole range of associated rhythmic, dynamic, and color material offered a rich source of ideas, and the twelve-tone notion of Schoenberg—or some modification of it—suggested a way of handling this material without necessarily adopting a specific idiom. Furthermore—and in spite of Webern's success with small forms—it offered a way of re-creating large forms, which was hardly possible with most of the neo-tonal, non-functional diatonic idioms. Historically, the creation of the large form was precisely coincidental with the growth of functional tonality with its potential for incorporating significant small-range motion and detail into a network of long-range relationships growing out of the tensions and interconnection of horizontal and vertical events and of structural contrasts, extensions, tensions, and resolutions. Many of these big formal tensions were inevitably lost in a non-functional tonal style which tended to build on repetition, juxtaposition, and rhythmic articulation. The rather arbitrary imposition of the skeleton of classical "sonata form" on neo-classic works was a stopgap solution at best. Indeed, some of the most successful neo-tonal structures—works like Stravinsky's *Symphony of Psalms* that go far beyond a mere motion from one tonal area to another—come surprisingly close to serialism. What Schoenberg had found was a new way of articulating long-range structures through a rich and suggestive range of musical ideas; and the impact of this was far-reaching. As the characteristic diatonicism of the 1930's began to wane, and as the associated esthetic notions of a new simplicity, a new "practicality," and of musical nationalism and populism began to be played out, an increasing number of composers began to concern themselves with chromaticism, with chromatic line and harmony more and more detached from tonal processes. There is a discernible psychological-historical pattern in the gradual aural acceptance of chromatic ideas and processes as "natural"; the pattern is reflected in the cycle of acceptance and influence of this century's major composers, which ran chronologically about like this: Stravinsky and Hindemith, Bartók, Berg, Schoenberg, Webern.

CENTRAL EUROPE

Schoenberg had many pupils besides Berg and Webern but none of comparable stature. The first important composer outside of the Schoenberg circle to adopt the twelve-tone technique was Ernst Krenek. Krenek, who was born in Vienna in 1900, was not a Schoenberg pupil and

---

[1] Boulez's famous polemical article "Schoenberg est mort" was a rejection of the assumption that expressionism and "neo-classic" post-expressionism are necessary concomitants of twelve-tone technique; it was not merely an attack on Schoenberg's music.

had made his mark earlier with the opera *Jonny spielt auf*, a lively, dissonant, but tonal work touched by jazz. In the 1930's, Krenek began using twelve-tone technique—notably in his big opera, *Karl V*—and, for a number of years, he alternated or intermingled tonal and twelve-tone ideas. After the war, Krenek's music became more and more strictly twelve-tone and more and more concerned with numerological method. A musician of great natural fluency, Krenek long personified a link between the Hindemith tradition and that of Schoenberg and Webern; the latest of his long list of compositions similarly link the Schoenberg-Webern tradition with more recent techniques of serialism.

The accession to power of the Nazis in 1933 and the Austrian *Anschluss* in 1935 forced Schoenberg to leave Central Europe and abruptly put an end to the teaching and performance of twelve-tone music. The Nazis demanded a simple art with a popular base of support; the new simplicity of composers like Orff and Egk was a powerful anti-twelve-tone force in German-speaking countries. Nevertheless, after the war, a number of middle-generation composers—Wolfgang Fortner, Rolf Liebermann, Boris Blacher—cautiously adopted some form of dodecaphonic writing. The French-Swiss composer, Frank Martin (b. 1890), should also be included with this group since a great deal of his work and activity has been associated with Central Europe; his gradual infusion of twelve-tone techniques into a basically tonal style—mainly for structural strength and a broadening of scope—is typical.

The break between the older and younger generations in Germany is very marked. Most of the younger composers—Karlheinz Stockhausen (b. 1928) is the best-known and most important—actually started their musical careers as ultra-twelve-tone composers *à la* Webern and developed from that point. Some of the younger German composers who have become known since the war have continued to develop a twelve-tone idiom in a fairly direct line of descent from the Viennese; the best-known of these is Henze, whose work remains closely identified with expressionist techniques: chromatic and twelve-tone in a dissonant-melodic style worked up into large-scale theatrical and symphonic works. Henze's music represents a conscious attempt to create a free-flowing, serious, popular-practical twelve-tone style—a latter-day chromatic Hindemith, as it were. Significantly, Henze's turn towards political radicalism has widened his creative approach and led him into new areas of social concern and theatrical experimentalism, but in terms of a kind of post-expressionist *Gebrauchsmusik*.

ELSEWHERE IN EUROPE

Schoenberg had a number of foreign pupils—the Greek Nikos Skalkottas (1904–1949), the Norwegian Farten Valen (1887–1952), the Ameri-

can Adolph Weiss (1891–1971), the Spanish-British composer Roberto
Gerhard (1896–1970), and others—who introduced twelve-tone ideas outside of Central Europe, but most of these composers worked in an ob-
scurity only partially dispelled by recent revivals of interest in their work.
The first Latin composer to use twelve-tone materials in a distinctive and
personal way was Luigi Dallapiccola, an Italian whose only direct relationship with the Viennese was through a brief contact with Webern. Dallapiccola began to write twelve-tone music in the late 1930's under the
combined influences of Webern, early Italian lyric tradition, and the so-
called "hermetic" movement in contemporary Italian poetry. Later Dallapiccola moved briefly towards a more highly charged, complex style
(the opera *Il Prigioniero* of 1944–1948 was influenced by Berg and
Schoenberg), but in general his music represents a distinctive development and extension out of the Webern esthetic—always remembering
Webern's strong orientation towards vocal and lyric style. Dallapiccola's
twelve-tone technique is generally orthodox and in itself not very complex, but there is a special interest in the way the material is manipulated,
much in the manner of a strict counterpoint constructed on given schematic principles or expressive plans: groups of triads, elaborate canonic
part-writing, twelve-tone ideas arranged in conjunction with numerical
or schematic patterns often of literary or symbolic significance. Dallapiccola has always been oriented towards vocal music and, to a lesser extent, towards the theater; literary and philosophical notions—derived
from Italian "hermetic" poetry and a commitment to the theme of personal and intellectual freedom—have played an important part in his
work. Dallapiccola approached twelve-tone technique through the increasing use of chromatic contrapuntal methods based on small serial
nuclei in *Tre laudi* of 1936–1937 and in *Canti di prigionia* for chorus and
percussion orchestra of 1938–1941, one of the composer's most important
works and one of his first to break definitively with "neo-classic" tonality.
A major turning point is apparent in the war-time settings from the Greek
(translations by Ungaretti) for voice and instruments; quiet, intense, and
persuasive, these small lyric works form simple, clear, twelve-tone structures. The large post-war theater works, *Il Prigioniero* and the ballet *Job*
(1950) are a deep plunge into the world of expressionism—undoubtedly
facilitated by far greater contact with the music of the Viennese. Both
these works are effective and powerful theatrical and human statements
which gain strength, not from Dallapiccola's typical allusive lyricism
(here much subordinated) but from a brilliant adaptation of twelve-tone
ideas set forth in broad theatrical strokes. With the partial exception of
the large-scale *Canti di liberazione* of 1955 (again a work with a "freedom" subject treated in terms of a simple, broad twelve-tone music for
chorus and orchestra), the later works return to a lyric-elliptical style aris-

ing now, not from the theme of awakening consciousness of early antiquity (the Greek lyrics), but from the nature mysticism of medieval Italian religious poetry and the German Romantic lyric. Many of these aspects of Dallapiccola's work are synthesized in a recent major work on Greek mythology, the opera *Ulisse* (first performed in 1968).

A number of the younger and middle–generation Italian composers with a basically diatonic and neo-classical outlook have introduced twelve-tone materials in their work. Goffredo Petrassi, whose earlier work was strictly neo-tonal in a Stravinskyian sense, has been using twelve-tone and serial material, first in a loose manner and without breaking the tonal bonds, later as a dominating factor. Petrassi's recent music abandons direct tonal techniques and approaches avant-garde serialism—which in Italy, as elsewhere, had its point of departure in twelve-tone technique.

Both the musical style and the direct techniques of the Viennese school have had a relatively small overt influence in France. The conductor and composer René Leibowitz (1913–1972) was one of the first non-German composers to begin using twelve-tone ideas, and his book *Schoenberg et son école* (1947; in English, 1949), one of the first on the subject in a non-German language, was influential; however, his position in French music has been one of extreme isolation. Olivier Messiaen (b. 1908) has used twelve-tone technique to his own purposes, abstracting serial ideas without the style or esthetic of the Viennese, and this approach has proved to be the more fruitful. Pierre Boulez (b. 1925), who studied with both Leibowitz and Messiaen, began using twelve-tone techniques in the 1940's, and his early works—the first two Piano Sonatas, the *Sonatine* for flute and piano, *Livre* for string quartet, *Le visage nuptial* for voice and orchestra, and others—show the transition from post-expressionist influence to something new.

The transfer of Schoenberg's pupils Roberto Gerhard and Egon Wellesz (b. 1885) to England, the work of the Hungarian-British composer Mátyás Seiber (1905–1960), and the teaching and writing of the theoretician Hans Keller had an influence on the development of English music somewhat analogous to that of the European composers who came to the United States during the war. The first British composers to use twelve-tone technique were Elisabeth Lutyens (b. 1906) and Humphrey Searle (b. 1915), the latter a pupil of Webern although stylistically much closer to Berg. Other important twelve-tone composers in Great Britain include the Scottish composer Iain Hamilton (b. 1922), Alexander Goehr (b. 1932), and Peter Maxwell Davies (b. 1934). Davies evolved a very personal, lyrical twelve-tone style based on medieval and early English music; some of his works are specifically intended for vocal and instrumental performance by children and are thus among the rare examples

of twelve-tone music not necessarily intended for professional performance. More recently Davies has incorporated pop and theatrical elements in a striking expansion of stylistic outlook.

Twelve-tone ideas have permeated every corner of Europe. The
Swedish composer Karl-Birger Blomdahl (1916–1968), originally a neo-
classicist, developed a twelve-tone line of thought in a series of instrumental works of note. His best-known work, the "space-ship opera"
Aniara (1959), combines twelve-tone, pop, and electronic elements. Even
Eastern Europe, long closed to non-tonal, highly chromatic, or experimental music, has accepted twelve-tone ideas. The first break with an
effective censorship took place in Poland where, since 1958, all forms of
modern technique have received wide acceptance. After an initial impact of Bartók and Hindemith, the introduction of twelve-tone ideas
materially changed the entire course of Polish contemporary music. A
key work in this development was the *Funeral Music* (1958) of Witold
Lutoslawski (b. 1913), dedicated to the memory of Bartók and one of the
first Polish works to make use of twelve-tone technique. Lutoslawski's
music has developed through a chromatic, twelve-tone symphonic phase
into a freer kind of avant-garde style laid out in broad rhythmic and
color planes and blocked out in levels of intensity and timbre. Most of the
younger Polish composers as well as Lutoslawski himself have moved
well out of the area of closely controlled twelve-tone style and idea, but
the block-like manipulation of large instrumental and orchestral intensities and timbres laid out in broad masses and dramatic juxtapositions has
remained characteristic of recent Polish music. The direct techniques of
twelve-tone music remain influential in the music of the older generation
and in the work of a few of the important younger men: notably Tadeusz
Baird (b. 1928), whose derivation from the Viennese is quite direct, and
Kazimierz Serocki (b. 1922), who turned towards and then away from
the rather static, dramatic-theatrical style of young Poland towards a
new, ongoing, developmental symphonic character often employing open
or flexible materials but characterized by control.

Outside of Poland, the most important modern music center in
Eastern Europe has been Yugoslavia, where a number of younger composers have been using contemporary ideas for several years; the best-
known of these is Milko Kelemen (b. 1924), who has worked through the
typical stylistic evolution from Bartók to Boulez with twelve-tone technique as a turning-point in between.

The situation all over Eastern Europe, however, has been in flux
and, with the exception of Albania, there is no country in that part of the
world where the impact of rapid change was not felt. Within a period
that could almost be measured in months, avant-garde techniques—even

extreme ones—were taken up in nearly all of the major Eastern European centers. Twelve-tone technique has been adopted by composers even of the older generation in Czechoslovakia, Hungary, Rumania, and elsewhere. The Soviet Union has remained more isolated, but similar changes (at a more evolutionary pace, perhaps) are taking place there. Already over a period of years a number of Soviet composers have been working with twelve-tone and other contemporary materials, but this music has remained little known and little performed in or out of Russia. Among the best-known are the Muscovite Andrei Wolkonsky (b. 1916) and the Kiev composers Eddy Denisov (b. 1929) and Valentin Silvestrov (b. 1937), whose twelve-tone chromatic styles suggest roots in Scriabin as well as Schoenberg and Berg. Among the younger generation are the Moscow composer Alfred Chnitke (b. 1934), who has been influenced by Boulez, and a Latvian group including Arwo Pärt (b. 1935), who has created static color structures of considerable effectiveness.

THE UNITED STATES

The strongest line of continuity between the Viennese and latter-day twelve-tone composition is to be found in the United States, where Schoenberg settled in 1933 and remained as a teacher until his death in 1951. Schoenberg taught composers as disparate as Leon Kirchner and John Cage; and indirectly, through the teaching and influence of a composer-teacher like Roger Sessions, twelve-tone ideas became a dominant part of American music. In the 1920's Sessions had developed a distinctive, rich, and contrapuntal neo-classical style modified in the 1930's and 1940's into a characteristic, dense chromaticism of an expressive and individual character. This style, a personal way of speaking which, in works like the Violin Concerto (1935), the Symphony No. 2 (1945), and the opera *The Trial of Lucullus* (1947), can be easily differentiated from Viennese chromaticism, gradually absorbed constructive elements of row technique. Later works—particularly the Sonata for violin solo (1953), the Piano Concerto (1956), the *Idyll of Theocritus* for voice and orchestra (1956), the Symphony No. 4 (1958), and the opera *Montezuma* (1947–1962)—are dominated by row material which adds constructive strength and solidity while actually reinforcing the sense of stylistic identity and individuality. The primary impulse of Sessions's music—and in this he resembles Schoenberg—is contrapuntal; it is the characteristic web of long, shaped lines which gives a typical sound to the music. But Sessions's line is also concrete in conception, vocal in shape, and dependent on a complex sense of phrase accent and motion which gives a dynamic impulse to the music remarkably parallel to the way in which classical harmonic progressions performed the same function.

This characteristic linear chromaticism dominates the work of a large group of American composers, many of whom studied with Sessions; Andrew Imbrie (b. 1921), Seymour Shifrin (b. 1926) and Leon Kirchner (b. 1919) are outstanding examples. Composers like Ben Weber (b. 1916) and George Rochberg (b. 1918) have been working on essentially independent but parallel lines.[2] Chromatic idioms (mainly but not exclusively twelve-tone) based on a "narrative," ongoing phrase structure and some kind of contrapuntal, developmental form succeeded "neo-classicism" or "neo-tonality" as the mainstream of American concert music—equivalent, in effect, to the abstract expressionism that dominated American painting.

These large-scale directional-developmental or narrative forms which replace the old functional tonality by some kind of row thinking stand in contrast to a number of important recent works which interpret twelve-tone ideas in terms of static, suspended structures which interlock in various cyclical patterns; these have, in fact, a relationship with certain "neo-classic" structural (as opposed to stylistic) notions, now newly propounded in terms of the chromatic material. The late music of Stravinsky belongs here, along with a number of parallel (and, in some cases, earlier) twelve-tone pieces by American composers whose work has been identified with his, notably Aaron Copland and Arthur Berger. Copland's involvement with chromatic techniques goes back to the 1920's; his *Piano Variations* of 1930 employ very closely worked and effective serial techniques based on a four-note row that is, in type, not at all unlike certain ideas used by Webern. Copland returned to this kind of serial, chromatic material in 1950 with his Piano Quartet and again with the *Piano Fantasy* of 1960 and the *Connotations for Orchestra* of 1962. They are strongly twelve-tone in sound and method although expressing characteristic Copland techniques of layers and planes, angles, and juxtapositions; these conceptual principles even carry over into a non-twelve-tone work like the *Nonet for Strings* of 1960. Berger, whose earlier music was strongly "neo-classic," developed a technique for projecting long-range linear motion—chromatic and contrapuntal—in terms of big blocked-out static structures which themselves interlock through internal twelve-tone relationships. In his first works of this kind (e.g., the *Chamber Music for 13 Instruments* of 1956) these techniques are specifically adapted to neoclassic rhythmic and phrase structures. Later (in the String Quartet of 1959, for example), this "neo-classicism" disappears or is absorbed into

---

[2] Rochberg's more recent work, however, uses quotation-collage techniques.

larger patterns; the detail is chromatic, highly inventive and serial-twelve-tone; the big forms remain sectional and additive in the neo-classic sense but are made organic by being interpenetrated by the row and the row-sound.

Stravinsky's original involvement with row technique was with the serial-order principle—the tenor solo in the *Cantata* (1951–1952), the Septet (1952–1953), the Shakespeare songs (1954), and *In Memoriam Dylan Thomas* (1954) are based on rows, but they are not twelve-tone. Only later and through his specific interest in a technical-structural idea—not altogether unrelated to quasi-serial techniques he had earlier developed for detail patterns and even (as in the *Symphony of Psalms*, 1930) for longer-range relationships—did Stravinsky begin to work with the full chromatic material. The score for the ballet *Agon* actually sums up the process as part of its own developing form: it begins diatonically, becomes chromatic and twelve-tone, and eventually returns to the diatonicism of the opening. A similar and even more wide-ranging process takes place in *Canticum Sacrum* (1956), a work which moves from Gregorian intonation to dodecaphony. After 1958, however, Stravinsky's music was strictly twelve-tone although, to be sure, always in a very distinctly Stravinskyian way. *Threni* (1958), a large-scale work for soloists, chorus, and orchestra, is completely organized in twelve-tone fashion not only in matters of detail but in the way the larger plan relates to that detail; for example, points of major articulation are often as clearly organized with respect to one another as are the smaller events in between. The result—particularly in the choral and vocal writing—has the effect of a series of unyielding statements (big choral declarations, *a cappella* solo voices in canon, etc.) with a sparse ornamental detail which, in effect, represent a transformation into twelve-tone thinking of Stravinsky's characteristic underlying formal and esthetic sense. Stravinsky's dodecaphonic music is neo-twelve-tone in the same sense that his earlier works are neo-tonal— "neo-classic" or "neo-baroque." *Movements* for piano and orchestra (1958–1959) stands in the same relationship to the music of Anton Webern as the *Dumbarton Oaks Concerto* and *The Rake's Progress* do to the music of Bach and Mozart. Neither in the latter nor the former case is there any question of a model but rather of the materials of a discourse whose actual forms—propositions and conclusions—are, as always, quite personal and original.

After *Movements* Stravinsky again turned to vocal and vocal-dramatic materials in a series of spare, aphoristic works—*A Sermon, A Narrative, and a Prayer; The Dove Descending Breaks the Air*, for *a cappella* chorus; a short work in memory of President Kennedy; the television dance-drama *The Flood; Abraham and Isaac*, a Biblical setting in Hebrew for baritone and orchestra; the *Requiem Canticles*. Virtually all of these unite a special permutational twelve-tone technique, a pointed thinness and brevity, a kind of abstracted religious mysticism expressed in a contemporary twelve-tone stylization. Stravinsky's unexpected turn towards the twelve-tone idea, treated in his own personal manner, was a remarkable demonstration of the essential unity underlying apparently dissimilar and contradictory twentieth-century art.

BIBLIOGRAPHICAL NOTES

An extensive bibliography of writings on twelve-tone, serial, and electronic music by Ann Basart was published by the University of California Press in 1962. Roman Vlad's *Storia della dodecafonia* (Milan, 1958) is one of the few general sources which discuss the diffusion of twelve-tone ideas; however, it contains nothing about American music and is not translated. Boulez's "Schoenberg Is Dead" and other early essays on the impact of twelve-tone music and ideas are contained in his *Relevés d'apprenti* (Paris, 1966), later issued (New York, 1968) in a poor translation as *Notes of an Apprenticeship*. The best sources of information on the diffusion of twelve-tone music after World War II are various music journals, notably *Melos* (Germany), *The Score* (England), and the American *Perspectives of New Music*.

part five

The Avant-garde
and Beyond

TWELVE

INTRODUCTION:
BEFORE WORLD WAR II

The cycle that began after World War II, although in part a continuation of earlier motifs, in part parallel to the first half century, is far from a recapitulation of earlier events. The second half of the century still has some years to run and it is hardly possible to offer any really definitive synthesis. But it seems as though an "avant-garde revolution," the second of the century, begun well within the traditional Romantic conventions of alienation, individuality, originality, progress, and avant-gardism, may in fact be evolving something genuinely new—a "post-modern" art of the late twentieth century.

What distinguishes the second from the first half of the century is, above all, the intrusion of technology. With the development of magnetic tape, the long-playing (and, later, stereo) record, and FM radio, as well as inexpensive, high-quality recording and playback equipment, the burden of musical communication has shifted from live performance to recording. No aspect of musical life, from the study of traditional music to the dissemination of new musical ideas and the impact of mass media and pop culture, has remained unaffected by these changes. Technology has not only provided important new tools; it has changed the nature and the experience of the musical public. In effect, technology makes the entire experience of mankind available as raw material and—potentially and, increasingly, in actuality—part of the common shared experience.

This remarkable situation, in conjunction with the larger movements of social change, provides the background against which artistic innovation has taken place. In some ways, these changes have been more striking in Europe where classicism, populism, political events, and the war effectively ended the old avant-gardism, marked off an era, and compelled new beginnings. Nevertheless, European post-war avant-gardism has already been accepted as part of the mainstream of European culture. The American situation is quite different and more complex. Experimental music in the New World has a long and quite continuous history and a more erratic and individualistic record of achievement; it has provided new music with some of its most important creative energies and offers genuinely new possibilities for cultural renewal.

The development of new musical ideas since World War II has, in spite of great diversity, taken certain characteristic forms: the isolation of the individual acoustic event; the extension of the sound material to include the entire possible range of aural sensation; the absolutely equal esthetic (though not necessarily equal artistic, psychological, or psychoacoustical) validity of all possible material in all possible relationships (duration or loudness, for example, being potentially equal in significance to fixed pitch). Every level of control is possible, from total pre-determination to improvisation to indeterminate indeterminacy, and choices within these may be determined at any level, at any time before or during (if not after!) the performance; all relationships (including none) are possible.

The first years after the war were marked by these discoveries, rationalized through some form of serialism or intentionally de-rationalized through the introduction of non-predictable or performer-option elements. These apparently contradictory approaches—sequential in European music but simultaneous in America—were reconciled or synthesized in the 1960's, largely through the intervention of media and technology. The re-evaluation of communications media, live performance, and the social role of music again raised the old questions of context and content. Everything is possible but nothing can be meaningful in and of itself. There were two significant reactions to this situation: minimalism, where each single experience is extended to occupy an entire universe, and its natural converse, maximalism—multi-level form, happenings, multimedia, music theater—where ranges of experience are in and of themselves subject matter, and where meaning and context again become issues, social context and concern again become relevant to the development of new forms of expression.

If certain cyclical patterns seem to repeat themselves, the turn of the wheel never really brings us to the same place. Nevertheless, before examining the development of what is new and distinctive about post-war music, it is worthwhile to sketch the relationships with the past and to discuss here those earlier composers whose work seems to be linked most closely with recent developments.

SOURCES

As already suggested, post-war music is in part the continuation of motifs begun early in the century and interrupted by the achievement of closed, settled forms in between-the-wars European music. The freely atonal and "expressionist" works of the Viennese and Stravinsky's pre-World War I work have tended not only towards the development of new, non-tonal materials but also towards organic, non-developmental forms on the static, additive Stravinskyian model or on the associative on-going form created by Debussy, Strauss, and Schoenberg. The tendency towards miniaturism exemplified by Webern has been especially significant not only for brevity and concision of form but also for the way individual events are broken down and isolated into clear, differentiated packets of sound with identifiable characteristics. This has suggested the possibility of restocking and rebuilding the entire process of creative thought from its basic elements. The order principle of twelve-tone music, extended to articulate all levels of musical thought, has been decisive in the development of a great deal of post-war musical thinking.

There were other antecedents. The Futurists gave concerts of noises before World War I and the painter Russolo built a noise machine. The Dadaists gave performances which included musical and sound manifestations of various kinds; Marcel Duchamp's *Erratum musical* of 1913 consists of random isolated pitches without any indicated durations. A long and continuing impact of literary and intellectual movements has been felt from the French symbolists down to surrealism and Brechtian theater. The tradition of abstraction and individualism, derived from Romantic views about the artist and society, was a continuing potent influence until recently. The brief but notable challenge of *Gebrauchsmusik* and the social involvement of the 1930's—a strong reaction against the isolated and alienated position of the artist—put only a dent in the generally accepted view of art music in Western culture and produced only a relatively limited group of works of importance; nevertheless, they also anticipated a later turn of the wheel.

In addition to these connections with European modernist culture, there are still more direct connections with the American experimental tradition. American music has always been essentially syncretic, tracking and merging a whole variety of cultural source material; technological development, non-Western ideas, ethnic sub-cultures, folk and pop culture have all helped form a distinctive American experience which has had continuing significance for new music. The global impact of American commercial culture may be a reflection of American economic power, but the development of alternatives or antidotes—beyond a mere retreat into traditionalism—has had a significant testing ground in the New World. Even the young anti-American European radical is, in part, "American" in his culture. This is really only a way of saying that, increasingly, we all live in a single super-culture and that we all face common problems.[1]

IVES

Charles Ives was the first important Western composer to stand essentially outside the mainstream of European culture, and he was the first to propose—with no direct influence of technology—the totality and unity of the human experience as a subject matter for art. Ives could do this because, although he was brought up on New and Old World culture, he kept an essential distance from received tradition and its dominant professional activities. This is the essence of Ives's "amateurism" and the source of his originality and unique position.

Ives worked far from the European centers and, in many cases, years ahead of his European contemporaries. He composed proto-serial and proto-aleatory music; he invented block forms and free forms; he used tone clusters and structural densities; he wrote in poly-meters and poly-tempi; he composed spatial music and music that could be realized in a multiplicity of ways; he anticipated recent improvisatory works-in-progress, assemblages, and "pop-art" ideals—in short, just about every important development of the last sixty years and some of the most notable of the last twenty. Yet Ives was also aware of the past, and he used aspects of American and European tradition throughout his creative years. In one sense, he stood so far outside of these traditions (although he understood them perfectly well) that—unlike Schoenberg and

[1] But see discussion at the beginning of Chapter 17.

Stravinsky—he did not have to overthrow them and then labor mightily to rebuild. He knew and used what he needed in just the same casual, determined way he used any idea or material that was appropriate or relevant to what he had to say. Ives felt no "historical compulsion" to abandon tonality (or anything else); his music turns away from narrative and process in the conventional sense; its tendency is inclusive; it absorbs or even revels in contradictions. Like Whitman, Ives could contradict himself, he could contain multitudes.

Nothing in human experience was alien to Ives, but that does not mean that he was a "primitive." There is a myth which depicts him as an untutored pioneer in the New England wilderness; a visionary but a kind of musical Grandma Moses; a rugged individualist working in complete isolation, utterly lacking in technical skill and sophistication but totally original in a rough and ready way; a kind of inspired *naïf;* a phenomenon of nature. In actual fact, Ives's father was a well-known bandmaster who did many experiments in acoustics and temperament. Ives studied with his father in his hometown of Danbury, and later at Yale with the distinguished Horatio Parker. He had extensive practical experience with his father's band, arranging for it and playing with theater orchestras and on church organs in New Haven and New York. All of Ives's mature life and most of his composing years were spent, not in the wilderness, but in New York where he embarked on a double career as an extremely successful insurance broker and a composer. Most of his music was actually written between his arrival in New York in 1898 and the early 1920's; he spent the later years of life arranging, putting in order, and preparing for performance works from the enormous mass of material he had produced earlier.

None of this is meant to detract from Ives's stature as an innovator or as an individualist; quite the contrary, it should emphasize his real achievement by taking it out of the realm of nature mythology and emphasizing its origins in conscious decision and choice. For example, Ives was always able to use tradition—classical tonality, say—in exactly the same way he used his own new tonalities, poly-tonalities and non-tonalities, as a kind of special case, as it were, of his total experience of meaningful sound. It was this range of activity, this totality of experience that interested Ives and it was out of this totality of experience—out of simplicity and complexity, coherence and contradiction—that he made his pieces. One of his best-known pieces, *The Unanswered Question* (1908), shows his technique of deriving a completely new form out of simple, contradictory elements. A small group of strings—it can be merely a string quartet—is seated off-stage or away from the other instruments; it provides an obsessive, endless rotation of a simple "chorale" sequence of triadic harmonies. On another level, entirely detached from the strings and without any specific rhythmic co-ordination, a trumpet reiterates a questioning phrase. Opposite, flutes (possibly mixed with an oboe and a clarinet) respond to the trumpet question, toss it around, and eventually get into a terrible tangle. There is, in the end, no answer, no resolution; only the question unchanged and the distant string "harmony of the spheres" fading out to infinity.

This tiny conception is full of prophetic Ivesisms: the literary idea which generates a form; the unification of seemingly contradictory material through the very exploitation of the fact of contradiction; the easily perceptible external references; the spatial arrangement of the instruments; the projection of distinct layers of sound with informal vertical arrangements. What is not so obvious is just how all these elements come together to make an expressive form which communicates on a subtler level by no means equivalent to the verbal descriptions (see Appendix; Example 12-1).

The Ivesian view of art and life has to do with the value of a poetic idea realized as a human action or activity. In spite of all his presumed impracticality (but many of the old difficulties of performance, of notation, and of general comprehensibility have vanished over the years), Ives thought of his music as a kind of non-passive, performance-practice activity; he meant it primarily to be performed, only secondarily to be listened to. He seems to have had the idea that audiences might, at some point, sing along or that someone might jump up with a flute or a harmonica and join in. Ives wanted to transform even the passive state of reception into positive involvement, which accounts in part for the intentional use of familiar and popular music to produce a shock of surprise or amused recognition. Yet, on the other hand, he hardly even "composed" music in the usual sense. During his creative years, he poured out a continuous stream of musical expression—works for chorus and organ, five symphonies, four sonatas for violin and piano, two string quartets, many piano works including the massive "Concord" Sonata, a large number of songs, and extremely important works for chamber orchestra or chamber ensemble: the sets of *Tone Roads* (1911–1915), *Three Places in New England* (1914), *Central Park in the Dark* (1898–1911), *Over the Pavements* (1913). There is no question that Ives knew what he wanted in these works—he claimed to have tried many of his ideas out in practice during his theater orchestra and organist days and, by accounts, he could show what he wanted on the piano. On the other hand, what he wanted was often intentionally unclear or imprecise, and he himself changed the way he played his music over the years. His idea was to involve the performer in the activity of creating the music, and the works themselves form a kind of continuous stream of musical expression, portions of which have coalesced—indeed all are still coalescing—into individual scores.

Ives disliked and distrusted the conventionalized rituals of public music-making; he wanted to get back to some underlying realities about human activity, about the physical reality of human beings communicating immediate and almost tangible experiences—even experiences of complexity, contradiction, and incoherence. He wanted a speaking kind of music, a music that could be jotted down to convey fresh impressions and thoughts, that could flow with the naturalness of plain speech; a music that could somehow get across that impenetrable barrier between art and life, not to "express" nature but to flow along as part of it. On the one hand, he wrote music that was and is difficult, every part a separate and individual activity; on the other, he wrote things that are easy and banal. He was wildly visionary; one music runs exaltedly or humorously into the next, and in some cases only with the greatest difficulty have performable pieces been separated out into a practical, usable state. Yet there is nothing abstract about any of Ives's work; all of it is conceived, not as paper music, but as matter for action. He wanted performers to decipher illegible and complex new notations, but he also wanted them to understand his ideas and ideals and act freely within them. He wanted to speak to those who understood, yet he also thought that anyone could understand and he wanted everyone to participate. He was not himself a "phenomenon of nature," but he wanted to think of his music that way. He wanted to break down the distinctions between man and nature, between art and life, and to integrate them into some all-embracing experience. His last piece was to be a "Universe" Symphony to be played and sung in the fields and mountains by thousands—indeed, by all of humanity.

On one hand, Ives's music has had a direct and continuing influence and can be linked quite directly with certain recent avant-garde ideas. On the other hand, he was also a kind of traditionalist—if one realizes that Ives and his father were the only important musical representatives of that tradition! The tradition was, of course, that of Whitman, of Thoreau, Emerson, and the New England transcendentalists, and Ives set himself the job of creating, single-handed, a musical equivalent. This tradition, above all others, had to find its starting points in some kind of expression that was at once personal, free, and spontaneous, close to "natural" expression. Ives's range runs from hymn tunes and ragtime to complex, atonal polyphonies; he had to compose out the entire tradition from one end to the other. At the same time, he was able to encompass his vision of the totality of human experience within a personal utterance that was also an evocation of some Golden Age in which art and life were—or would be—naturally and inextricably woven together.

OTHER INNOVATORS; VARÈSE

The period of the 1920's was one of extensive exploration in American music, and the intensity and importance of the activity have scarcely any parallel in the European music of the time (a similar kind of activity seems to have existed in the young Soviet Union, but years of Stalinism all but obliterated even the very names of pioneers such as Rosslavetz). The creation and assimilation of new ideas was a primary aim, and the strong musical voices were recognizably those dealing most directly with new materials and new ways of organizing sound: Edgard Varèse (1883–1965). Henry Cowell (1897–1965), Carl Ruggles (1876–1971), George Antheil, and, of course, Ives. The works of Wallingford Riegger (1885–1961) and Adolph Weiss, Leo Ornstein (b. 1895; a Russian-born American who specialized in thick cluster dissonance and static accentual forms), John J. Becker (1886–1961) and Ruth Crawford Seeger (1901–1953; her husband, Charles Seeger [b. 1886] was an important theorist of new resources and Mrs. Seeger's remarkable String Quartet of 1931 is, as an example, full of proto-serialism) extend and diffuse the experimental tradition well into the 1930's and 1940's. Copland's music of the 1920's and early 1930's was strongly influenced by the current avant-garde ideas; it is curious to realize that the position of Roger Sessions was, with respect to the American modernist movements of the day, quite conservative. Ideas such as tone clusters, new scalar and rhythmic formations, new instruments, and, especially, new technological means were very much in the air. In an entire issue devoted to new "mechanical" and electric means, the journal *Modern Music* clearly anticipated the idea of *musique concrète* ("Recorded Noises—Tomorrow's Instrumentation") as well as electronic synthesis ("electrical musical instruments" or "eminos").

Some of these pioneers have remained essentially isolated figures without—until now at least—significant influence. Antheil made an international reputation as a wild man and was sponsored by no less a personage than Ezra Pound, but his sensational *Ballet mécanique* (1925) for percussion, player pianos, and airplane motors now seems mildly attractive, overlong, and rather tame in a manner obviously derived from Stravinsky's *Les Noces;* its importance has been eclipsed by much more remarkable percussion works such as Varèse's *Ionisation.* Antheil's later music, much of it written for Hollywood, was tonal, conservative, and unimpressive. By contrast, Ruggles remained the classic type of American rugged individualist: late-developing, uncompromising. His rare, dense, personal, chromatic music forms a distinct kind of American expressionism. Unlike the European expressionist, whose approach is psychological and often suggests anxiety and alienation, Ruggles was a visionary who strove for the sublime, always remembering that the path upwards is not a little rough and torturous. His titles themselves suggest the intense character of the vision: *Angels* (1920), *Men and Mountains* (1924), *Portals* (1926), *Sun-Treader* (1933), *Evocations* (1937–1945), *Organum* (1945).

This tradition of American individualism survives in the personalities of composers like Henry Brant (b. 1913) and Harry Partch (b. 1901). Brant, Canadian-born, active as a jazz arranger, now teaching at Bennington College, anticipated many recent ideas with his open rhythmic structures ("polychronic," that is, using independent, multiple meters and tempos) set into large, freely co-ordinated spatial counterpoints which derive ultimately from Ives. Brant creates out of the character of the instruments, their physical disposition, and the acoustical properties of the space in which they are enclosed; typically, he distributes instruments around a hall, with various groups working individually on flexible material in a free, even, unco-ordinated stereophony. He has also proposed a kind of collective performance-practice ideal and has suggested a method of teaching music through creative activity.

Partch is, to some degree, associated with the West Coast percussion movement of the 1930's and 1940's discussed later in this chapter. And his major importance undoubtedly lies in his remarkable, ritualistic music-theater works: *The Bewitched* (1957), *Revelation in Courthouse Square* (1961), *Delusion of the Fury* (1963–1969). But it is impossible to put Partch in any of the standardized modern music categories; he has little to do with any of them. Essentially self-taught, he lived for years as a wanderer and a recluse. Later he built a studio in an abandoned shipyard in the San Francisco area where he constructed instruments of his own devising. Then, after a period at the University of Illinois, he settled in Southern California where he has been able to work with younger people, training them to play his instruments and act out his theater rituals in a kind of communitarian performance ideal. Partch, not Ives, is Rousseau's "natural man" among American composers. He had to construct or reconstruct everything for himself. His instruments bear picturesque names such as Cry-Chord, Mazda Marimba (made of light bulbs), Cloud Chamber Bowls, The Harmonic Canon, and Spoils of War; they are striking both to hear and to look at. At the same time, he has created new tunings and scale patterns based on microtonal divisions of the octave. He has developed techniques of repetitive, ongoing polyrhythm, wide ranging, chant-derived vocal style, appropriate new notations as well as significant new music and theater forms. Partch's work has practically nothing to do with the main currents of Western modern music. It has distant points of origin in Greek mythology as well as in folk and non-Western music, but it is uniquely his own, a kind of composed ethnic music created not by a whole culture but out of individual creative need.

Partch's use of microtonalism (the division of the octave into more than the conventional twelve tempered chromatic steps) is connected with his theories about "natural" tunings, with his "ethnic" style and his instrumental creations. An interest in microtones—generally connected with very different ideals—appeared earlier in the century; it seemed the logical next step after the exploitation of the total chromatic. Among the composers who worked with microtones in more than a passing way are the Czech Alois Hába (b. 1893), who has apparently since abandoned it, the Mexican Julian Carrillo (1875–1965) and the Russian Vyshnegradsky (b. 1893).[2] More recently, problems of tuning and microtones have attracted the attention of several younger composers including Ben Johnston (b. 1926) at the University of Illinois (where Partch was formerly in residence) and John Eaton (b. 1935), who has used them in conjunction with live-electronic performance. Microtonal materials and techniques have been most extensively used in electronic music. In instrumental and, especially, vocal music they require greater refinement on the part of performers and audience than has been generally forthcoming; at any rate, they remain essentially undeveloped resources.

The most direct connections between the American avant-garde scene of the 1920's and the recent post-war period can be found in the work, personality, and ideas of Edgard Varèse. Varèse was born and educated in France, worked briefly in Germany, and came to New York in 1915 with a vision of artistic new worlds already amazingly fully formed. He was perhaps the first composer to conceive of sounds as objects with sculptural, spatial configurations held together by rhythmic energy. The traditional idea of developmental process and variation plays virtually no role in his music, which is composed of planes and volumes. His starting points, perhaps included the experiments of the Futurists and certain "cubist" aspects of *Le Sacre du printemps*. But Varèse's esthetic position was vastly different from that of his contemporaries, and he stands apart as one of the most original figures of twentieth-century music.

The development of new resources based on technology—an ideal perhaps derived in part from his contact with Busoni in Berlin before World War I—was part of Varèse's vision from the very beginning. However, his first mature works in the new style—*Amériques* (1917–1922), *Hyperprism* (1922), *Octandre* (1924), *Intégrales* (1924), *Arcana* (1927)—are compositions for chamber or large orchestra which make striking use

---

[2] Bartók, Bloch, and others used "quarter-tones" but only as special inflections of the traditional half-steps.

of winds and brass along with large percussion sections. The "melodic," fixed-pitch content is reduced to small, insistent groupings of single notes or two or three cells strikingly articulated by rhythm and accent. The vertical, "harmonic" element consists of highly dissonant, static structures filling out various segments of the total chromatic and framed by the expanded use of percussion. Melody, harmony, and timbre (the terms are hardly valid in the traditional sense) are assimilated to rhythm and accent, and the fixed, invented musical shapes are thus built up in a highly unified manner. These powerful, static building-blocks, held together by rhythm—percussive energy—are piled up in great, spatial juxtapositions which define Varèse's new conceptual musical space. Enormous amounts of energy are created by these works, but the tensions are internal. There is no sense of motion in the conventional sense at all but rather a play of kinetic and potential energies which give the impression of holding together complex, unyielding physical sound objects set, as it were, into a dynamic musical space.

If timbre and accent and rhythm are aspects of melody and harmony in traditional music, the situation is reversed here. Indeed, there is often a kind of continuum with fixed pitch at one extreme and pure rhythm and accent on the other; but there is constant interaction and even flow between these fixed extremes. Pitch is no longer the ongoing, developmental, all-powerful generator of form but it is by no means abandoned, even in an all-percussion piece like the famous *Ionisation* of 1931. Thus the sirens represent the use of pitch on a continuum, and the entrance of piano clusters and bells near the end are structurally essential in a work which puts color, rhythmic form, and accent in the first plane (see Appendix; Example 12-2). Only a few years later Varèse wrote a wholly successful work based on a single, pitched instrumental line, the well-known *Density 21.5* for solo flute.

During the 1920's Varèse was a major figure on the American scene, organizing and directing an important series of new-music concerts which introduced new European and American works in New York. The International Composers Guild and its successor, the Pan-American Composers Guild, were closely associated with the work of Varèse, Ruggles, Ives, Cowell, and others. Concerts directed by Leopold Stokowski, Nicolas Slonimsky, and others, were presented in New York, California, Havana, and several European cities. However, this intense activity subsided in the 1930's when, under the influence of populist ideologies, avant-garde ideas and forms were set aside.

During this period, Varèse expended most of his energies in the fruitless attempt to spur the development of a creative sound technology for the realization of large-scale musico-dramatic concepts. A science-fiction opera dealing with attempts to contact extra-terrestrial intelligence was turned over to the playwright Antonin Artaud; a libretto is extant but little or no music survives. Of a projected "Symphony of the Masses" with André Malraux—one of its forms was to involve simultaneous performance in various parts of the world connected by radio communications—nothing remains but a fragmentary piece for chorus. One completed work of the 1930's, *Equatorial,* was scored for the Theremin and later revised for Ondes Martenot—both early attempts at electronic musical synthesis. Significantly, however, both *Equatorial* and the large-scale unfinished *Nocturnal* (completed after the composer's death by his pupil Chou Wen-chung) make important use of the human voice in conjunction with large instrumental forces. These works bring to the foreground an aspect of Varèse's work not often discussed; his exploration of very deep-seated and elemental areas of the human psyche. Varèse's work, which looks forward in so many respects, also looks "backward"—not into the historical past, but to unexplored recesses of the human mind and very basic, elemental forms of human expression.

Varèse's music is non-linear, non-process, non-narrative in form; its creation of sound objects and musical space are quite distinct from most of the music of his contemporaries but is fundamental to much of the music of recent decades. Varèse specifically and conceptually anticipated the new percussion music as well as the basic form of tape and electronic music. After World War II, with the widespread diffusion of magnetic tape and the development of tape and electronic equipment and studies in Europe and America (see Chapter 13), Varèse himself was finally able to realize some of the visionary concepts he had conceived so many years before. Fittingly, he provided the *musique concrète* movement with its first masterpieces: *Déserts* (1954) for tape, winds, brass, and percussion, and *Poème électronique,* commissioned for the 400-odd loudspeakers that sent sound spinning around the inside of Le Corbusier's Philips Pavilion at the 1958 Brussels Worlds Fair. These powerful montages—Varèse's own preferred term was "organized sound"—are worked out of recorded sound images, altered, rhythmicized, juxtaposed, overlaid and intercut, the whole built up into new spatial structures of great originality, breadth, and scope. *Poème,* although designed for a continuous 360° sound space, is overwhelming even in its stereophonic form, realized by the composer for the purposes of recording. The spatial concept is not merely a matter of the physical arrangement of the sound sources; it is actually built into the juxtapositions of aural images, slowly turning and colliding in cataclysmic spatial encounters.

With Varèse the notion of a continuous musical space, proposed intellectually by Busoni in 1907 and, in another sense, by Ives at the same time, becomes a reality. Varèse's work not only anticipates but actually merges with the new post-war music.

COWELL: NON-WESTERN INFLUENCES

Henry Cowell was the most direct representative of the Ives "tradition" in the 1920's, the most important link between Ives and the latter-day avant-garde, and himself one of the most prolific innovators of the century. Cowell's work is a vast accumulation of new materials and ideas. The most famous of these, the "tone cluster," is simply an agglomeration of adjacent fixed frequencies in which, however, the over-all impression is that of a texture rather than of a chordal sonority consisting of separable fixed-pitch elements. The "cluster" occupies an intermediate ground between fixed pitch and noise; it is made up of fixed frequencies, but the confused interaction of the upper partials of these frequencies produces an indeterminate effect closely related to noise. Cowell's *Mosaic* for string quartet and *26 Simultaneous Mosaics* for five players are remarkable early examples of open form. He also did extensive and important creative investigation in the field of rhythm and was perhaps the first person to propose—and realize in a piece of music—the concept of deriving rhythmic–durational relationships from the ratios of harmonic vibrations (2:1, 3:2, 4:3, etc.). Cowell also developed a great number of new instrumental resources—most notably, a great variety of timbres plucked, scraped, strummed, and scratched out of the insides of the piano—and he pioneered in new notational techniques appropriate to his new resources (see Appendix; Example 12-3). His later work was largely concerned with materials drawn from folk, "ethnic," and non-Western sources treated in terms of Western instrumental and musical organizations; again an anticipation of contemporary concerns and an illustration of the developing notion of ranges of experience.

Cowell's work provides an immediate connection between the experimental activities of the 1920's and the rather special, quiet, East-oriented American movements of the 1930's and 1940's. These developments, centered in Cowell's home state of California, had two closely related aspects. One was the absorption of strong influences from the East; the other, related to new Cuban and Mexican music, was the extensive use of percussion instruments and ensembles. The most important composers associated with these developments were Cowell, Partch, Colin McPhee (1901–1964), Alan Hovhaness (b. 1911), Lou Harrison (b. 1917), and John Cage (b. 1912). Cage and Harrison actually collaborated on *Double Music*, a percussion work with a notable Eastern influence. Harrison's work, after encounters with the influence of Ives and Ruggles, has taken him back to this area; his recent work involves Eastern instruments, adaptations of Eastern instrumental and vocal styles, and the use of non-tempered tuning. Cage's early involvement with this movement, his experiments with rhythmic serialism and recording technology, and his involvement with Eastern philosophy led him to challenge the traditional Western supremacy of pitch organization. He went on to challenge the relationship between one sound event and another and, ultimately, even the need for conscious determination and control of such events.

BIBLIOGRAPHICAL NOTES

Duchamp's *Erratum musical* is given in Robert Lebel's *Marcel Duchamp,* translated by G. H. Hamilton (New York, 1959).

For Ives, see his own *Essays Before a Sonata and Other Writings* (New York, 1961); also in the *Three Classics* cited previously. An important sourcebook is *Charles E. Ives: Memos,* ed. John Kirkpatrick (New York, 1972). Henry and Sidney Cowell's *Charles Ives and His Music* (New York, 1955) and the author's "Charles Ives, American" in the August 1968 issue of *Commentary* cover Ives's life, work, ideas, and contributions.

Cowell's *New Musical Resources* (New York, 1930; reprinted New York, 1969) and the essays he edited under the title *American Composers on American Music* (1933; reprinted New York, 1962) are basic documents for the American 1920's and 1930's. Other material on or from this period would include Virgil Thomson's writings, notably *The State of Music* (rev. ed., New York, 1962) and *American Music Since 1910* (New York, Chicago, San Francisco, 1970–1971), Paul Rosenfeld's *Musical Impressions,* ed., Leibowitz (New York, 1969), as well as the issues of *Modern Music* and the *Copland on Music* volume already cited. Pound's *Antheil and the Treatise on Harmony,* originally printed in 1927, has been reissued (New York, 1968); Antheil's own *Bad Boy of Music* (New York, 1945) is an anecdotal autobiography. Partch's *Genesis of a Music* (Madison, Wisc., 1949) has been reprinted (1973). For Ruggles, see the author's article in the September 1966 issue of *Stereo Review.*

There is surprisingly little material on Varèse. Fernand Ouellette's *Edgard Varèse* (tr. New York, 1968) and Louise Varèse's memoirs *A Looking-Glass Diary* (New York, 1972), an issue of the French-Canadian review *Libertés,* ed. Ouellette (September–October, 1959), studies in *The Musical Quarterly* by Chou Wen-chung (April, 1966), and the author's article in the June 1971 issue of *Stereo Review* are some of the major references.

Peter Yates's *Twentieth-Century Music* (New York, 1967) is most valuable for its treatment of the American pioneers.

THIRTEEN
TECHNOLOGICAL CULTURE
AND ELECTRONIC MUSIC

The expansion of audio technology, the creation of *musique concrète*, the concept of a totally rationalized music, and the introduction of indeterminate elements into performance were almost simultaneous events. Suddenly composers seemed to turn back to that exploration of materials, techniques, and new perceptive forms which had marked the early years of the century. The movements of the late 1940's and 1950's returned to the discovery of new kinds of experience and new ways of experiencing, all propounded in rigorous forms—serial or indeterminate— pushed to their logical and physical extremes, much in the manner of controlled experimentation.

There are many parallels with the pre-World War I situation, but there are also many differences, notably the tremendous development of electronic technology. Among the tools and media that became widely available after World War II were magnetic tape, the long-playing record, improved recording technology including multi-track recording, two-

and four-channel playback, FM radio, various signal generation and modification equipment, and component sound reproduction. The availability of a variety of new means for creation and dissemination of new music has had a tremendous cultural impact. Technology has created a remarkable extension of common shared experience, an availability of (admittedly transformed) sound events, and the means for the quick dissemination and dispersal of new ideas. Attention is turned towards and then away from the minutiae of musical experience. As a result, the meaning of notation and the role of live performance have been drastically re-evaluated. The availability of new sounds, although significant, is nevertheless the least important result of the introduction of electronic technology. Total control, infinite repeatability, the widening of experience to include all possible sound and music, and the development of new modes of communication—these have been more important, particularly in suggesting strikingly new ways of dealing with the old questions of creation and communication.

THE BACKGROUND

The initial aim of technology was to transmit, store, and reproduce the live experience of sound; towards this aim the essential recording and playback devices were developed. Sound was coded for amplification, long-range transmission, or storage as electrical energy. But this energy could also be created with generators and used to drive loudspeakers directly; the result was sounds whose only existence was in the form of emission from a loudspeaker. The early work in this field was directed towards the invention of performance instruments such as the Hammond organ, the theremin, and the Ondes Martenot, all developed before World War II. The earliest sound experiments of Cage, Pierre Schaeffer, and Pierre Henri were with disc recordings; however, it was the invention and availability of magnetic tape that made the electronic music movement a reality. Tape is a faithful, pliable storage device which itself can be edited and manipulated in a variety of ways. Improved recording techniques as well as the various generators and sound modification devices offered the means for shaping sound much as a sculptor shapes his material. For the first time in music history, the composer was enabled to work directly in his medium without the necessary aid of performing interpreters. So-called "pure" electronic music is based on the fact that a loudspeaker can be driven to produce sound by electromagnetic impulses derived (with or without the use of tape storage) from electronic generators. These generators produce impulses ranging from the simple pulse of a sine wave (producing a "pure" sinusoidal tone) to the complex, random oscillation of all the audible frequencies (producing "white noise"). By contrast—although as we shall see the distinction has been rendered obsolete in practice—the use of recorded "real" sounds, no matter how manipulated, falls into the category of *musique concrète*.

Most tape/loudspeaker music shares certain basic techniques: the superimposition of layers of sound through simultaneous recording and overlaying, and the alteration of sound characteristics through the use of electronic filters, reverberation, tape loops (providing endless pattern-repetition), control of intensity, change of tape speed (producing transposition up or down to the limits of equipment response). Tape can be chopped or spliced in limitless combinations and juxtapositions, affecting the character of single sounds or whole structures. Sound transformations involving the finest distinctions or the most gradual rates of change may be juxtaposed with the most violent contrasts, and the extremes can be mediated by every possible gradation in between.

All of these early, basic techniques were considerably modified by the development of electronic music synthesizers, built especially for sound production (or "synthesis") and modification. The R.C.A. Synthesizer, still in use at the Columbia-Princeton Electronic Music Center in New York, was the first. Later generations of synthesizers have come into common use as the equipment, now transistorized, became more compact and less expensive. Synthesizers were originally designed for studio work, generally in conjunction with storage devices, mainly magnetic tape. More recently, however, they have been used in live performance, and units specially designed as performing instruments have become available.

The synthesis of loudspeaker sound through the use of computers was the logical next step in this direction, and, in spite of the high costs involved, studies are going on in this area. Computer generation of sound is a complex problem since, unlike the studio or synthesizer situation where the composer works directly with his medium, the computer tends to be twice removed from the final result (the output as transduced by a loudspeaker or stored on tape for replay). Computer synthesis may allow every level of pre-control from the simple synthesis of isolated sounds to a set of rules under which the computer itself "composes." In theory, at least, composers may someday compose computer programs with the information—the composition or the conditions for a realization—simply available for performers on demand. However, it is far from clear that this abstract idea of musical and creation and performance will ever have any cultural impact.

PRINCIPAL CENTERS

Although esthetics based on technology have played and continue to play a role in the history of recent music, tape and electronic music cannot be considered as a movement. It is a paradox that the single most widely influential medium of post-war musical life has produced no single "style" or "school"; the influence has been rather cultural, conceptual, and technical. In a real sense, technology is a set of tools as well as a cultural condition and, therefore, its relationship to the culture that produced it is one of continual feedback.

The closest approach to a tape-and-electronic movement is *musique concrète*, first realized in 1949 at the studios of the French national radio by Pierre Schaeffer and Pierre Henri. A number of important composers have worked at these studios including Varèse, Yannis Xenakis and, among younger French composers, Luc Ferrari. Although the long-range value of the work produced in Paris has been challenged, the *musique concrète* ideal—images of the external world juxtaposed, overlaid, fragmented, enlarged, dissected—remains important.

The Columbia University Studio, founded by professors Otto Luening (b. 1900) and Vladimir Ussachevsky (b. 1911) in 1952, tended from the very first to use live-recorded sound in conjunction with tape techniques. Luening and Ussachevsky were the first, after Varèse, to explore the important area of tape and live sound. In 1959, with the acquisition of the R.C.A. Synthesizer and the participation of Milton Babbitt of Princeton University, the studio became the Columbia–Princeton Electronic Music Center; it remains the principal center for tape and electronic music in the United States. Composers who have worked there include Varèse, Ussachevsky, Luening, Babbitt, Luciano Berio, Charles Wuorinen, Jacob Druckman, Alcides Lanza, Walter Carlos, the author, and others. Two composers closely associated with the studio are Mario Davidovsky (b. 1934), an Argentinian now living in New York and known for his adroit tape-live combinations, and Bülent Arel (b. 1918), who has founded electronic studios at Yale University and the State University of New York at Stony Brook, Long Island. Electronic music studios are now common in universities and colleges across the country.

The first and most important of the European electronic music studios was founded in Cologne, Germany, in 1951 by Herbert Eimert (b. 1897) with an emphasis on the purely electronic production of sound. This studio is closely associated with the work of Karlheinz Stockhausen. The most important of the numerous and often ephemeral studios that sprang up in these years—in Stockholm, Amsterdam, Warsaw, Tokyo, and elsewhere—was the Studio di Fonologia at the Milan radio station in north Italy. The studio was directed by Luciano Berio (b. 1924) and Bruno Maderna (1920–1973). The electronic work of Berio and Maderna—and also that of the Belgian Henri Pousseur (b. 1929)—although originally identified with the serial style of their instrumental music, was characterized by a close, empirical experimentation with new material. With a few exceptions, most of the works to come out of Milan have the character of exploratory essays in the discovery and transformation of materials. This was fairly typical of much of the early work in the medium. Many composers became interested in electronic music as a source of new sounds; others were looking for control. What they discovered was the continuum, the range of experience available in every domain. The unexpected result for some was a turn away from the tempered scale and a turn away from a simple twelve-tone approach—an expansion or even rejection of serialism. Nearly every serial composer who worked with electronics returned to live music with some modification of his older approach. Some abandoned predetermined, fixed, and closed forms as not being suited to live performance; tape could do it better. Most enriched their approach to performance in some way; nearly all combined live or recorded performed elements with the purely electronic textures. It is striking that the most significant tape and electronic pieces of the 1950's and early 1960's used the human voice—on tape or live with tape —as an essential part of the conception: Stockhausen's *Gesang der Jünglinge,* Berio's *Omaggio a Joyce* and *Visages,* Babbitt's *Vision and Prayer* and *Philomel.*

On the whole, the importance of the pure, fixed forms characteristic of the first electronic music has dwindled, and technological means have been absorbed into the mainstream of new music, not as a thing apart but as an essential part of a larger view. Cage, right at the start, managed to find ways to use tape in multiple montages to produce variable forms. It was also Cage, with his associates David Tudor (b. 1926) and Gordon Mumma (b. 1935), who first began working with electronic extensions of live sound. Such extensions have, of course, been the norm in pop music for many years, but their acceptance in non-pop was curiously delayed. Electronic extensions may amplify live sound, project it in space, or modify it in any number of ways. These techniques, first used independently by the Cage group, later by the author, by Stockhausen, and by others in the mid-1960's, have provided the basis for a new kind of live performance ensemble specializing in the electronic production and projection of sound. Examples of such groups include the ensembles founded by John Eaton and William O. Smith (b. 1926) in Rome; the Musica Elettronica Viva with Frederic Rzewski, Alvin Curran, Richard Teitelbaum, and others; Sonic Arts (Robert Ashley [b. 1930], David Behrman, Alvin Lucier [b. 1931], Gordon Mumma); and others. These groups use existing electronic equipment including synthesizers and tape playback along with especially designed circuitry to produce or modify electronic as well as more conventional vocal and instrumental sound. Live electronic performance of one sort or another has come to dominate new music performance in America in recent years and has achieved a good deal of importance in Europe as well. Technology, which at one time was thought to replace live performance, has in fact ended by re-invigorating it.

BIBLIOGRAPHICAL NOTES

Electronic Music: A Listener's Guide by Elliott Schwartz (New York, 1973) is a thoughtful, popular overview by a composer with broad interests and a great deal of insight. Hugh Davies's *Répertoire international des musiques électroniques* (Paris and New York, 1968) is a catalogue of music; Lowell M. Cross's *Bibliography of Electronic Music* (Toronto, 1967) lists over 1,500 works on the subjects. For *musique concrète,* see *Sept Ans de musique concrète* (Paris, 1954) and the special issue of the *Revue musicale,* No. 236. Stockhausen's "The Origins of Electronic Music" (*The Musical Times,* 112, July, 1971) gives his view of that subject. *Die Reihe,* No. 1, is devoted to electronic music; many other articles on it have appeared in *Perspectives of New Music, High Fidelity, Stereo Review,* and other publications. For computer music, see *Experimental Music* by Lejaren Hiller and Leonard Isaacson (New York, 1959) and *The Computer and Music,* ed., Harry B. Lincoln (Ithaca, 1970).

FOURTEEN

ULTRA-RATIONALITY
AND SERIALISM

With some validity, the history of Western composition since the Renaissance might be described as a continuing process of articulating the inarticulate. Gradually and increasingly, unorganized or purely conventional aspects of musical performance—phrasing, dynamics, articulation, timbre—were brought under notational control. Schoenberg's twelve-tone method, an attempt to organize the total chromatic material, is in part an extension of this control process. The relationships between background and foreground, harmony and melody, in Classical-Romantic music are essential to the success of that music. Schoenberg consciously attempted to make these relationships explicit with his twelve-tone idea; in his later music and, in particular, in the music of Webern, this process was extended to include the rhythmic, dynamic, and even timbral domains. What had long been the prerogative of the performer or lay within the domain of "tradition" now became part of the articulated compositional process. The notion of bringing all the elements or dimensions of musical discourse to the foreground and of rationalizing them seems to have occurred almost simultaneously in Europe and America.

BABBITT AND AMERICAN SERIALISM

The first works in which linear succession, harmonic simultaneity, duration (including rhythm and tempo), dynamics, articulation, register, and timbre are all strictly derived from a single, all-inclusive premise were written in 1948 by Milton Babbitt (b. 1916). Most of these techniques are worked out in his *Three Compositions* for piano; they are fully realized in his *Composition for Four Instruments* and *Composition for Twelve Instruments* of the same year. With Schoenberg and even Webern, the twelve-tone idea remained essentially a process or, to use Schoenberg's own term, a method. With Babbitt, it is most definitely and carefully a "system" in the strictest sense. The row becomes a "set" of values and relationships, absolutely and strictly defined not only in terms of structure but also of operational process. Thus the twelve-tone material represents the totality of possible relationships inherent in every aspect of the musical material, and the actual unfolding of each piece is a process of permutation within which all these potential relationships are revealed.

In the late 1950's, Babbitt began working at the newly re-organized Columbia–Princeton Electronic Music Center with the R.C.A. Electronic Sound Synthesizer. With the Synthesizer, a sophisticated instrument specifically constructed for the production of electronic sound, every aspect of both pitched and non-pitched sound—duration, quality of attack and decay (dying away), intensity, tone color, and so forth—can be set out with precise definition, and any sound can be tested immediately and, if necessary, readjusted down to the finest possible gradations. Babbitt's interest in electronic techniques has not been so much in matters of new sounds as in the possibilities of control, and his electronic works— *Composition for Synthesizer, Ensembles for Synthesizer*—have been primarily concerned with new ways of organizing time and form perception.

As with others of his contemporaries, Babbitt's electronic experience seems to have affected the character of his "live" performed music, which has taken on a new vitality and color. Works like *All Set* (1957) for jazz ensemble, *Partitions* (1957) for piano, and *Sounds and Words* for soprano and piano combine his typical clarity and care with a new richness and lively virtuosity appropriate to the conditions of live performance. Babbitt has also twice combined live performance with tape in works for soprano and synthesized tape: a setting of Dylan Thomas's *Vision and Prayer* (with a purely synthesized accompaniment) and *Philomel*, to a specially written text by John Hollander using live voice, recorded and altered vocal material, and purely electronic sound. The Greek legend of Philomel—a woman who was raped, had her tongue torn out and then, through the pity of the Gods, was turned into the nightingale—is rich in metaphoric material, which is emphasized by the musical and structural qualities of Hollander's poem. Language becomes a kind of musical expression, while the music becomes articulate and precise, almost like language. Inarticulateness and the quality of musical experience are rationalized and, as in all of Babbitt's work but with the greatest force in this one, a certain range of perception, carefully planned and controlled, is used quite literally to "express" complex, non-verbal thought processes (see Appendix; Example 14-1).

Babbitt has had a strong influence as a teacher and theoretician, primarily in the United States. The most skillful of his pupils—Donald Martino, Henry Weinberg, Peter Westergaard—have developed individual means and styles of considerable originality within the premises of total rationalization and control, and Babbitt's influence can be seen also in the work of composers like Charles Wuorinen, Harvey Sollberger, and others connected with the Columbia group. In the end, Babbitt's influence seems most significant not so much in specific matters of method or style as in the more general diffusion of concepts of technique and intellectual responsibility.

EUROPEAN SERIALISM

The first "totally organized" piece of music to be written in Europe was the etude, *Mode de valeurs et d'intensités,* one of a set of piano pieces written by Olivier Messiaen in 1949. Messiaen has a particular place in recent music both as the father of the European avant-garde and as a highly original figure in his own right. He is a professional organist in the tradition of Franck and Widor and a professed Christian mystic with strong pantheistic overtones to his thought. His position in European music has certain parallels to that of Varèse, who may have influenced his concepts of sonority and of static, spatial form. An influence of impressionism and even a touch of a rather (intentionally?) vulgar popular harmony is present in his earlier work. Later, he absorbed influences from some of the younger composers he himself had influenced. He developed a personal system of rhythmic modes derived from East Indian practice;

other techniques, notably the use of plainsong, derive from European medieval music. He has also made extensive use of transcriptions of bird song in works like *Oiseaux éxotiques* and *Catalogue des oiseaux*. From the rather insistent religiosity of his early works, often bordering on banality without any trace of redeeming irony, and the completely inward, brooding, meditative quality of his *Quartet for the end of time*— written in a German concentration camp—Messiaen's music has evolved into a distinct and unique amalgam of disparate elements. His studies in twelve-tone music, the serial innovations deriving from his work with rhythmic modes, and the influence of his pupil Boulez helped bring about this synthesis. *Chronochromie, Couleurs de la Cité Céleste, Turangalila,* and *Et Especto Resurrectionen Mortuum*, written for the 700th anniversary of the Rheims cathedral, are works of great spiritual intensity and, like the later works of Varèse, fully belong with the new post-war music.

Messiaen's importance as a teacher and as an influence on the younger European composers has been very great. After the war, he was one of the few European musicians who taught twelve-tone technique, the first to relate pitch serialization with organized rhythm, and almost the only one who was entirely free not only of the prejudices of the tonal system but of the orthodoxies of the Schoenberg followers as well. And he was the teacher of Pierre Boulez and Karlheinz Stockhausen and thus influenced directly the course of post-war European avant-garde music.

The most powerful impulse in the initial development of new ideas in post-World War II Europe was the re-appearance of twelve-tone technique. Whereas the development of twelve-tone ideas was fairly continuous in the United States, it was completely cut off in Europe by the crises of the 1930's and the war. The first task of the younger European composers—and, for that matter, many of the older ones—was the rediscovery of the one technique that seemed to offer a means of expressing new ideas in new ways; hence the great importance of a handful of teachers like Messiaen and of the newly created international school and festival at Darmstadt, where the long-suppressed music of Schoenberg and Webern could be heard and its techniques studied. Although the Schoenberg models were important, it was finally Webern who seemed to offer the way out of expressionism and the possibility of building a new music from the simplest and barest of premises: the younger European composers began as Webernites. Their initial premises were the individual, isolated sound event and the rational, organizing power of the serial principle; they did not hesitate to draw the most extreme conclusions from these simple propositions. The twelve-tone idea in pieces like Boulez's *Structures* for two pianos or Stockhausen's *Kontrapunkte* is not a method (in Schoenberg's sense) nor a complex system (in Babbitt's sense) but rather a total generating principle through which a new and complete identity of materials, means, structure, and expression could, hopefully, be achieved. The difficulty with this identity was always that it remained, even in the best works, a mere play of numbers arbitrarily translated into various musical facts, without a real organic base in perceptive experience. But it also gave rise to the characteristic European "serialism" with its idea of a fixed scale of values.

In serialism's simple early form, the twelve-tone arrangement of pitches was paralleled by an arrangement of twelve durations, a fixed grouping of twelve dynamic values, and so forth. All of the possible points of intersection of these values could then be plotted; the result was the piece.[1] The reign of this strict and narrow interpretation of serial technique was in fact rather brief, although literally dozens and even hundreds of totally organized, post-Webern serial pieces were written, nearly all for small combinations of instruments and nearly all based on a highly rationalized arrangement of isolated, "pointillist" events and textures, often surrounded by generous amounts of highly organized silence.

The initial impulses towards this refined, ultra-rational post-Webernism came from Messiaen and Boulez in Paris; a second group of composers in northern Italy—Luciano Berio, Bruno Maderna, Luigi Nono—came out of the Webern-Dallapiccola line partly under the influence and tutelage of the German conductor Hermann Scherchen, one of the few musical personalities whose activity links the Viennese School and the post-war avant-garde. But the most influential architect and theorist of European serialism was (and remains) Karlheinz Stockhausen. Stockhausen's initial concerns were the complete isolation and definition of every aspect of musical sound and the extension of serial control into every domain. The latter point is important: Stockhausen envisaged the possibility of serializing and thus pre-controlling even such matters as the density of harmonic, vertical masses; the number of musical events occuring in given time segments; the size of intervals and the choice of register; the types of attacks and articulations employed; the rate of change of texture and tone color. Often the technique and the formal ideas far outrun the actual materials; in the *Klavierstücke I–IV* (1952–1953), for example, there are combinations and refined distinctions which cannot be meaningfully realized. Later, Stockhausen was to return to performed music with new ways of applying serial technique to the

---

[1] It is not quite accurate to say, as some commentators have, that this is music in which analysis precedes composition. The analysis is quite equivalent to the piece.

necessities of live performance; in the early 1950's, however, electronic music seemed to offer the solution to the serial dilemma.

The use of electronic media had a very specific importance in Stockhausen's work: it offered him the possibility of creating new forms out of transformation and rate of change. Stockhausen's earlier instrumental works use material based on values arranged in fixed steps—sometimes conceived in terms of arbitrary and unidiomatic distinctions. In his electronic music—in particular, in his *Gesang der Jünglinge* of 1956—he could break away from the discreteness imposed by the use of individual instruments and by the tempered scale and literally break down conventional distinctions between noise and pitch, between clarity and complexity, between simple statement and transformed event, between pure electronic and recorded vocal sound, between gradualness, even between sound and silence. Later, partly under influences from the United States, Stockhausen was to discover a way of re-interpreting these principles in terms of "live," performed music; in a way, it was the electronic experience that was decisive. In 1959, Stockhausen wrote a tape piece, *Kontakte*, which is entirely structured on great continuous sliding transformations of every possible aspect—every dimension or, to use the term in vogue, "parameter"—of musical sound. *Kontakte* also exists in a version with two piano and percussion performers, in which even the gap between purely electronically produced and live sound is closed. Nearly all of Stockhausen's later work uses one form or another of electronic sound processing and in works like *Mikrophonie, Mixtur,* and *Hymnen* electronic transformation is the essential aspect of the form.

BIBLIOGRAPHICAL NOTES

Ann Phillips Basart's *Serial Music: A Classified Bibliography of Writings on Twelve-Tone and Electronic Music* (Berkeley, Calif., 1961) covers what might be called the classical period of the subject. Milton Babbitt's formulation of twelve-tone structure as a system is scattered in several highly technical articles in *The Score, Perspectives of New Music, Journal of Music Theory,* and *The Musical Quarterly.* Perhaps the most accessible expositions are those in *The Score* (December, 1963; reprinted in *Twentieth-Century Views of Music History,* New York, 1972) and *The Musical Quarterly* (April, 1960; entire issue reprinted in paperback form as *Problems of Modern Music,* New York, 1962).

For European serialism, see *Die Reihe,* especially Nos. 3 through 5; *Contemporary Music in Europe,* eds. Lang and Broder (New York, 1965;

reprinted 1967); Ulrich Dibelius, *Moderne Musik 1945–1965* (Munich, 1966); also Stockhausen, *Texte* (Cologne, 1963), and Boulez, *Notes of an Apprenticeship* (New York, 1968; translation of *Relevés d'apprenti*, Paris, 1966).

FIFTEEN

ANTI-RATIONALITY
AND ALEATORY

The appearance of "totally organized," totally rational music and the systematic abandonment of conscious, pre-set composer control were precisely coincidental in time. John Cage came out of the Ives-Cowell line and his early music is, in some respects, the end rather than the beginning of a development; it is, like much of Cowell's work of the 1930's and 1940's, concerned with non-tempered sounds, with percussion and with Oriental ideas. Cage's famous prepared piano is a kind of one-man percussion ensemble (often closely related in sound to the Javanese gamelan). A more prophetic idea was the use of phonographic test records to produce a kind of proto-electronic music. Eventually Cage abandoned not only steady-state pitch phenomena but also rational control over many aspects of the musical event. He threw dice,[1] used the *I Ching*, plotted

[1] *Alea*, Latin for dice, is the root of the word "aleatory," loosely used to describe various kinds of music in which chance elements, randomness, and indeterminacy figure in the "realization" in performance. Another adjectival form is

152

star charts or the imperfections on a piece of paper—not to give the performers freedom, but to de-control the conscious manipulation of sound. He produced a pair of tape-collage pieces (among the earliest tape pieces anywhere) as well as his famous *Imaginary Landscape* for twelve radios, random noise assemblages whose subject matter is a fixed time span within which aural objects—any aural objects (including other music) in any combination—may occur, plucked from the real world by random, intentionally irrelevant methods and put in random juxtaposition. Fixed time segments and some kind of graphic, schematic, or diagrammatic notations—newly invented or plotted for each piece—are characteristic of the live performed pieces. These notations are basically programs for activities; they renounce any specific control of actual sound results but merely define the limits of choice, the possible field of activity, and the impossibility of prediction. Scores or parts may be played separately, together, or not at all. Instruments are objects to be acted upon; sounds are a series of unpredictable disturbances and interferences. The graphic representation becomes partly an end in itself, a significant catalyst in an ongoing relationship between creator, performer, and listener. Musical performance becomes a kind of existentialist activity in which the notions of "musical composition," of "performance," of "communication," and of the "work of art" itself are destroyed or drastically altered; in which the real, determined world and the unreal, accidental world of "art" merge; in which the listener becomes directly involved in an activity in which the old distinctions and relationships are meaningless. Ultimately there need be no activity at all—only an open piano and the contemplation of 4′33″ of nothing at all. Cage's famous silent work, the classic and pure piece of non-music (1954), may be taken as a frame for the natural sounds of life, a segment of time isolated and defined in order to trap, for a moment, the experience of the haphazard, "real" world. Or it may be taken as the zero point of perception where total randomness and aleatory meet total determinism and unity in the literal experience of nothing.

Cage is not perhaps to be considered as a creator in the ordinary sense—but then he has done a great deal to change that "ordinary sense." He has been and remains one of the most influential figures in avant-garde arts since the war, and aspects of his work have generated whole esthetics of graphic notation; of performance as gesture; of chance, choice, and changes; of "neo-realist" use of accidental or chosen sound objects from the exterior world. Electronic music suddenly seemed to make the whole question of perfect order and rationality in performed

---

"aleatoric"; this is decried by some critics on the grounds that "aleatory" is already an adjective presumably derived from the French *aléatoire* meaning "chancy" or "risky." As usual, usage outruns etymology.

music irrelevant. It is in the nature of human activity that a precise action can never be repeated and that no event can ever recur; it seemed logical, particularly to the European dialectic mind, that irrationality and randomness should be built in as qualifications for the construction of a new instrumental and performed music. Actually, of course, irrationality and randomness are no more the essence of the human condition than is man's capacity to impose or conceptualize order in the external world. When a mathematician wants true randomness he turns to the machine and computer, and related techniques have been used, notably by Yannis Xenakis (b. 1922), to generate random statistical patterns—bunches of unpredictable events sprayed over a given field—which are subsequently translated into instrumental sound values.

An obvious corollary to the de-rationalization of composer control was the increased importance given to the performer's role in determining the details or the actual shape of a conception in performance. Already in the early 1950's, a number of composers—Earle Brown (b. 1926), Morton Feldman (b. 1926), Christian Wolff (b. 1934), comprising a New York school of "action music" close to but distinct from Cage—began to open up spaces within which multiple possibilities could be realized at the moment of execution. New notations were invented for these purposes, not only to indicate graphically the limitations of the space within which the performer could operate but also to re-engage the interpreter in a kind of dialectic vis-à-vis the score. The notations generally have exactly the opposite significance from the scientific, graphic indications which they often externally resemble. Scientific notations are ways of representing the precise course of observed events, generally on a continuum. Most of the musical graphics are, on the contrary, only generalized guides intended merely to outline or suggest to the performers the areas in which choice and chance are permitted to operate. Thus Feldman indicates, within a typically soft and spare range of sound events, general areas of attack, pitch, or register, the exact choice being left to the performer; the sound events are carefully isolated and disassociated from one another. Intentional disassociation—statement without relationship, evolution, or process—is a fundamental, underlying idea. Brown's *December 1952* is a series of horizontal and vertical black rectangles inked on a white sheet, indicating only some very general co-ordinates; within these, all choices are possible and equally valid. It is important not to confuse this music with improvisation; there is no question here of performance tradition or spontaneous invention within some given pattern but only controlled-choice situations in which any rational basis for decision has been intentionally removed or minimized.

These techniques of performer choice and of automatic chance mechanisms are also applied to the actual sequence of events in a performance and, thus, to larger "structure." By the application of an inexhaustible series of devices—shuffling pages, selecting fragments, performers interacting with one another, performers ignoring one another, live performance pitted against tape, and so forth—a conception is designed that will, on each reading, result in a new juxtaposition of the parts. In theory, there will be some constants from one performance to the next that will define the basic conception throughout all its transformations, but in some cases this constant would seem to be only the program for action itself.

Cage's earlier chance compositions tend to be fixed, principally in some kind of determined time span (details open, over-all space closed); after Cowell, Brown seems to have been the first to propose open form (details fixed; sequence variable). Later on, Cage also adopted the notion of multi-directional structures, applying this to diagrammatic programs of action; a work like his *Piano Concert* consists of a piano part, whose elements can be played in any order desired, and an orchestral part, to be realized by any number of players (including none) on any number of instruments, playing parts made up of pages of which any number may be played (including none), with or without other instruments. Beyond the free-will, existentialist music of chance and changes, Cage moved on into a vaster area of activity and gesture. He attached contact microphones to instruments and scratched record pick-ups and mike heads, clogging the lines of amplified communication with violent, random electronic "distortion"; he sent electronic feedback whirling through speaker systems and across the thresholds of perception and pain; he smoked cigarettes and swallowed water, contact mike at the throat, volume at full blast. Typically, he has left the exploration of complex and multiplying noise levels and indeterminacies to others and has moved logically onwards (he has always been more of a dialectician than his interest in Oriental ideas would lead one to believe) to a kind of ritual theater in which the act of performance becomes a way of drawing together meaningless and unordered bits of real life. *Indeterminacy: New Aspect of Form in Instrumental and Electronic Music* is, in spite of its grand title, a set of ninety funny stories—accompanied, interrupted, or blotted out by piano and electronic activities taken from the *Piano Concert*—slowly recited or gabbled through to make each story fit a one-minute space. His *Theater Piece* is a big amalgam of action and gesture indeterminately organized in a determinate time space.

HPSCHD is a multi-media work realized with Lejaren Hiller, based on a musical dice game attributed to Mozart and including computer read-outs, chunks of traditional music, and various visual elements.

From 4'33", the programmed absence of planned sound, Cage has come to programming excerpts from the totality of possible experience (give or take a possibility or two).

A good deal of this kind of activity is defined in a negative way by excluding certain ranges of possibility or, in some cases, by reversing the traditional premises. This is clearest in Morton Feldman's music where, instead of organizing sounds in relationship to one another, the elements are carefully disassociated. In traditional music (including earlier modern music) the essential character comes out of the way the music goes from one note to another. In Feldman's it is the isolated sounds themselves that are the essential experience, intentionally unrelated and disassociated from one another, thus creating a new time sense, previously unknown in Western music. In many Cageian and post-Cageian works, there is a set of activities regulated by a set of limitations, often with an intentional disassociation between the nature of the activity and its possible results in sound. Instead of being conceived as sound, performances may be based on visual definitions, programs of activity, ideas of non-sound or silence. Instead of defining time, the compositions are themselves defined by the random passage of time, extending to indeterminate or theoretically infinite length. Instead of a music of definable identity, we have conceptions whose essence is lack of identity.

In spite of their seeming opposition, serialism and indeterminacy have certain things in common. Both were, in their pure state, essential, relatively brief phases—a clearing of the ground, as it were, before reconstruction could begin. Both came out of philosophical attitudes about music and art—serialism contemplating the activity of the mind and its internal order, in Western determinist style; indeterminacy contemplating an Eastern-influenced philosophy of activity in the indifferent external world. In the end, Cage's use of chance or randomness was the least important aspect of his work; his conception of art as a human activity and his opening up of the external universe as subject matter for an art that had become almost entirely interiorized will stand as his major contributions.

The influence of Cage and his "school" (if one can use this terminology any more) has been very great in all the arts in the Americas, in Europe, and even in Asia.[2] This influence has ranged from the simple use

---

[2] A curious return of a compliment, since Cage and the "New York School" have appropriated ideas from the Orient. Japanese (and also Korean) composers have participated actively in musical developments of recent years. The best known of the Japanese Cageians is Toshiro Ichiyanagi. Many of the other Japanese, the Matsudairas (father and son), Toru Takemitsu, Toshiro Mayuzumi, and Kazuo Fukushima, as well as the Korean Isang Yun, have tended towards an adaptation of European serialism tempered by Oriental elements and chance, indeterminate, open-form, or even gestural materials derived from the "New York School."

of random noise techniques and chance procedures to various projects for a "neo-realist" theater of gesture and objects. Stockhausen used some kind of aleatory or open-form procedure in a whole series of works beginning with his *Klavierstücke XI* of 1956 (made of short piano segments which can be put together in different ways) and *Zyklus* of 1957 (a percussion piece written in a graphic notation and open for various realizations on a simple ground plan). Virtually all European avant-garde music of the last few years has been affected in some way. Mauricio Kagel (b. 1931), an Argentinian now living in Germany, has been specifically involved with the character of performance as gesture and activity. Others, including a number of young Germans and an Italian group working in an area close to "pop art," have used actual pre-existing sound objects as well as sets of activities and gestures for the materials of paste-up neo-realist collages. Stockhausen himself has written a Cage-like (but structured) theater piece (*Originale*) and there have been a number of random gestural-theater ventures of one sort or another. In the United States, "action" activity groups like 'Fluxus' in New York and exponents of a kind of mobile, kinetic music like the 'Once' group in Michigan have paved the way for a wide acceptance of the idea of activity—musical, meaningless or otherwise—as a way of life. Pop art, happenings, multimedia, minimalism, concept art, and contemporary music theater all owe something, or trace their origins, to Cage; the impact of his ideas is now so generalized that one can only describe them as having entered the mainstream of twentieth-century art.

BIBLIOGRAPHICAL NOTES

There is no clear line of distinction between Cage's writings and his musical works; see his collections *Silence* and *A Year From Monday* (Middletown, Conn., 1961, 1969; the former in paperback, Cambridge, 1966); a new collection will be out in 1973. A full Cage bibliography would be immense; material on his work and ideas has appeared in many languages and in many kinds of publications dealing with contemporary culture. The major study on Cage is edited by Richard Kostelanetz (New York, 1970; with a very extensive bibliography); see also the catalogue of his works put out by his publisher (C. F. Peters), which is, in the Cageian tradition, something more than a catalogue (New York, 1962). His *Notations* (with Alison Knowles; New York, 1969), a collection of manuscript pages by more than 250 composers together with a typographical arrangement of their comments about notation, constitutes at once documentation of an important subject and at the same time a typical Cage project. Peter Yates's *Twentieth-Century Music* (New York, 1967) is particularly valuable for its comments on the American individualist or experimental tradition and Cage's place in it.

On the Fluxus group and related phenomena, there are a number of collections of events, proposals, and other matter; one anthology (called *Anthology*) was put together by LaMonte Young and George Brecht. The *Something Else Press Newsletters*, ed., Richard Higgins (New York and Vermont) and other publications as well as various issues of *Source* magazine document this period and these ideas.

For the European view of aleatory, open-form, and related ideas, see later issues of *Die Reihe* and the *Darmstädter Beitrage*. Boulez's "Alea," originally presented as a paper at Darmstadt in 1957, is published in translation in the Fall–Winter, 1964, issue of *Perspectives of New Music;* the Fall–Winter, 1965, issue includes "Indeterminacy: Some Considerations" by Roger Reynolds. "The Significance of Aleatoricism in Twentieth-Century Music" by Anthony Cross, originally published in *The Music Review* (London, 1968) has been reprinted in *Twentieth-Century Views of Music History,* ed. William Hays (New York, 1962).

SIXTEEN

THE NEW PERFORMED
MUSIC: AMERICA

In a sense, it was possible to grasp the real impact of electronic music only when its limitations began to be understood. Anything can be reproduced or synthesized on tape except the act of performance itself. The result was that the experience of working in the studio led composers back to the performance situation with a new understanding of that medium. If total control was part of the genius of the electronic medium, then this was no longer a necessary goal for live performance. Since no two live performances can ever be identical anyway, it seemed to make sense to make variability and choice a part of the music. Since an essential element in the performance act is the personality and ability of the performer, performer choice, virtuosity, and freedom could be built in from the start; open form and graphic notations flourished. Other influences from the tape and electronic experience were equally important. The notion of working with the sound material on a continuum could be applied very well to the live situation. Tempered-scale restrictions need no longer be universally observed. New techniques, new sounds, new extremes of range and virtuosity could be explored by composers working closely together with a new breed of performers. The richness and virtuosity of instrumental and even vocal performance were sought out and developed to a remarkable degree with the performer—himself sometimes a composer—as a collaborator in the realization.

Some of the conditions of this performance situation are the following: (1) control (the tension growing out of the necessity to put the right finger in the right place at the right time) interacting with freedom (the flexibility of actions whose precise value is determined only at the moment of performance); (2) interaction between composer and performer as well as between performers; (3) interaction between the musicians and the performing space and, possibly, between the live performance and electronic transformation through amplification, modification, and playback; (4) performer choice, improvisation, and controlled virtuosity set at the limits of performer possibility; (5) exploration of the limits of form perception.

This "new virtuosity" was not mere embellishment but an organic part of the musical substance itself. A unified set of actions and gestures functions as a source of thematic ideas which form relationships—between performer and score; between real (i.e., clock) time and psychological time; between fixed units of measure and open cadenza; between control and complex precision on the one hand and the open play of color and virtuosity on the other; between the uniqueness of the individual performers (in character, in material, even in space) and the overall unity of the conception; between the requirements of what can be perceived and new ideas of concept, activity, and substance extended in every direction and dimension to the most extreme limits.

This is no longer a music of fixed goals but of tranformations which take place in every dimension and throughout the range of perception. These transformations become ways of acting and experiencing, and relating action and experience, i.e., of knowing. In a sense, the aim is actually to alter, extend, and redefine the quality of our experience and the limits of our ability to perceive and understand.

In Europe, some change of direction could already be seen in the mid-1950's: Boulez's *Le Marteau sans maître* (1955), in which a complex poetic and conceptual form replaces a "merely" serial one; Nono's *Il Canto sospeso* (1955–1956), with its use of *engagé* texts (letters from the partisan underground) set for large, multi-layered orchestral and vocal forces; Stockhausen's *Zeitmasse* (1956), with its alternation of controlled and flexible situations. Change is evident in Milton Babbitt's *All Set, Vision and Prayer,* and *Philomel,* works which, although they remain faithful to a vision of total rationality and control, also relate to the character of the live performance situation and the virtuosity of the performer. The appearance of a new generation of performers—Bethany Beardslee, Cathy Berberian, David Tudor, Paul Jacobs, Severino Gazzeloni, Paul Zukofsky, Siegfried Palm—skillful in the traditional ways but open to the extention of techniques and ideas, was essential. The evolution of a new generation of conductors—the composers Foss, Boulez, Maderna, as well as Andrej Markowski, Michael Gielen, Michael Tilson Thomas, and others—completed the cycle.

THE NEW VIRTUOSITY

Not all of the composers involved in the new performance practice were veterans of twelve-tone serialism, aleatory, or electronic music; the presence of an active, younger generation of American performers, a certain currency of ideas and personalities, and a more unbroken tradition of new-musical and experimental activity and performance gave a certain distinct "third stream" character (to use in a wider sense Gunther Schuller's term for the jazz/non-jazz merger) to much new-musical activity in the United States. In this respect, the work and influence of two older composers, Stefan Wolpe (1902–1972) and Elliott Carter, and a number of younger Americans must be considered here.

Wolpe, like Varèse, was born and trained in Europe where his early work was connected with radical musical and political movements. After a sojourn in Palestine in the late 1930's, he came to the United States where, after World War II, he evolved a mature, radical, and highly influential abstract expressionist style. In this sense Wolpe's work is parallel to that of certain highly influential emigrés connected with New York School painting—Josef Albers, Hans Hoffman, and William de Koening. Wolpe's experimental work of the 1940's and early 1950's—*Battle Sonata* for piano, Quartet for trumpet, tenor, saxophone, percussion and piano, *Enactments* for three pianos—is connected with jazz and American performance practice on the one hand and with Cage, Tudor, and the nascent New York action-painting, action-music avant-garde on the other. His later work combines a striking individuality and assertiveness with a development of organic form and a concept of ordered freedom which is related to but quite distinct from either European or American serialism. Works like *In Two Parts* for flute and piano, *In Two Parts* for six players, and *Piece for two Instrumental Units* take shape from the constant interplay of oppositions of clarity and complexity, simplicity and density, careful articulation and freedom. Wolpe's forms, like Varèse's, accumulate as great static objects, but the ideas and the small-range motion are packed with intense, revolving detail. Many of these works are built on tiny, cell-like structures which retain their essential, immovable identity through every kind of registral, rhythmic, dynamic, and color shift; the larger result is an accumulation of potential energies which twist, turn, combine and recombine, destroy and reconstruct an apparently unyielding material. Nearly all of Wolpe's work is closely involved therefore with a complex use of the energies produced by the act of performance and, as much as anything else, it is this flow of form-making energy which gives his music its unique character.

Wolpe taught at the Third Street settlement in New York, at Black Mountain College in North Carolina, and privately. Most of the older American avant-gardists did little or no teaching; Wolpe was for many years one of the few who espoused new ideas. As a teacher, as a source of new ideas, and as a highly original composer, Wolpe exerted a major and not yet fully documented influence on the course of new music.

The concept of cumulative form, deriving from the work of Varèse and Wolpe, had two major influences. One, essentially East European, flows through the work of the sometime Varèse collaborator Yannis Xenakis (b. 1922), the Hungarian György Ligeti (b. 1923), and the new Polish school, notably Kryztof Penderecki (b. 1933). The other stream is connected with the building-block structures of a number of American composers, most notably Ralph Shapey (b. 1921) and George Crumb (b. 1929). Shapey, perhaps one of the most underrated contemporary composers, can also be associated with New York School painting although for a number of years he has been directing a contemporary music ensemble in Chicago. Like Boulez, Maderna, Foss, and Schuller, Shapey has been active as a conductor, and there is a closeness to sonorous material in all his work. Shapey's music—*Discourse* for flute, clarinet, violin, and piano of 1960–61 can serve as a typical example—uses large, contrasting, block-like ideas set forth in broad planes and constantly turning and returning in great, overlapping, phased cycles. Shapey's ideas are highly charged patterns, melodically simple, often highly dissonant, and strikingly articulated with rhythmic energy and accent. Within a static structure of balanced, inflexible, and immobile units, there is a kind of internal play of energies resulting from the continuous redefinition of a fixed material which remains set in a constant state of tension. Occasionally these accumulated energies are let loose in an explosive manner: in *Rituals* for orchestra, this actually takes the form of improvisational elements; elsewhere, this release is expressed by a more controlled pile-up of instrumental and percussive energies.

Shapey's output is considerable and encompasses a variety of traditional and non-traditional instrumental and vocal/instrumental media. A number of his works, notably the Violin Concerto, *Rituals*, and *Ontogeny* for orchestra, are organized into larger cycles of large scope. Shapey's music represents a major extension of the old idea of originality, individualism, personal expression, and a kind of visionary power as the artist's true domain. In a sense, all his work is a representation of a kind of personal willfulness and protest—the act of individual will imposing itself on a not always very receptive mass society. It is against this background that Shapey's rather startling recent decision to stop composing and withdraw all his works must be understood.

The music of George Crumb stands rather apart from that of his contemporaries in its special feeling for sonority, its exploitation of unusual, invented, or even familiar and referential gestures, its ritualistic and mystical qualities, its essential simplicity and intense poetic sensibility. Crumb's static forms and juxtapositions are derived from the Varèse tradition and relate to certain European music, mainly East European and French. His extreme sensitivity to timbre and isolated sound grows out of the most rarefied forms of post-Webernism; his simplicity, block form, and use of repetition suggest a Stravinskyite turned minimalist; and his sense of time is not unlike that of Morton Feldman. These points of reference may suggest influences, but in fact Crumb's independence and individuality make it difficult to categorize his work. Whereas, for example, Feldman tries to do away with the linear, developmental aspects of time to focus on the "it-ness" of the sound experience itself, Crumb is engaged in a larger and much more difficult task: the suspension of the sense of passing time in order to contemplate eternal things. This preoccupation with time is characteristic of Crumb's work from the several compositions titled *Madrigal* and *Night Music* (1963, 1964) to instrumental works like *Eleven Echoes of Autumn* (1965), *Echoes of Time and the River* (1970), *Four Processionals* for orchestra (1967), the vocal *Ancient Voices of Children* (1970), and the more recent ritualized chamber pieces utilizing masked performers and amplified instruments (e.g., *Black Angels* for electric string quartet, 1970). Many of these works use texts or fragments from Federico Garcia Lorca, often spoken or whispered by the instrumentalists. All of them share the very special sense of ritual which is Crumb's particular contribution to the contemporary live performance idiom.

The other major, and older, American whose work must be considered here is Elliott Carter. Carter, who was born in New York in 1908, studied at Harvard and with Nadia Boulanger, and was one of the few younger composers who was close to Ives; also, although his earlier work reveals a rather complex American neo-classicism, there are many musical and intellectual strands which connect him with Varèse, Ruggles, and the American experimental tradition. At the end of the 1940's and early in the 1950's Carter began to expand his vocabulary in the direction of a non-twelve-tone instrumental chromaticism. Works like the intense First String Quartet (1951), based on long, contrapuntal lines, and the more decorative and elegant Sonata for flute, oboe, cello, and harpsichord (1953), with its new element of ornamental virtuosity, grow out of the interaction of complex parts; the *Eight Etudes and a Fantasy* for woodwind quartet (1952) constitute a set of close-up studies of simple and very precisely defined material; the most remarkable is a study on a single pitch. By the *Variations for Orchestra* of 1955 and the Second String Quartet of 1959, Carter had achieved an identification of the material, the performing situation, and the individualization of the players through a form which is non-serial yet controlled, flexible and "invented" yet completely organic. In the Second String Quartet, the four players are separated in physical space and completely individualized in their musical way of speaking; the parts are related by a common virtuosity—a kind of highly ornamented fantasy style in which the "embellishments" and colors are not merely decorative but organic and essential—and yet each has distinct characteristics of pitch, rhythm, and dynamic. The totality of the piece is a confluence of divergent currents which retain their identity while remaining essential parts of the larger flow. In the *Double Concerto* for piano and harpsichord of 1960–1961, the two solo instruments are set off against one another, each with its own small ensemble of winds and strings, plus a huge battery of percussion which literally frames the piece in highly articulated noise. The pitch content of the piece emerges from and eventually returns to a more undifferentiated state of percussion "noise," and these transitions are, so to speak, mediated by the soloists who perform on what are, in effect, pitched percussion instruments. The same integrated opposition which exists between pitch and noise on one level operates, on another plane, between interval pattern and rhythm; and these in turn generate a big structure of changing, "modulating" tempos. Again, as in the Second String Quartet, the parts are distinguished by complementary pitch and rhythmic content. The total impression becomes that of a sum of disparate elements—a sum of rhythms, for example, which generates a higher-level pulse that ultimately determines the overall motion. The rhythmic groupings and phrase articulations, taken through wide changes of register and timbre, carry out the association of pitch, texture, and rhythm; just as there is a sum of rhythms, there is a sum of textures, lines, and harmonic conglomerations which integrates highly differentiated material and derives a new and expressive form from them.

The "tradition" of Varèse, Wolpe, Carter, and Shapey forms a New York School of a distinct character, and their influences are carried forward in the work and activity of a group of composers associated with Columbia University: Charles Wuorinen (b. 1938), Harvey Sollberger

(b. 1938), and Chou Wen-chung (b. 1923 in China). Chou was one of Varèse's few formal pupils and is his musical executor; he completed his teacher's last major uncompleted work, *Nocturnal,* from the surviving sketches. His own music represents a fusion of conceptual ideas derived from the East, Western serialism, and Varèse's idea of block or cumulative form. Serialism plays an important role in the music of Wuorinen, who, with the flutist and composer Sollberger, founded and directs the Group for Contemporary Music, which was active for a decade at Columbia and is now sponsored by the nearby Manhattan School of Music. Wuorinen, who is also a skilled pianist and conductor, is a prolific composer whose earlier work is closely connected with his own performing interests and abilities; his *Piano Variations* (1963) includes, besides fistfuls of notes articulated in the usual way, the brushing and slamming of the keys with fingers, palm, and fist; plunking, hitting, and scratching the strings directly inside the piano; and so forth. This earlier, wilder, more intuitive style has gradually been replaced by a more elaborated and studied approach that owes a great deal to Babbitt and twelve-tone serialism (thus somewhat reversing the evolutionary sequence found in European avant-garde music). This style, which can be heard in Wuorinen's recent Concerto for amplified violin and orchestra, his music theater piece *The Politics of Harmony* based on Chinese legend, and many other chamber and symphonic works, develops a very highly controlled and intellectualized series of modes controlling extremes of density, register, virtuosity, forward thrust and immobility, violent energy and violent calm.[1] Sollberger's *Chamber Variations* (1964) similarly grows out of an extraordinary virtuoso instrumental technique characterized by a tension of contrasts and the unified opposition of extremes, tightly controlled at first, then ultimately decontrolled, in every dimension and with extreme precision.

Many of the younger American composers are themselves expert instrumentalists or conductors. One can speak of a new performance-practice involving the closest interaction between the creative and performance processes. Chicago and New York ensembles have already been mentioned. Other important composer-performance centers in the 1960's included a group at the University of Illinois—Kenneth Gaburo (b. 1926), Lejaren Hiller (b. 1924), Ben Johnston (b. 1926), and Salvatore Martirano (b. 1927)—working with a performance ensemble, a new-music chorus, an electronic studio, and a lively performance situation. Gaburo and Mar-

---

[1] Ironically, Wuorinen won the Pulitzer Prize for a purely electronic work, *Time's Encomium* (1968–1969), realized on the RCA Synthesizer at the Columbia-Princeton Center. However, Wuorinen, whose interest in the electronic medium stems from the total-control philosophy of Babbitt, is not primarily an electronic composer; the use of technology remains secondary in his work.

tirano both extended the idea of solo virtuosity into choral ensemble music. Martirano's *O, O, O, O, That Shakespeherian Rag* (1959), a setting of Shakespeare for chorus and instruments, is built on a complex of singing, speaking, trilling, hissing, whispering, and shouting; the instrumental frame (informed by a virtuoso performing technique evolved to a point close to jazz) is at once contradictory and essential, equally free and planned, in a structure which is both controlled and dramatic. His *Ballad* for pop singer and ensemble, *Underworld* (1965, a theater piece), and *L's G A* for actor, film, and tape extend a virtuoso solo style in the direction of a wider consciousness, close to multi-media and music theater.

Gaburo, who founded and directed the new-music chorus at Illinois, has reconstituted this activity at the University of California at San Diego. California, now a major creative and performance center, has revived the performance-practice traditions of the 1930's: Partch is still active in Southern California, and the Cageian tradition is still very much alive. Robert Erickson (b. 1923), originally from the San Francisco area but currently active at San Diego, has been working out new performing situations which combine improvisation and written scores; he has also been active in the continuing development and construction of new instruments and instrumental types. Other California composers working in a performance-practice area include Larry Austin (b. 1930), Charles Boone, Pauline Oliveros (b. 1932), and Morton Subotnick (b. 1933). Subotnick, one of the pioneers of multi-media and synthesizer work, has more recently been working with game and theater forms; similarly, the concept-art and theater work of Austin and Oliveros take us into new areas (see Chapter 18).

Perhaps the first and best-known ensemble for non-jazz improvisation was that of Lukas Foss, who founded the Improvisational Chamber Ensemble in Los Angeles in the late 1950's. Foss's idea was—in the absence of an improvisatory performing tradition in music other than jazz—to invent the conditions (basically the limitations) within which a new kind of improvisation could take place. The importance of the Ensemble was not so much its demonstration of the possibilities of spontaneity and "discovered form" as the corroboration of a new vitality in creative performance based on the character of the instruments and the skill and personality of the players. Significantly, Foss's own creative work—up until then closely identified with American neo-classicism—underwent a striking evolution at this time. *Time Cycle* (1960), a twelve-tone work for voice and instruments, has several versions, some of which can include actual improvisation. *Echoi* of 1963 is directly involved with post-serialism and performer choice; indeed, it has the character of a set of free and exceptionally successful improvisations. The forms are in fact controlled, yet they give the impression of growing out of the character of the detail

—which is, in turn, an outgrowth of a genial conception of the pleasures and possibilities of the live performance situation.

After Foss's appointment as music director of the Buffalo Symphony, the activity of the Ensemble lapsed. But, with the collaboration of the State University and the Albright-Knox Gallery and the Symphony, Foss organized a major new-music center in Buffalo. This center, which emphasized close relationships between performer and composer, produced an ambitious and wide-ranging program of new-musical performance involving the entire spectrum of new ideas in Buffalo, in New York, and on tours. Foss's own work typically absorbed and synthesized most of these new trends. His *Baroque Variations* is a meditative or hallucinatory experience of eighteenth-century music far removed from "neoclassicism." *Paradigm* re-introduces texts and repetition in a manner that owes something to the minimalists (see Chapter 18). *Geod* employs four orchestras disposed in a 360-degree area, each playing a different kind of material—in effect, an environmental work using traditional forces. All of Foss's recent music reveals his exceptional ingenuity and musical facility; his work is always conceived very close to the act of performance itself, and this gives it a concreteness, a sense of reality, and a sense of spontaneity and inventiveness that is never far from the improvisatory performance-practice ideal.

"THIRD STREAM"; THE NEW PERFORMANCE PRACTICE

The only important living tradition of improvisation in Western music is that of jazz—now a complex form that has evolved very rapidly. In a sense, jazz has recapitulated in a matter of decades a cycle that took "classical" music two or more centuries to complete (and there is evidence that a similar cycle is taking place in rock over a period that can be measured in years). Jazz is now "art" music like any other; hence it is understandable that as modern "concert" music approaches the conditions of jazz—in improvisatory freedom and instrumental virtuosity—so modern jazz and post-jazz have been approaching the conditions of avant-garde music. A brief note here cannot do justice to this important development, but the names of a few of the outstanding innovators in the field should be mentioned, notably those of John Coltrane, Ornette Coleman, Cecil Taylor, Eric Dolphy, and John Lewis. These musicians and others are distinct personalities, but their identification with the controlled richness of a complex, modern performing style, with a tremendous instrumental virtuosity and a wide harmonic and melodic range is common and basic to all. The free, extreme explorations of still

younger musicians—Albert Ayler, Archie Shepp, Sun Ra, the Jazz Composers Orchestra—shake off most conventional ideas of jazz "sound" entirely and approach the conditions of other new music; often their
music relates to traditional jazz only in its impromptu, intuitive, ecstatic
qualities.

Breaking down the "hardening of the categories" that divides the
various forms of pop, jazz, and non-jazz from each other has long occupied thoughtful musicians from Ives to Copland, Gershwin, and Weill.
Gunther Schuller (b. 1925), himself a performer and conductor active in
several areas, has long advocated an interaction and synthesis of styles.
Schuller, whose basic orientation is a kind of American twelve-tone expressionism, has explored stylistic cross-cuts (*Seven Studies on Themes of
Paul Klee* for orchestra, 1959), spatial polyphony (*Spectra* for multiple
orchestras), and a kind of modern instrumental *Gebrauchsmusik* (many
chamber and ensemble pieces for standard and non-standard combinations). But he is best-known for the pieces which incorporate jazz or improvisatory elements: *Abstraction* for jazz group and orchestra, an opera
(*The Visitation*) based on Kafka's *The Trial* but set in the American south,
and other works. Schuller, who coined the term "third stream" for this
intersection of styles, has carried it to some degree into his written-out
twelve-tone music, which grows out of a spontaneous and idiomatic instrumental invention that often opens up to allow for the image, if not
the actual substance, of improvisation.

In spite of Schuller's own work, his sponsorship of a number of
younger men, and his recent activity as president of the New England
Conservatory (where both jazz and non-jazz traditions are represented in
an active teaching and performance scene), a real "third-stream" movement has not materialized to any notable extent. In fact, the impact of
rock (see Chapter 18) has, to some degree, taken the play away from the
experimental jazz musicians, and musicians like Miles Davis (from the
jazz side) and The Soft Machine, Frank Zappa, or Emerson, Lake, and
Palmer (from the rock side) have re-invigorated jazz tradition with electric instruments and an approach using strong rock/blues elements.
Nevertheless, if understood in a wider and more general sense than usually employed, the "third-stream" concept remains useful. Music, like all
of the arts in technological society, no longer flows in one or two main
currents and—to give the argument a somewhat more dialectic cast—the
merging of seemingly opposing streams or traditions continues to play a
role in producing the new syntheses that are increasingly important in
late twentieth-century art.

The music of Earle Brown has developed in the direction of a very
distinct and notable performance-practice synthesis growing out of the

experience of aleatory and open form. Brown, who studied the Schillinger system[2] and was long active as a recording engineer, was one of the original Cage group about 1950; he produced some of the first work to use graphic notation, open form, and performer choice. Out of this he evolved a kind of "action music"; the analogy is with New York School of "action painting," with the important difference that the ultimate goal is the performance activity itself and not the production of an object. This music is not aleatory (chance plays little or no role in it), and it is not improvisational in the traditional way (which uses fixed or periodic forms with improvised details). The basic principle is that of controlled improvisatory freedom arrived at through the interaction of the musicians at the moment of performance. Works like *Available Forms 1 and 2* (1961–1962; for chamber and large orchestra respectively) are made up of fixed details which can be "improvised" into a form. The performers make their decisions by reacting, within a specified technique, to each other as well as to the flexible character of the materials. In *Available Forms 2* a more or less standard symphony orchestra in a normal seating pattern is divided into intermeshed groups, each of which responds to the cues of an independent conductor; each conductor chooses material at the given moment by responding to the immediate situation and to the choices of his confrère. As with any improvisation, the results can be extremely variable depending on, among other things, the skill and sensitivity of the performers; when everything is working well, there is a sense of lively, organized spontaneity, a kind of controlled incoherence of great vitality, and, from time to time, a real impression of "discovered" form arising from the interaction of an effectively conceived musical action and gesture (see Appendix; Example 16-1).

Brown's approach to structure—best described as open or kinetic form and often compared to the mobiles of Alexander Calder—is a satisfactory meshing of the desire for control and need for performer flexibility and freedom; it has had a particularly notable impact on the course of European serialism. Brown has more recently returned to fixed, larger forms within which, however, graphic notation permits flexibility in detail. The composer-performer collaborative process is always important in his work.

One of the natural results of the new performance practice and the emphasis on composer-performer collaboration has been the formation of performance and improvisation ensembles. Besides the Foss group and other California activity already mentioned, there have been a number

---

[2] Josef Schillinger (1895–1943) attempted to produce a mathematical synthesis of music and musical theory; ironically, his influence was much greater in the pop and jazz world than in other areas of new music.

of collaborative organizations formed in the United States and in Europe. *Musica Elettronica Viva,* already mentioned in another context, went so far as to permit members of the audience to "sit in" or even take over the performance activity.

Open form, the new performance practice, and improvisation were foci of certain kinds of new-music activity not very long ago but they are no longer at center-stage. This is not because these ideas are no longer "viable" but because, as with many important new ideas, they have passed into the new-music mainstream.

BIBLIOGRAPHICAL NOTES

The author's contribution to *The New American Arts* (ed., Kostelanetz; New York, 1964; paperback, 1967) is an amplification of the material in this chapter. Various issues of *Perspectives of New Music* offer further information about the composers discussed here. *Flawed Words and Stubborn Sounds—A Conversation With Elliott Carter,* by Allen Edwards (New York, 1972), and two articles in *The Musical Quarterly* (Richard Franko Goldman, 1957; Kurt Stone, 1969) concern Carter's music and ideas.

The following selected list of works on jazz and its history is intentionally large since this important subject has not been treated here: Leonard Feather, *The Encyclopedia of Jazz* and *The Encyclopedia of Jazz in the Sixties;* Rudi Blesh, *Shining Trumpets: A History of Jazz* (2nd ed., New York, 1958); Nat Hentoff and Albert J. McCarthy, *Jazz* (New York, 1959); André Hodeir, *Jazz; Its Evolution and Essence* (New York, 1956); Gunther Schuller, *Early Jazz, Its Roots and Musical Development* (New York, 1968); LeRoi Jones, *Black Music* (New York, 1970).

See also H. Wiley Hitchcock, *Music in the United States,* a companion volume in the Prentice-Hall History of Music Series.

SEVENTEEN

POST-SERIALISM:
THE NEW PERFORMANCE
PRACTICE IN EUROPE

There are many good arguments against any continuing separation of European and American music—or, for that matter, of a separation from either of them of Asian music. Communications systems are now effectively global, and influences travel quickly; there should be, presumably, no reason for provincialism anymore, and avant-gardism is an international, although distinctly Western, phenomenon. Nevertheless, the old social and economic structures continue to exist, and influences continue to radiate from the powerful economic centers; what we call internationalism is sometimes only a form of cultural imperialism. Furthermore, as the inevitable reaction to that sets in—and there is an important need for artists once again to work on the community level—localism, barely banished, may well return.

In any case, it is still useful to continue with a certain categorization of new music. Not only are there meaningful distinctions between Old World and New but we can, if pressed, discern clear national differ-

ences between, say, Stockhausen, Boulez, and Berio—differences that
certainly have something to do with national character. It is a moot point
whether it is the connections or the differences which are more important;
every successful work of art or artistic experience, even the most "advanced," partakes of both the particular and the universal.

STOCKHAUSEN

After the middle 1950's, the character of new European music
began to change drastically. Totally controlled serialism, growing out of
the identity of the isolated musical event, gave way to a new idiom based
on transformations of densities, colors, and textures; on the "statistical"
(i.e. controlled chance) arrangement of events; on multiple, open, or
"chance" forms. The systematic development and application of such
ideas in European music is largely due to Karlheinz Stockhausen. Stockhausen argued for the controlled use of multiple realization as a new conception of performed music, and he argued that such new techniques
were in themselves new forms; a work like his *Momente* (1958) is conceived as a complete set of possible realizations for what he designates
as the "moment" form—the scheme, so to speak, for an infinite number of
possible actual realizations. In effect, the basis of these new forms—one
to a piece, with Stockhausen—is an extension of the concept of serialization into every dimension of the musical conception; even the amount and
quality of specific compositional control over the performers is arranged
on a serial scale of values ranging from total notated control to extreme
variability. Performer action may be designated by graphic notations that
delimit fields of wide or limited choice, elaborate and loose densities of
note-spattering or very closely unified sound structures, with transformations through all possible values in between. Similarly, Stockhausen began
to use a basic material which ranges away from pitch towards a complex
use of "noise"—that is, patterns of unfixed or random frequency content—
and away from all types of simple steady-states to complex superimposi-
tions of oscillating patterns. He serialized density and complexity themselves; he serialized periodicity (that is, cyclical and repeated structures)
and a-periodicity (or asymmetrical and non-repetitive structures); he
serialized the concept of transformation and change, the disposition of
sounds in physical space, and the perception of clarity and complexity,
comprehensibility and confusion; he serialized ways of perceiving; and
he serialized the construction of time and the ways of acting—of "performing"—in time. Out of all this, Stockhausen derived a characteristic
notion of form: the unique set of propositions in each piece which relates

these various kinds of serialized activity. Beginning in 1956 with *Zeitmasse* and continuing with *Klavierstück XI, Zyklus, Refrain* for three keyboard-percussion players, the theater piece *Originale, Gruppen* for three orchestras, *Momente* for chorus, keyboard, percussion and brass instruments, and *Carré* for four choruses and four instrumental ensembles, each conception is a specific representation of very carefully defined formal, serial techniques, each developed uniquely for the particular conception. Thus *Momente* is based on an enormous range of performing activities including all kinds of playing, banging, singing, speaking, hand-clapping, foot-shuffling, whispering, and babbling, all arranged in varying degrees of control and randomness, clusters and isolated tones, densities and simplicities, clarities and confusions. Even the communication of the texts (which must be translated into the language of the local country) is serialized with regard to comprehensibility. All of this material is arranged into a series of events or "moments"—not isolated sounds but complex occurrences of a given duration—which, by an arbitrary arrangement of the pages of the scores and parts, may be placed in any order. Finally, even any given sequence of these events or "moments" is further complicated by a system of interpolations—insertions or "tropes," one might say —in which material from certain events may be anticipated or recalled during the performance of others.

In one sense, all of Stockhausen's work has been based on a series of propositions about sound material and ways of acting on this material— not so much about form as about ways of forming. Thus the microphone and amplification techniques in his recent work are used, not, as in similar American works, to project a faithful or distorted image against live sound, but to extend and project the relatively fixed and discrete actions and events of a live performance onto a broader continuum in which every sound possibility is extendable and capable of being merged into any other sound possibility. *Mikrophonie I* (1964) is a work for a single tam-tam set in motion by four performers in every conceivable way; two of the players hold microphones which are brought towards and away from a vibrating gong or even actually put into contact with and rubbed against it; these amplified vibrations are further taken up by performer-technicians who transmit them to a pair of loudspeakers under all kinds of electronic-filter transformations. The piece is built—like all of Stockhausen's works—directly out of its techniques, out of its ways of forming and of acting on its materials. Stockhausen has synthesized and systematized— and occasionally created—technique with the ultimate aim of regulating all possible ways of acting on all possible materials. This total, anti-dualistic attempt at composing out the unity of experience approaches an almost mystical view of life and art.

The idea of a music based on transformation appears in Stockhausen's work in *Kontakte* (1959–60) for percussion, piano, and electronic sounds. In the *Mikrophonie* pieces and the two versions of *Mixtur,* acoustical and instrumental sounds are "modulated" (in the electronic rather than musical sense) by various devices. In *Telemusik, Hymnen,* and *Prozession,* Stockhausen uses folklore, national anthems, conversations and radio broadcasts, and even his own earlier music as the subjects for extended transformations on a Wagnerian time scale. In *Kurzwellen* the material is taken, *à la* Cage, from whatever signals are picked up on short-wave radios; only the method of transposing is specified. In these works, Stockhausen approaches an "American" performance-practice style, but always elaborating and codifying rather than merely adopting the intuitive or "action" approach typical of his sources. In *Stimmung,* a work for vocal ensemble based on a single chord, Stockhausen is elaborating an idea of La Monte Young, surrounding the elements of a sustained, finely tuned, evening-long pedal with all kinds of other verbal and vocal elements. These works approach a pure performance-practice style with little written music; *Aus den Sieben Tagen,* like certain American works of the 1960's, has only verbal instructions. At the same time, Stockhausen returned in *Mantra* to a totally composed, almost traditionally serial work—without, however, giving up the principle of transformation.

There is in Stockhausen's work a kind of reverse pantheism which seeks to internalize all possible experience in a kind of endless present; the wholeness and simultaneity of the experience and the transformation suggest a kind of mysticism seemingly at variance with his own earlier ultra-rationality. More clearly than any of the other Europeans, Stockhausen has responded to technological innovation and the impact of new media and has sought the basis for a new music of size and scope growing out of the varieties of contemporary experience filtered through his extraordinary capacity to absorb and transform.

Stockhausen was and remains the dominant figure in Central Europe as the source, transmitter, and codifier of new ideas. Composers working in related areas include the Swede Bo Nilsson (b. 1934), one of the first to serialize open-form and chance techniques and one of the first Europeans to use amplification; the Italian Franco Evangelisti (b. 1926), who has worked with graphic techniques and the consequences of certain systems of transformation and randomization and, more recently, with improvisation; and the Polish-Israeli-Austrian composer, Roman Haubenstock-Ramati (b. 1919), and the Austrian Friedrich Cerha (b. 1926), with their clusters and densities of sound, twisting and turning in open, spatial arrangements. Two important, independent figures are the Belgian Henri Pousseur and Mauricio Kagel. Pousseur, like Stockhausen, has widened the notion of serialism to include the familiar as well as the unfamiliar, the periodic as well as the a-periodic. His major work, *Votre*

Faust, is a theatrical collaboration with the French new-novelist Michel Butor. Pousseur's extensive critical and theoretical writings document the shift in new-musical thought from what we can call a "positivist" point of view—logical, internally consistent—to a "structural," linguistic and even anthropological approach.[1] Kagel, who lives and works in West Germany, is even more directly involved with a kind of gestural theater, with music as activity, with the elaboration of complex, invented accoustical phenomenon, with an interaction between music and everyday or external phenomenon. Pousseur represents a link between Central Europe and the Latin countries; Kagel, like Stockhausen, links Old and New World ideas.

BOULEZ

Surprisingly the first important post-war European manifestations of twelve-tone and serial technique developed in countries that had previously been the most hostile to them: France and Italy. In a special and remarkable way, the twelve-tone idea had a very particular appeal for a certain kind of French rationalism which, rather than imposing a total vision of order on the world, German style, seeks to rationalize the relationship of man to his experience of the world. Pierre Boulez, a pupil of Messiaen, began as a twelve-tone *enfant terrible* and became, for a brief moment, a totally organized, totally serial super-rationalist. His early twelve-tone works of the late 1940's—the Second Piano Sonata (1948), the *Sonatine* for flute and piano (1950), the *Livre* for string quartet (1949) —find their rationale not only in the Viennese operations of an expressive twelve-tone method but also in the relationship of this method to a virtuoso content built on timbre, texture, dynamic accent, and an ongoing form. Later, with *Polyphonie X* for 18 instruments (1951) and the first book of *Structures* for two pianos (1951–1952), Boulez committed himself to a completely systematic and pre-determined conception of a total

---

[1] Philosophical positivism can be connected with determinism and certain aspects of serialism. Opposed to it is "structuralism," an important philosophical theory in analytic and cognitive psychology, linguistics, and anthropology connected with the names of Carl Jung, Wolfgang Kohler, Noam Chomsky, and Claude Lévi-Strauss. The structuralist attitude, reached independently in several fields and supported by recent work in neurobiology, is opposed to behaviorism in holding that certain knowledge is innate and that information reaches the mind only through the transformation of sensory data into patterns that match our mental structures. This point of view, which has importance for all contemporary arts, has influenced the ideas of Pousseur, Berio, and others. Ironically, Lévi-Strauss has attacked certain new-musical ideas, with Pousseur acting as the principal advocate for the defense.

material. But these works raise more problems than they solve. *Structures I* is the classical monument of totally organized serial technique in the European avant-garde music of the early 1950's, but its method of making relationships is at once too easy, too numerological, and too irrelevant to the real issues of organic form to be convincing. (A second book, written later, is an intentional antithesis to the closed, classical, unidirectional rationality of the first). In general, the authority *Structures I* possesses seems to stem from Boulez's own considerable personal authority as a pianist and performing musician.

Le Marteau sans maître is, by contrast, one of the first avant-garde European works to escape the narrow confines of a strictly interpreted serialism. In some ways a continuation of Boulez's earlier twelve-tone music, it also marked a development of ideas descended from the "new" music of the first decades of the century, now informed by a generalized serial technique and a newly rationalized conception of form whose aim was the effective control of fluctuating masses, colors, densities, and intensities of sound. After *Le Marteau*, Boulez extended this conception in still other directions—notably in the use of performer choice and multidirectional forms. But *Le Marteau*, a group of vocal settings surrounded by instrumental "commentaries," already contains the basic patterns and many of the modes of thought which became dominant in his later works: the Third Piano Sonata, *Pli selon pli* (*Portrait de Mallarmé*) for voice and orchestra, and *Doubles* for orchestra (all composed over a period of years beginning in the late 1950's). These works are by no means the free, improvisatory, post-serial fantasies they have sometimes been made out to be. They all contain related but free-standing sections or movements, each based on independent and preconceived forms or formal plans of action. The sections were written and often performed separately as a series of steps in a "work-in-progress" conception: even the present form of *Le Marteau* is a revision dating from 1957; several sections of *Pli selon pli* were rewritten after being composed and performed separately; *Doubles*, already reworked, is a movement from a projected larger work. The intentionally ambiguous, open relationship of the parts to the total scheme is built into the conception; the whole might be compared to a system of planetary bodies discovered, one by one, to be moving around a center of gravity according to fixed relationships yet in a multitude of different actual juxtapositions. The forms themselves originate in a special conception of the relationship of the composer to his material, to the world of experience, and to the act of creative communication. These modes of creative thought, often constructed on very specific literary, poetic, or psychological premises, are conceived as ways of acting on a vast and pliable material which is poetic, even in a sense discursive, but never really narrative or directional in character. After

Le Marteau (which is still a series of closed and fixed shapes), Boulez developed ideas of embellishing and of moving on, around, and through a chosen material as revealed in the act of performance. Actually, the compositional process seems to be exactly the reverse: that of imagining a concrete and idiomatic material which will function as the poetic realization in time of a preconceived plan of action.

Unlike most of the European avant-garde composers, Boulez was involved with electronic music only very briefly, and he has always been engaged—as a pianist and, particularly, as a conductor—with music as a performing art.[2] An involvement with the physical, tangible, even sensuous qualities of the musical material and with the poetic and psychological significance of the activity of producing it has, aside from his brief encounter with strict serialism, given Boulez's music a distinct character within the general flow of new ideas in Europe. His forms are preconceived and rationalized, but they never uniquely generate or predetermine the character of the material; rather, they seek to reveal themselves through the quality, fantasy, and imaginative rightness of the ideas. Hence the impulse—rare among avant-garde composers—to revise and rewrite, to seek the clearest, the richest, the most meaningful realization of the conception. The forms may be open and flexible, but they do not rest on the operations of a chance, a statistical, or even an improvisatory method; instead, they seek to reveal the multiple possibilities—the poetic facets, so to speak—of the creative imagination. Boulez is very much involved with the significance and impact of personal statement, with the performance situation as a mode arising out of an invented and seemingly open and flexible material which is, however, realizing and revealing a hard strategy underneath—a ground plan, a path, a map that is in itself a rational, poetic realization of the relationship between the acts of creating and performing, as well as experiencing, a work of art.

Boulez's antecedents are Debussy and Messiaen; he is a composer of distinctly French style and thought, often close to the clarity and fluidity of the French language itself. Nevertheless, his outlook is essentially cosmopolitan, and for various reasons he has chosen to live and work outside of France. His influence, now very widely diffused, is hard to pinpoint except in France itself, where a group of younger composers may fairly be called *Boulezistes*. Of these, the most important and independent are André Boucourechliev (b. 1925) and Gilbert Amy (b. 1936). A number of other French composers—notably Luc Ferrari and the

---

[2] A recent work, . . . *explosante/fixe* . . . (1972–1973), uses an electronic distribution of sound in space very similar to the original version of the author's *Foxes and Hedgehogs* (1964–1967); the aim in both works is to extend and transform the live performance situation.

musique concrète group, Michel Philippot, and Barraqué—have produced work of individuality outside of the direct Boulez influence.

XENAKIS AND EASTERN EUROPE

Yannis Xenakis, born in Rumania of Greek parents and long resident in Paris, studied music with Messiaen and architecture with Le Corbusier; he worked with Le Corbusier and Varèse on the Philips Pavilion at the 1958 Brussels World's Fair. With *Métastasis* of 1953–1954 he began to apply mathematical probability theory to the composition of music. In essence, *Métastasis* and, in varying ways, *Pithoprakta* of 1955–1956 and *Achorripsis* of 1956–1957 are orchestral ensemble works built on sliding, shifting masses and densities whose definition is derived by a "statistical" probability method. Later works—*ST/10-1,080262* of 1962, *Eonta* for piano and brass of 1963, *Strategy* for two orchestras of 1964—extend this conception of the rationalization of the irrational in all domains through the use of electronic computers. With Xenakis, the use of these techniques has to do, not with any kind of "automatization" of the creative process, but rather with the search for new materials and new forms. Esthetically, the music is big in scale, violent in density and intensity of character, and strongly involved in an idea of the re-creation of the meaning of the act of performance. *Strategy* is a piece for two orchestras and two conductors who literally compete with one another in an attempt to realize a given set of preconditions. Xenakis always defines his conditions precompositionally and in the strictest terms, even when he is dealing with so-called irrationalities. (If Cage's is "music of the absurd," this is "music of the surd.") For better or for worse, the ultimate reality of the music (even when miscalculated from a psychological point of view) is to be found in the solution—the engagement with the performing material—as realized on real instruments in real time.

Xenakis inherited from Varèse a concern with volumes and densities of sound and, in effect, helped create a kind of subdivision of European music devoted to changing color and density. This style is also associated with György Ligeti, a Hungarian expatriate working in Vienna, and with the new Polish school, notably Krzysztof Penderecki. New ideas have, by now, appeared in the work of composers in all the Eastern European countries, including the Soviet Union, but Yugoslavia and Poland have led the way. The turning point was the bloodless Polish "revolution" of 1956 and the remarkable declaration, by the Polish intelligentsia, of cultural independence from the prevailing policies of artistic and intellectual direction in Eastern Europe. Since that time, Poland has quickly developed what is undoubtedly the most remarkable modern-music life in all of Europe and an important and individual creative production as well. The most striking fact of musical life in Poland in recent years has been the amount of contemporary music performed—in festivals and in concert—and the size and involvement of its public. Virtually all modern and avant-garde ideas from the West have been well-represented in Poland, and Polish composers have available to them an immense variety of resources including a well-equipped electronic studio; well-trained, experienced orchestras; ensembles and soloists with ample rehearsal time at their disposal; and a sympathetic and involved audience. These facts are important in understanding the new Polish music in its variety, its extensive use of resources, and its strong, direct character. Older Polish composers, notably Witold Lutoslawski, Kazimierz Serocki, and Tadeusz Baird, have moved from the development of twelve-tone and serial ideas towards a rich, intense, thoughtful kind of expression, informed by latter-day avant-garde ideas. The younger group—Penderecki, Boguslaw Schäffer (b. 1929), Henryk Gorecki (b. 1933), Wojciech Kilar (b. 1932), and Wlodzimierz Kotonski (b. 1925)—can be characterized by their direct engagement with the *matière sonore*, virtually stripped of everything but its immediate impact as sound. Works like Penderecki's *Threnody: to the Victims of Hiroshima* (1960) and his *St. Luke Passion* (1966) create intense, dramatic effects with their use of tone clusters, free choral babbling, Gregorian motifs, striking contrasts, and even major triads. Their weakness is that the entire effect lies on the surface—but it is a surface of great, intense effect.[3]

The range of new Polish music is large, and composers like Schäffer, involved in an experimental work of Cageian and post-Cageian dimensions—extreme ideas carried to extreme conclusions (one piano work lasts indefinitely until the last member of the audience leaves)—really belong in the final section of this book. On the other hand, the music of Gorecki and Kilar, born of the remarkable richness of the percussive-white-noise Polish language, are mainstream European avant-garde; they achieve a significant and expressive identity between means and materials that deserves to be better known in the West.

ITALY

A close involvement with a new and wide-ranging material and an interest in psychological, linguistic, or dramatic form arising out of the character of musical performance and communication is typical of the recent Italian music, notably that of Nono, Maderna, and Berio. All three

---

[3] There are connections between the music of Penderecki and, on the one hand, that of Carl Orff; on the other, that of the minimalists (see Chapter 18).

were identified with the Central European serial group of the early
1950's, and all worked with electronic means at the Milan studio and elsewhere; but all of them have since become closely involved in the projection of poetic, dramatic, or even specifically philosophical-verbal
ideas through the medium of a new-performed music. In the case of
Luigi Nono (b. 1924), these ideas have a specifically social orientation;
in the contemporary non-literary arts, Nono is an artist with a strong
commitment to relate artistic revolution to the social revolution of
our time. The artistic significance of the realizations of this point of
view is debatable. The opera *Intolleranza* (1960) is a curious hodgepodge
of contradictory notions; *La Fabbrica illuminata* (1964), a kind of Orwel-
lian anti-capitalist, anti-Stalinist sound-study of the factory of the future,
gains strength from its dramatic, impressive tape babble of voices but is
nearly destroyed by its climactic, agonized cry, "factory as concentration
camp." The problem is crucial for Nono, and not only because of his
views of the social value and impact of avant-garde ideas. Nono's instrumental works, although possessing a certain importance, lack the imaginative, concrete, and personal push, the impulse towards expressive form,
that one finds in his vocal and vocal-dramatic works from *Il Canto sospeso*
(1955–1956), a relatively early serial setting of letters by condemned anti-
Fascist resistance partisans, to the more recent dramatic and semi-dramatic works for voices, instruments, and tape.

　　The commitment of Maderna and Berio has been not only to a view
about the social value of art but also to the quality of the new material
and the significance of the act of producing it. In addition to being active
at Darmstadt, both composers were with—were for a time in fact directors
of—the now moribund electronic studio at the Milan radio station. The
electronic experience everywhere profoundly altered attitudes towards
serialism and the role of performed music; in Milan, the studio became
almost a kind of escape hatch for composers who felt compelled to adopt
serial controls but were anxious to find a new, substantial musical matter.
The electronic realizations of Maderna and Berio in particular have the
character of improvisations arising out of a direct and fresh experience
of the materials. Both composers came back to vocal and instrumental
music with something of this attitude, to which was added an intense
faith in the expressive and dramatic power of action and gesture as well
as the musical form-building potential of word and language.

　　Maderna's opera *Hyperion* (1964), though defective as an over-all
conception, illustrates these musical and philosophical tendencies very
well: the "protagonist" is a flutist who spends the first ten minutes of the
work quietly unpacking piccolo, flute, alto flute, and bass flute; when he
finally gets around to the actual act of performance, the sound that
gushes forth is in fact an enormously amplified percussive fortissimo (on
tape). The piece has a complex choral part—also on tape—with a babbling-

of-tongues text made out of isolated words taken from many different languages. There is an instrumental ensemble part and, finally, a long and sensuous—almost Bergian—solo soprano song at the end. In a work for solo flute by Maderna, the flutist must perform against the pre-recorded image of his own playing.

Berio's work is notable for its involvement with language and linguistic structure as well as its important development of music theater and social-gestural content. This is true even of his instrumental works, but it is obviously more evident in his vocal and dramatic works. *Omaggio a Joyce* (1958) is a tape piece made entirely out of the sounds of a James Joyce fragment. *Visages* (1961) combines electronic sound with a structure of high emotive vocal sounds, images, and gestures. *Circles* (1960) is a live setting, for voice and percussion, of poems by e. e. cummings in which the physical movements of the performers become part of the acoustic and visual space of the piece. *Passaggio*, commissioned by La Scala, and *Opera*, written for Santa Fe, are anti-opera operas dealing with the very function of art and theater in our culture. *Laborintus II*, on a poem of Edoardo Sanguineti, was written for the 700th anniversary of Dante and is, in effect, a culture-shock piece. *Sinfonia*, written for members of the Swingle Singers with orchestra, has one movement made out of the sounds of the syllables of the name "Martin Luther King" and another which contains a symphonic movement by Mahler entire, imbedded in a context of quotes, references, and original remarks. The need for dramatic context and form and the concern with verbal and language problems—sound as language, language as sound, the relationship of meaning to sound, of linguistic to musical structure, of content to sound—are strikingly illustrated in Berio's work. The involvement with significance and gesture has important antecedents not only in new music but also in linguistic and anthropological structuralism and in the tradition of Brechtian epic theater. Berio's organic and dramatic forms, his concern with content and context and his integration of sound, language, and conceptual structure are a continuing source of influence and ideas and—except for his use of traditional media—carry us beyond modern music.

BIBLIOGRAPHICAL NOTES

The best sources for information on European serialism and post-serialism are the various European periodicals already mentioned. Extensive material on Stockhausen has been published in German, notably the *Texte zur elektronischen und instrumentalen Musik* in the DuMont Dokumente series (Cologne, 1963) and vol. 6 of the Kontrapuntke series (Rodenkirchen, West Germany, 1961). For Boulez, see the composer's *Pensez la musique aujourd'hui* (Mainz, 1963), translated as *Boulez on Music Today* (Cambridge, 1971). Pousseur has published two important volumes, *Fragments théoriques I sur la musique expérimentale* (Brussels, 1970) and the difficult *Musique, Sémantique, Société* (Tournai, 1972). Xenakis has written about his ideas and theories in *Musiques formelles,* translated as *Formalized Music* (Bloomington, Ind., 1972); the book is even more difficult than Pousseur's. The crisis of serialism can be surveyed in a series of articles, with contributions from both the Old World and the New, in the French review *Preuves* over a period of several months from fall to spring, 1965–1966.

Jonathan Cott's conversations with *Stockhausen* (New York, 1973) convey the composer's increasing concerns with perception, communication, and anti-dualistic views of the unity of human experience right up to and including its outer fringes. Stockhausen remains the key figure in European music for the transmission of ideas, and a great deal of his recent thought is contained in this volume.

EIGHTEEN

BEYOND MODERN MUSIC

The serial and the chance music of the early 1950's, apparently con-tradictory, shared certain premises; both were deductive, experimental in a strict sense. There are a limited number of pre-compositional hypoth-eses, negatively defined by a rigorous exclusion of possibility, and the music is, so to speak, deduced from the unique set of premises. The premises are simple and limited; the deductions are thorough, extreme, and encompassing; they are, in a sense, equivalent to the piece.

Taken in sum, this music affirmed (or perhaps only re-affirmed) the principle that each conception had to establish its own unique premises; the actual content of a work and the relationships (including non-relation-ships) of its parts as they unfold, are acted upon, or intersect in time are defined uniquely. In short, instead of each work being an instance of its class, each work creates its own class (of which it may be the only mem-ber).

This kind of art grew out of and required a certain separateness and specialization as a kind of ongoing "research" activity, well-subsidized and, by and large, played out for an increasingly restricted audience of adepts. The very impact of recording technology and media—so important in the development of new musical ideas—also had a tremendous effect on the social context of new music-making and made the specialist position increasingly difficult to maintain. If mass culture breeds commercialism, the art-for-art's sake position leads to elitism and academicism. The twentieth-century pendulum has swung back and forth between these extremes, the Scylla and Charybdis of the modern composer. It is against this background that a still meaningful "third-stream" question can be defined. Increasingly, composers and other thoughtful musicians, rejecting the alternatives of commercialism and academic isolation, have found it necessary to re-assess the cultural and social context of new music-making, and new music can hardly fail to be affected.

Recording technology—comparable to the camera in the visual arts—is the essential factor that creates new cultural and perceptual situations. The open microphone, like the open camera, creates not so much a frame as a window, an opening on the world. The class of which an individual work is an instance becomes everything that can be recorded. Any experience is now available; its significance can only depend on its use. This totality of experience is not merely a new or larger fund of materials and processes but actually part of the context out of which each new work grows. This suggests that there is a new totality of forms and perceptions which come out of a universalized experience but which are re-established in particular by each work. In a sense, this seems to resemble and re-establish the traditional cultural situation, but now widened, broadened, and universalized by technology.

As the full impact of technology becomes felt throughout musical culture, the old institutionalization of music becomes less and less serviceable. One result of this is that composers have begun to organize their own performance ensembles for the dissemination of their music, in many cases creating and building new electronic and non-electronic instruments for their purposes. It has become increasingly difficult to separate the creative act from the activity of making music; that separation is only possible in stable cultures with highly responsive institutional forms. In the same way, music and all the arts, after years of carefully nurtured isolation and abstraction, have no longer been able to escape the impact of social upheaval and change. In a very real sense, the most recent developments mark the end of "modernism" since they pose the very fundamental question of what is art, functionally as well as formally.

Many sources and symptoms could be cited but only those connected with music itself will be mentioned here. The importance of Cage's work and activity cannot be over-emphasized. The happenings and pop-art movements of the 1960's, often only peripherally related to music, owe a great deal to Cage and other artists working in his orbit. Cage was long active as a teacher at Black Mountain College, an influential experimental school in North Carolina, and at the New School in New York City. Many visual artists, poets, and others studied with Cage—for example, Allan Kaprow, the man generally credited with "inventing" happenings. The activities of composers or near-composers on the edge of the cross-cultural activities of the 1960's—George Brecht, LaMonte Young, Jackson MacLow, Richard Higgins, Philip Corner, Yoko Ono, the Fluxus group—were an important part of the performance scene in New York, independent of the "music world" as such but nonetheless significant. Related to these activities—and also descended from Cage—was a kind of performance-practice music mixing live and electronic media, one that was conceived in free, spatial terms with performers acting rather than performing on their instruments and every possibility carried to its extreme—mixed, transformed, and even distorted to the limits of perception. Its practitioners included the Once group in Michigan (Gordon Mumma, Robert Ashley, Roger Reynolds, George Caccioppo); some West Coast musicians (Pauline Oliveros, Ramon Sender, Larry Austin); some of the University of Illinois and Buffalo personnel; one or two expatriates (Frederic Rzewski and the Rome group); and a number of Europeans (Boguslav Schäffer in Poland, Piotr Kotik in Prague, the Nuova Consonanza group in Italy, Dieter Schnebel, Hans Otte, Michael von Biel in Germany, Luc Ferrari and the GERM group in France. An important part of Mauricio Kagel's work belongs here (*Acustica* for invented instruments or sound sources), and a whole series of works by Stockhausen (*Telemusik, Hymnen, Mixtur, Aus den Sieben Tagen*) helped spread the influence of these ideas. A great deal of this music could be characterized as "junk music"—equivalent to junk sculpture—in which otherwise useless and discarded bits and scraps from the junk heap of aural experience are arranged and de-ranged. Much of this music was pitched at some outer edge: close to the threshold of bearability, often harsh and ugly, occasionally vulgar, banal, or pornographic (but never passionate), curiously objective and detached, extended in time and environmental in effect. From this point it was only possible to push ahead to a new synthesis or to pull back and internalize.

The period of all this activity was surprisingly brief—a few years at the most—and its constituency is now widely scattered. These various activities had certain things in common. A tendency to mix the arts and media, with musicians and other artists working collectively, was important; so was the already-noted development of non-linear, non-dramatic, environmental forms (performances could and did continue for hours). There was also the need to ignore history (thereby gaining the freedom to use it or not) and to open windows on the world (thereby ending the long reign of abstraction and abstract expressionism). If we except the recordings—essentially realizations of performance-practice pieces and, by and large, difficult to listen to—nothing much seems to have survived; as in the comparable Dada period early in the century, the musical pickings are slim. But this was an important and essential transition, and out of it has come what is, in effect, post-modern music, the contemporary music of the late twentieth century.

MINIMALISM AND CONCEPT ART

It may seem surprising that a conceptual art and an art that rejects all forms of dualism should have arisen from the complex situation just described, but on reflection it becomes clear why this was so. The need to return to the simplest, most basic elements was already felt by Webern and the serialists; clearly, minimalism is a reaction to twentieth-century information overload, to the buzzing, blooming confusion. It is, in one sense, a form of escape, but it is also a deepening of experience in certain highly limited perceptual areas—"head" music in more than one sense. Most of the practitioners of minimalism disclaim the popular association of their music with the so-called "drug culture," but the typical combination of intellectualization, pattern perception, slow change, and inner rhythm suggests a music that pushes into relatively unexplored areas of consciousness. The analogies and interactions with non-Western musics are still clearer.

In a sense, minimalism is the logical result of an art, first proposed by Cage, which is radically non-historical (in content, at least, if not in the way it came to be). Ideas replace a historical or social context; the work of the performance is the carrying out of the idea as an activity or perceptive experience. Such "concept art" is an extension of the need for each work to create as well as realize its own premises; when there is no longer any common practice, all art becomes, in some sense, "concept" art. With Cage and many other artists of the 1960's, the notion had a very direct and encompassing application. There are activities by LaMonte Young (b. 1935) which consist of directions like "Hold this for a long time" or "Prepare any piece and play it." Performers are directed to sit on the stage and look at the audience, to burn musical instruments or to sit in their cars, blow horns and flash lights. We are on the borderline between minimalism and a neo-realism which takes us, through intermedia, multi-media, and music theater, in a very different direction.

The weakness of "concept" art from a purely musical point of view is its detachment from the actual in sound (which may be incidental) or from the social aspects of music-making (which cannot be incidental). There is a constant ambiguity as to where the center of interest actually lies: in the idea, in the activity, or in the result. John Lennon and Yoko Ono have a work—or an activity—in which fans blow open the pages of a Beethoven symphony and instrumentalists are directed to play whatever happens to fall under their eye. Alvin Lucier (b. 1931) has a piece in which a group of blindfolded performers equipped with a kind of sonar attempt to orient themselves by producing clicking sounds in the manner of bats; Mauricio Kagel has a somewhat similar work which uses blind-folded actors and canes. Another piece by Lucier amplifies the electrical energy emitted by the brain of a "performer" in a state of alpha sleep; there is another work based on the same principle by David Rosenboom (b. 1947). These are activities based on idea-situations; the result in sound may or may not amount to anything. We are again close to a kind of concept theater.

The work of the percussionist and composer Max Neuhaus is set nearer the "real" world. His *Public Access* works connect the audience with the performance via radio and listener response; the audience reaction is not only incorporated in the activity but influences its course. The Subotnick-Martin game pieces are even more specifically audience-involving; the piece is the playing of the game. In these and similar works, the connection between the audience and the artist's environment (one cannot really speak of a work in the old sense) is accomplished through the use of some kind of feedback technology.

There are many connections between such concept and environmental art and minimalism. The notion of a non-dualistic (or "monistic") art free of conflict or dialectic has recurred from time to time in the twentieth century; elements of it can be found in composers as diverse as Webern, Varèse, and Cowell. The cluster or density works of Xenakis, Ligeti, and the younger Poles use simple, non-dualistic structures in transformation rather than dialectical process; a good example is Xenakis's tape piece *Bohor I*. There are precedents for the influence of non-Western ideas in the work of composers like Partch (who often sounds like a contemporary minimalist); Cage's involvement with Zen Buddhist philosophy and his essential acceptance of the world "as it is" precludes conflict or dualism. Paradoxically, there are opposing principles involved here: one is that any and all experiences are equally valid; the other is that the single experience is valid in and for its own sake. It is from this latter point of view that Morton Feldman developed his unique art. Feldman created the first minimal art in the strict sense not only because of his use of simple, extended, isolated sounds but also because of his rejection of process and conflict of any kind and his insistence on the essential

"it-ness" of the sound. There are no levels here, no meanings within meanings, no symbology; only the thing itself in its quintessential purity. La-
Monte Young's extended performance pieces—a single chord, tuned and
retuned; a single electronic-and-vocal interval extended over vast lengths
of time, changing only minutely—represent an extreme penetration, to a
point where an enormous amount of mental energy is focused on an
absolute minimum of sensory data.

Principles of slow transformation, phasing, and cycling are most
highly elaborated in the work of Steve Reich (b. 1936). Reich's earlier
works include several tape pieces (*It's Gonna Rain* and *Come Out* [1966]
are best-known) based on loops, i.e., a short piece of tape whose end is
spliced onto its head, permitting endless replay of a short cycle. By slowly
changing the stereo synchronization and phasing of a short, spoken
phrase and by superimposing the changes on the previous "takes," Reich
produces huge, cumulative forms. Because the points of departure have a
high rhythmic energy, the results produce not merely a hypnotic aural
effect but a series of perceptual patterns and illusions, something like
that produced by so-called "op art." Reich's later works combine performance and recording (*Violin Phase*) or are scored out for performance
ensembles (*Four Organs, Drumming*), with the principles of cycling and
phasing extended to a more traditional musical and rhythmic material.
Drumming, in part the result of a visit to Ghana, is an extended work
that uses long, overlapping rhythmic cycles in constantly changing relationships with one another, set forth in a live–performance situation involving percussion instruments and voices.[1]

Some of the same concepts, adapted to still more traditional performance situations and materials, appear in the work of Terry Riley (b.
1935). *In C* (1964) consists of a few short phrases relating to a modality of
C and performed in repeated, overlapping cycles. In *Poppy Nogood's
Phantom Band*, Riley himself is the band; short fragments played on a
soprano saxophone are extended through tape-loop repetition. *A Rainbow
in Curved Air* adapts these cyclical techniques to a pop-derived material
and sound. Related works have been produced by Philip Glass and
Frederic Rzewski; Rzewski's *Coming Together* combines these techniques with significant verbal elements.

These activities, largely centered in New York, have been fur-
thered by a number of performance ensembles. The oldest and best-
known of these is Sonic Arts, already mentioned in connection with
live-electronic performance. Reich has his own performance group and so
do a number of other composers. David Borden and Steve Drews's Mother

---

[1] Reich rejects the term "miminal" as applied to his music and, without
further explanation, refers to it as "structural."

Mallard's Portable Masterpiece Company is a pop-oriented group organized for collective performance realizations—an important attempt to bridge a gap. On the whole, however, minimalism and the notion of collective performance, growing out of the interaction of individuals, do not quite jibe, and, in general, minimalism remains an art of strong personalities, the last and most extreme form of the old modern-art notions of heroic individuality, alienation, and personal style.

THE NEW POP CULTURE

No discussion of the vast changes in musical life in recent years can ignore the developments in pop music during the 1960's. Popular music produced major and lasting exemplars in the blues/jazz tradition but, with some notable exceptions, the pop song was, if not merely commercial and ephemeral, an interpreter's form. In the 1960's, however, it took on the characteristics of an art form. Rock-and-roll, essentially black and populist in origin, with its heavy beat and sexual connotations, was fused with various other elements: folk and country music, gospel, blues, jazz, Eastern music, and even electronics.

A new quality of texts with subject matter of current concern, some rhythmic sophistication (set off by the simple beat), and a greater scope were combined with a high level of melodic invention by the best of the new breed of composer-author-performer. Pop musicians made extensive use of the new technologies: electric instruments, live amplification and synthesizers, an increasingly sophisticated and original use of the multi-track recording medium. The "Hit Parade" or "Top 40" mentality which long dominated pop music was circumvented by using "classical" means of dissemination—the long-playing or stereo album, FM radio, live appearances in new-style performance locales and college-circuit concerts.

The new pop music, the vogue for pop art and popular culture, and the social upheavals of the 1960's all were simultaneous events and the new rock—Dylan to San Francisco to the Beatles—made strong inroads on the "classical," the collegiate, and even the artistic, intellectual audiences. The vitality of pop music made a tremendous impression. Rock was "relevant," a music of social change and revolution. It triumphed everywhere and the very future of "classical" music was considered to be in doubt.

In fact, rock rather quickly passed through its own classical period, the end of which was symbolized by the breakup of the Beatles. But all music had been affected, and certainly "classical" music cannot ever quite be the same. Even (or especially) at the height of the rock culture of the 1960's, there was a remarkable rapprochement between pop culture and "art" which will continue to be an important factor in the future evolution of new music. The old categories—neo-classical and expressionist, serial and aleatory, closed-form and open-form, chance and ultra-rationality, classical and pop—seemed limiting and irrelevant. Many pop musicians, brought up outside of the cultural establishment, were not at all concerned or even aware of the fashionable do's-and-don't's which traditionally afflict the creative course of the art and music world. A good deal of the impetus came from England and was pioneered by the Beatles: it continues there to some degree with Pink Floyd and Emerson, Lake & Palmer as well as John Lennon and Yoko Ono (currently resident and working in the United States). The Beatles, whose music is entirely adapted and syncretic, extended their range to include all forms of pop music from that of the English music hall to swing to rock-and-roll, mixed with elements of classical and chamber music as well as tape-and-electronic sound. They used recording technology to merge these styles, often in terms of larger works or concepts (*Sergeant Pepper, Abbey Road*), nearly always with great skill; indeed, technology and mass media were their real instruments, on which (with the help of producer George Martin) they played with such skill. Other important impulses came from California: from the San Francisco groups and Frank Zappa. Zappa's music is born out of a kind of pop-Dada mixture of rock, jazz, classical modernism (even atonal expressionism), camp and nostalgia, parody and protest, as well as a strong sense of music theater. Mass media—primarily recordings but also radio, television, and film—played an essential role in the development of these aspects of pop, enabling performers to build up audiences and extend their ideas in mixed and media forms. An interesting footnote is that multi-media techniques were easily and naturally adapted by pop groups as part of their performance presentation.

A consideration of pop music in the 1960's should include at least a mention of the so-called "acid" or "psychedelic" rock developed by groups like Jefferson Airplane, The Grateful Dead, Jimi Hendrix, and others. The electric sound of this music—a fusion of rock and blues with a widened electric guitar performance style and other electronic elements—and its use of the so-called "light show" approached the conditions of electronic music and multi-media. In this period, rock came closest to the experimental or avant-garde situation. At the opposite extreme was the folk music movement, born or reborn in the 1930's under the influence of ethnomusicologists like Alan Lomax and Charles Seeger (the father of folksinger Pete Seeger and a notable "convert" from avant-gardism) and carried into the very center of the 1960's pop movement by singer-composers like Bob Dylan. Ironically, Dylan helped give the folk movement mass appeal by converting to electric instruments and then helped to spur a reaction away from "hard" rock by incorporating country music in his album, *Nashville Skyline*. The blues revival and the new mass appeal of country music launched a kind of "neo-classical" or revival movement in pop music, now extended to early rock-and-roll and even to early jazz and pop.

Pop music played a central role in many of the activities and movements of the 1960's, supplanting classical or modern music for some and yet, on the other hand, creating large new audiences who arrived at new music through the pop experience. Musicians working at both ends of the spectrum are characteristic of the period: Pierre Henri (b. 1927), who worked with the English group Spooky Tooth; Joe Byrd and John Cale, Cage disciples who went into rock; the English composer David Bedford and the American Robert Ashley, both of whom have worked with rock and pop groups; Emerson, Lake & Palmer, with their versions of Mussorgsky and Copland; Zappa, who studied classical music, was influenced by Varèse, and has written for chamber and symphonic combinations; Joshua Rifkin, who plays ragtime, arranges and conducts Renaissance music, folk/pop, and baroque-styled versions of songs by the Beatles, directs, and composes new music; William Bolcom, whose playing sparked the ragtime and old pop song revivals, and whose "unpopular" songs and mainstream contemporary music and music-theater pieces increasingly resemble each other; Stanley Silverman, an expert guitarist with both "classical" and jazz background, whose music theater pieces have strong pop elements; Michael Sahl, a "classical" and tape-music composer but active also as a pop pianist and arranger, whose recent work is a rich amalgam of pop vocabulary, minimalist texture, and traditional technique.

Pop music, in effect, filled a social role which modernist music, increasingly abstract and involved with a small, elite audience, could not fill. For better or for worse, it was pop—although far from exclusively—which related to the hippie movement, to the drug culture, to protest and politics. Certainly it was the specific example of pop music which forced many composers to re-evaluate the sense of their music and its role in modern culture.

Nevertheless, this was not—and is not—a one-way situation. Minimalism and multi-media form an essential part of the sub-cultural changes of the 1960's, and cross-influences are an important part of the picture. Furthermore, the pop movement itself is passing quickly through a cycle of classicism, romanticism, experimentalism, neo-classicism, and revival— the same cycle which jazz took a few decades and traditional music a couple of centuries to pass through. Popular music has come to be dominated by revivals and commercialism. Like any other expression of the culture, pop cannot really escape the essential social and musical conditions which produce it.

SOUND AS IMAGE: MUSIC AND LANGUAGE

Up to a certain point, most twentieth-century music can be described as a search for new forms of linearity, process, and narrative (to replace the old tonal forms) or a rejection of linearity in favor of abstraction, concept, and pattern forms. This corresponds quite closely in the visual arts to modern forms of figurative art (replacing the old perspective-based forms) and abstraction. Abstraction, atonality, non-linearity, serialism, and aleatory, revolutionary as they once seemed, still belong as categories in the Romantic tradition of high-art and art-for-art's sake. The Cageian reaction to this does away with the old notion of art and replaces it with activity and awareness; it tells us that art is what we think it is—a sunset perhaps or, as Cage once said, the sound of spores falling off a mushroom. The new pop is another kind of anti-art reaction, but it has only taken us back around again to the essential questions of culture, commerce, communication, and, in one or another sense, art.

The basic problems of art today are the re-integration of art into society and the question of art and meaning. These topics have been tackled before, in fragmented fashion and with varying success. They return now with new force, and we can see that they are not separate questions but aspects of a single larger situation.

Questions of meaning and music are particularly difficult and can hardly be dealt with at any length here. It must suffice to say that meaning and *verbal* meaning are not by any means identical and that music takes on coloration, character, resonance and thus, in some sense, meaning in a number of ways—through social context, performer personality, association with language and idea, interaction with other arts and media. Composers should have returned to these concerns in recent years, as we have already suggested. Before taking up the questions of media, multimedia, and music theater we must refer to the new techniques of musical imagery and music and language—basic resources in the formation of new and integrated musical and music-theater languages formed out of the new range of experience offered by technology.

Musical imagery, which appears sporadically in traditional music, often takes two forms: the reference to other, familiar music and the imitation of sounds of the external world. Examples include the quotations of other music in the banquet scene of Mozart's *Don Giovanni* and the bird calls in the slow movement of Beethoven's Pastoral Symphony.

However, these techniques are generally superficial and peripheral in traditional music. In a more recent period, Ives made use of quotation and stylistic reference, Messiaen has quoted chant and has imitated bird calls, and *musique concrète* has incorporated recorded noise and natural sound (although not always in recognizable form). But the specific use of musical reference in recent work represents an essentially new step, a kind of super-realism in which familiarity and association, strictly ruled out of serialism and most forms of aleatory, reappear; the juxtaposition of previously unassociated sound objects, the experience of the familiar along with the unfamiliar, the shock of recognition and the recognition of transformation produce new meanings and forms. Many analogies to work in other areas can be made, notably in modern "structural" linguistics and that most typically contemporary of art media, the film.

One of the first composers to make extended use of actual musical quotations (from 1965) was George Rochberg (*Contra mortem et tempus; Music for a Magic Theater*); it represented a very strong and conscious break with serialism in his work. Lukas Foss's *Baroque Variations* are an extensive series of transformations wrought on musical material by Bach and Scarlatti. The Pousseur/Butor *Votre Faust* contains, among other things, musical and literary palimpsests of earlier versions of the Faust legend. Stockhausen used a classical cadence in *Adieu* and various national anthems in *Hymnen*, all subject to his characteristic transformational activities. Both Stockhausen and Kagel wrote Beethoven "tributes." Berio's *Sinfonia* contains an entire movement of Mahler's Second Symphony surrounded by an ongoing musical commentary layered in by the composer. The references to traditional and pop music in William Bolcom's *Session IV* and *Black Host*, Michael Sahl's *Special Trash* and *Symphony*, and the author's *The Nude Paper Sermon* and *Ecologue* are stylistic rather than literal quotations but serve related purposes. The variations on "The Last Rose of Summer" which constitute the last movement of Sahl's *A Mitzvah for the Dead* (for violin and tape) are a kind of literal *double entendre:* the thing itself and the image of it at the same time.

The use of "second degree" transformation and the rich area that language and music have in common are closely related, and many of the same composers are involved in both areas. The traditional relationships of text and music are now viewed by some as a special case of a much wider field of relationships between words, language, sound, and music. Verbal meaning and structure—from the phoneme to word formation to narrative forms to non-linear verbal complexes—interact with sound and music on many levels: meaning and sound quality, clarity and complexity, linearity and non-linearity, clarity and confusion, comprehensibility and incomprehensibility. This attitude towards language appears in a number of Stockhausen's works from *Momente* to *Stimmung*, in Foss's *Fragments from Archilochus* and *Paradigm*, and in the work of several younger composers—Dieter Schnebel (b. 1930) and Hans G. Helms in Germany, Alvin Lucier, Robert Ashley, and others in the United States; it is essential in Berio's vocal and theater pieces and most of the author's work of the past decade.

The neo-realism of tape provides almost limitless opportunities for imagery and image transformation: of music (James Tenney's *Blue Suede Shoes* based on Elvis Presley), of language (Berio's *Omaggio a Joyce*), of noise (the author's *Queens Collage*, based on the "found sound" of an urban college campus and edited like a film). Still further along this line are certain "documentary" works in which the artist intrudes only to frame or define a certain sound environment: Alvin Curran's *A Day in the Country*, Luc Ferrari's *Un presque rien*, the listening exercises of Philip Corner, and the *Earth Music* series produced by the author for radio. In the first case, what we hear is art because it is transformed; the "meaning" is in the recognizability of the image and its transformation. In the second case, what we hear is music because (if) we experience it as music.

This is close to the Cageian view. We can, if we wish, go out into the country and listen to the birds. Music itself is only part of the larger environment—one kind of sound experience among many. The danger is that in saying this we are not really saying anything worth saying. Perhaps this understanding was lost and had to be regained, but once recaptured it becomes nothing more than a truism. From environmental art we can go not merely into the outer environment but also back into art. Environmental art—total, surrounding, involving, continuous, without beginning, middle, or end—evolved naturally as a response. And, by reaction, so did the new closed, dialectical forms of media and musical minimalism. Minimalism is exclusive; it is often defined by what it is not. Multi-media and music theater are inclusive; they are defined by what they start out with, i.e. (the possibility of) everything. They represent the attempt to re-invest experience with substance, not merely through sense bombardment but through a new intermingling of arts, media technology, and performance; through forms and structures—open or closed, cyclical or dialectical—which use the very range of contemporary experience as their point of departure.

MULTI-MEDIA AND MUSIC THEATER

Multi-media (mixed media, intermedia—the terms are used with somewhat varying meanings) refers roughly to an environmental art involving multiple sense impressions created or projected through technological means. It is a contemporary version of the old total theater concept, but instead of using closed, dramatic forms it is often extended in time and space on a continuum. The earliest major exposition of multi-media seems to have been the San Francisco Trips Festival of 1965 in which several composers participated, notably Morton Subotnick. Subotnick, who worked extensively with synthesizers, often combining tape music with live performance, collaborated with Anthony Martin, who is credited with the development of liquid projections and the so-called "light show." Subotnick and Martin later worked at New York's Electric Circus and collaborated on a number of multi-media and participatory works. Several important media and multi-media artists began as composers; for example, Nam June Paik, well-known for his collaborations with the cellist and intermedia entrepreneur Charlotte Moorman, and a pioneer in the new medium of experimental video.[2] Performance of multi-media and other technologically oriented works generally require rather special circumstances. The famous "Seven Evenings," which sparked a major technologically oriented art movement, were staged at a large armory in New York City. Out of them came the Experiments in Art and Technology group which sponsored performances and exhibitions. The art museum, gallery, and loft came to be places where new music—particularly with a technological or environmental orientation—could be "displayed." In San Francisco the planetarium had been used by the Vortex tape music group even earlier than the Trips Festival. The Electric Ear series, of which the author was a founder and, briefly, artistic director, was presented at the Electric Circus in New York; other rock clubs in the East and West—free-form institutions with pliable spaces, the needed projection and sound equipment, built-in electric performing ensembles and built-in audiences—were ideal for this sort of performance. The author's *Feedback*, with artist-filmmaker Stan Vanderback, is a structure for an environmental, participatory work on a large scale into which a huge range of live performance and media elements can be plugged. *Can Man Survive?* (commissioned for the centennial of the American Museum of Natural History) combines the cyclical forms of minimalism with the techniques and scale of multi-media, all focused on a basic subject and idea: the external environmental crisis as the analogue of an ongoing interior environment. Audience participation is an inevitable element in these works if only because of the 360° "surround,"

---

[2] Experimental television or "video" is an important and developing field with many analogies to electronic and tape music: use of tape, recorded images, electronic manipulation, and even the use of computers and the development of electronic video synthesizers. Not surprisingly, there has been some cross-over between the fields of electronic music and experimental video; 'The Kitchen,' a video theater in New York, has become equally well known as a performance center for electronic and other new music.

but also because the visitor must make his own form as he selects, focuses, concentrates, and moves through the environment. The multimedia concept proposed large-scale, collaborative, and participatory works, new performance situations and spaces, a high level of involvement for participants and audience alike, and the creation of a large, popular (i.e., non-elite) audience.

Happenings and multi-media, even in their earliest and crudest forms, are more than just ritualistic or sensory overloads of image and experience. They represent the range of experience and the impact of the cultural and technological situation that brought them into being. This range is represented by a slice of it—a cross-grain cut, so to speak—organized not through pre-compositional assumptions but through the act of mediating extremes. The range of perception and comprehension is the subject matter, and these media works, like their purely musical equivalents, are "about" the quality and nature of heightened experience, perception, thought, and understanding, "about" the nature of art and culture in contemporary life communicated throughout the range of human experience.

A great many of the traditional verities are challenged here: among them are the image of the alienated artist, "expressing" himself and the notion of personality and style as the starting point for, rather than a natural result of, the creation of works of art. Instead, the idea of environmental, ongoing, cyclical forms; the mixing of the media and the categories; the blurring of the distinctions between the functions of sound, music, image, movement, and theater; the close involvement of creators, performers, technicians, and public; the creation of total performing space; the use of sound, movement, and visual space on a continuum; the substitution of ranges of experience for "style"; the invention of ongoing systems and processes with balanced diversity—like a natural ecological system—replacing the old idea of the art work as a discrete product of a limited "monoculture"; the intermarriage of pop and non-pop; the close relationship between the inner artistic environment and the outer social (and natural) environment; the appearance of a new, large, and apparently liberated public—all these suggest major changes in the very notion and function of art.

In some ways, the "revolution" was premature. Multi-media is a big, expensive entertainment and, as social and economic conditions changed, it became less and less possible to find the needed support. Inevitably, overload for the sake of overload and quick commercialization of the superficial aspects cut into the initial interest and excitement. Nevertheless, there are certain processes of change, in art as in society, which cannot be reversed. Nothing in the multi-media premise has been invalidated. But the creation of new forms, new ways of thinking about and experiencing art, new connections, meanings, and institutions is a long-term project and cannot be manufactured by facile media "revolutions." Nevertheless, the difficulty of the task does not make it any the less important.

The composer's task has become something more than just the creation of new works of art. It has become necessary to create the situations, the spaces, even the institutions at the same time as the works which they are to communicate; in effect, the creation of new works and the renewal of musical culture are the same activity. It is in this light that we can understand the need for composer-performance ensembles, for new performance situations, and for new media.

Electronic media, themselves the source of new ideas and awarenesses, provide an important series of alternate media. These include radio, records, film, and various forms of television. Examples of works created by and through media include the author's *Voices* ("a capella" radio opera with the music-theater ensemble, Quog), *The Nude Paper Sermon* (commissioned for recordings and realized through multi-track and electronic recording techniques), and *Ecolog* (original television work with *Quog*, commissioned by the Artists' Television Workshop for educational television). Other examples include Stockhausen's *Telemusik*, originally realized for Japanese television, Mauricio Kagel's *Ludwig van* (film-video realization for German television), and Michael Sahl's *A Woman's Face* (a kind of pop opera realized with Ed Emschwiller for film). All of these works exist in more than one form, but in each case the media realization was the primary one. This is essentially a new situation and one that will continue to grow in importance. The potential of media in these respects is very great, and although the problems of working so close to mass, commercial media are very great, the challenges and potential are still greater.

In a sense, live performance and music theater have become two media forms among many, but they are media forms of a special character. While electronic media have been created for mass cultural purposes and have to be harnessed for artistic ends, live performance and theater situations exist essentially for artistic communication and must be re-created anew from the inside. The traditional concert and operatic media are perfectly appropriate for the works that created them; similarly, new performing institutions are needed for new works and ideas. Thus the importance of new performance situations like the WBAI Free Music Store and The Kitchen in New York, Roundhouse in London, the various festivals in Europe, and the new performing ensembles and spaces throughout the United States. Even Boulez has taken his new-music performance activities with the New York Philharmonic and the B.B.C. outside of the traditional concert hall.

The energies created by the multi-media experience flow naturally into new live and theater forms. Even the media works mentioned above are in fact forms of music theater. Other forms grew directly out of the re-evaluation of the concert situation. Many of Cage's concert performances approach theater and so do many rock performances. Cage realized a large-scale *Theater Piece* and so did Stockhausen (*Originale*). Kagel's *Sur Scène,* Ligeti's *Aventures,* some of the theater works of Berio and Sylvano Bussotti, the author's *Foxes and Hedgehogs,* Hiller's *Avalanche,* certain works of Austin and Oliveros are in effect dramatizations of the concert situation arising from certain kinds of culture shock and conflict. Martirano's *L's G A,* William Albright's *Tic,* and other works combining visual images, language, sound, music, and electronics are in effect multi-media pieces with theater forms. It is important to note that the distinction between environmental and dramatic forms does not depend only on the means employed. Environmental structures are open-ended—cyclical or ongoing—while closed and time-delineated forms may be regarded as dramatic. Both kinds have been used in concert, media, and multi-media performance, but theater situations have become increasingly important in defining the development of new music-theater ideas. The William Bolcom-Arnold Weinstein "opera for actors," *Dynamite Tonight,* and the Stanley Silverman-Richard Foreman collaborations —*Elephant Steps* and *Dr. Selavy's Magic Theater*—are closer to traditional musical theater in form if not content. The theater work of Kagel, Pousseur, and Berio (*Passaggio, Laborinthus II, Opera*) comes out of the modernist, serial tradition of European music with strong connections to more general currents of European intellectual thought: structural linguistics, new literary forms, Brechtian theater. In England, Alexander Goehr, Peter Maxwell Davies, and others have developed a kind of neo-Brechtian music theater related to both European and American ideas; Davies's *Blindman's Bluff* is a good example.

American work in this area is closely related to the ensemble and improvisatory activities of theater and dance groups like The Open Theater, Daniel Nagrin's Work Group, and La Mama. William Bolcom has worked with an improvisational theater group, Philip Glass with a dance-theater group called Mabou Mines. In 1970, the author founded the music-theater ensemble Quog for the ensemble study, creation, and performance of new media and music-theater ideas. The development of music-theater in ensemble form was an obvious and important step involving group study, workshops, exercises, performance games, interaction, and improvisation as well as creation and realization integrating movement and sound, music and language, dance and theater, image and idea; the collaboration between artists and performers in different areas and the creation of music-theater repertory are important long-range

goals. Major works with Quog include *Ecolog*, originally created for television but also realized in a theater version, *Saying Something*, and
Biograffiti. The development of a "third music theater" using the range
of contemporary resources and the formation of music-theater performance ensembles are two aspects of the same activity.

The return to music theater is one of those turns of the wheel that
has every aspect of inevitability about it. Until recently, vocal music and
theater were principal sources of new energies in musical evolution, and
the modernist emphasis on abstraction and instrumental music is probably only the exception that proves the rule. The new awarenesses
created by happenings and multi-media as well as the discoveries of
serialism, indeterminacy, electronic music, and aleatory are all grist for
the music-theater mill. The re-evaluation of live performance, the old
questions of form and content, context and meaning, even a certain
weight of history lend themselves to re-interpretation through music-
theater forms. In the broadest sense, music theater deals with the relationship between musical and non-musical experience. Its forms grow out
of conflict—the interaction of creator, performer, public, ideas, ranges of
experience. These forms are dialectical, creating oppositions, reaching out
to limits, mediating extremes. Many media may be involved; the medium
is not the message although the message must realize itself in terms of the
medium. It is probably not necessary at the present time to define it any
more closely than this; it is the works created in the genre that determine the form, not the other way around.

The era of exploration is over. All experience is now available raw
material for art—through 360° and on a continuum. What matters is what
is done with this raw experience. The old questions of context (the social
setting of the work of art) and content ("meaning" understood in a widened sense) must again be taken up. The best new art concerns itself with
the ordering of a particular universe of ideas and experiences from the
totality of possibilities within the psychological, poetical, and social realities of the act of performance, the meaning of non-verbal—or verbal/
non-verbal—communication, and the experience of sound. The total range
of experience and the act of communication are in themselves subject
matter. Forms arise out of a kind of dialectic of voice and instrument,
live and electronic, strictness and freedom, rational control and irrationality, fixed detail and improvisation, total unity and open form, symmetry
and asymmetry, periodicity and a-periodicity, pitch and noise, extreme
sound and silence, extreme register and extreme dynamic, maximum motion and stasis, high and low tension, thinness and density, complexity
and simplicity, clarity and confusion, intelligibility and incomprehensibility, expressive detail and big line, familiarity and purity, image and

abstraction, verbal sound and musical meaning, association and invention. Dramatic and musical forms arise naturally out of this dialectic process in which opposition and conflict may in fact lead to illumination and resolution. Structural forms based on opposition, or on resolution through a continuum which mediates extremes, provide a connecting link between musical form and development on the one hand and meaning, content, and context on the other. These are, without a doubt, the essential problems that confront the post-modern composer and, indeed, the future of music as an art form.

In a very real sense the age of modern music is drawing to a close. The music of the avant-garde, growing out of modern music, is in fact a transition to something new. The old categories are purely historical and no longer really relevant. For the younger composers and many of the older ones the barriers are down, the categories destroyed, the old battles over and done with. Any kind of statement is possible. All possible materials and all possible relationships between creator, creation, performer, and perceiver are possible (including none); but the significance of these possibilities is only to be found in the creative achievements themselves. The raw material of every piece is the total possibility of experience; the subject of the discourse is the quality and nature of experience, of perceptions and the way we communicate them in the context of an essentially social art. The best new art will reflect, on the one hand, the cultural and social situation that produced it; on the other, the structure of human perception and mind and, by extension, the biological history of the race and even some larger natural order.

The task is not an easy one but the best new music of the twentieth century has always proposed the most difficult, the most profound and universal, artistic problems and proceeded to resolve them anew. Today, more than ever, the problems, the materials, the premises and the forms, the context and content, the media, the expressive means and realizations, the psychological, artistic, esthetic, social, and human meaning of music must be unique to each experience and yet relate to some larger fund of experience and knowledge, established anew with each act of creation and realization and yet universally valid in terms of the scope and potential of individual and social experience and knowledge.

BIBLIOGRAPHICAL NOTES

The author's article "The Revolution in Music" in *The New American Review* No. 6 (New York, 1969; several times reprinted) deals with music and technology; his article on music theater in the *New York*

Times of December 24, 1972 will shortly be reprinted. The double number 268–269 of *La Revue musicale* (Paris, 1971) contains the principal papers delivered at the 1970 Stockholm UNESCO meeting on the subject of "Musique et Technologie." Leonard Meyer's *Music, the Arts and Ideas* (Chicago, 1967) is one of the few extended considerations of the state of contemporary musical culture in English; it contains an extensive bibliography. Marshall McLuhan's *The Gutenberg Galaxy* (Toronto, 1964) and *Understanding Media* (New York, 1971) are the classic statements of media impact on culture.

There has been a veritable explosion of writing on pop music. See Lillian Roxon's *Rock Encyclopedia* (New York, 1969), *The Age of Rock*, ed., Jonathan Eisen (New York, 1969), among others; also the periodical *Rolling Stone*.

Source magazine, while it lasted, was a good point of reference for new developments in music. The writings and anthologies of Richard Kostelanetz cover the upheavals of the 1960's in music and the other arts; the most recent is *Metamorphosis in the Arts* (New York, 1973). The author's forthcoming *Music in American Society* deals with the broad areas of new music, American life, and social change with particular emphasis on the current situation.

APPENDIX
MUSICAL EXAMPLES

The musical examples and discussions of them below are meant to be illustrative only—"examples" in the literal sense. They are intended to suggest the variety of twentieth-century music as well as approaches to further study by the student. In such study, it should be remembered that musical notation, even in its most elaborate and artistic twentieth-century forms, is only an approximate if convenient representation of the music, and not by any means equivalent to the music itself.[1] The reader should always assume that he is being referred to the music. Most of the music exemplified below, and much that is discussed in this volume's narrative,

[1] This accounts for the relative lack of examples from the second half of the twentieth century. The extensive use of original and bizarre notations—sometimes for purely visual effect, often for quite practical reasons—only serves to re-emphasize the purely pragmatic significance of musical notation. It is no longer true that "the score" is the equivalent of the music itself and, in many basic ways, recording has replaced printing as the means of "publishing" of new music.

has been recorded; however, since discographies date quickly, one has not been included here.

The numbering of the examples below corresponds to the book's chapters, and references within chapters, e.g., Example 10-3 refers to the third example cited in Chapter 10.

EXAMPLE 3-1. Debussy, *Jeux*. Quoted by permission of Durand & Cie, Editeurs-propriétaires, Paris.

Examples of symmetrical structures which are tonally ambiguous.

a. Four-note chromatic group filling in minor third (meas. 1-2).

Hn., harp.

b. Whole-tone harmonies, moving by major thirds (meas. 5-6).

Hn., harp, cel.

c. Major seconds in parallel motion; simultaneous, independent chromatic lines (meas. 25-30).

EXAMPLE 3-2. Stravinsky, *Le Sacre du printemps.* Copyright 1921 by Edition Russe de Musique. Copyright assigned to Boosey and Hawkes, Inc. Reprinted by permission.

Some uses of a basic block-chord structure.

b. At ☐14☐. Articulated version.

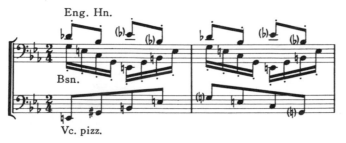

c. At ⑮ . a. and b. (as above) with new elements superimposed.

EXAMPLE 4-1. Schoenberg, *Three Piano Pieces*, Op. 11, No. 1. Quoted by permission of Mrs. Gertrud Schoenberg and Universal Edition.

Use of simple interval structures in early atonal Schoenberg. Closely related patterns—major third with adjacent half-step inside or outside (X), tritone with adjacent whole- or half-step (Y and Z)—generate the melodic as well as the harmonic material. Longer goals are also suggested; thus the opening melodic movement (X) outlines Z over the first three measures. Through the use of transposition and inversion (in the traditional sense, i.e., a minor second becomes a major seventh), all the intervallic material and almost all the chromatic steps are brought into play. These are all embryonic twelve-tone techniques, here used intuitively as a series of musical associations.

b. Opening Measures.

EXAMPLE 4-2. Webern, *Five Pieces for Orchestra,* Op. 10, No. 4. Quoted by permission of Universal Edition.

A brief analysis of a brief movement from Webern's "expressionist" period.

The piece consists of slightly more than two revolutions of the total chromatic cycle with miniature phrases of six, four, two, and five notes set among brief chordal structures and repeated notes. The opening harp sonority—G♭, D♭, F—is recapitulated in the fourth and fifth measures by the harp, clarinet, and celesta with the addition of another three harmonic elements, B, E, C (a re-arrangement and inverted transposition of a companion structure). This same figure also appears melodically in the mandolin (simultaneously with the harp chord) as the A♭, G, and E♭ of the opening phrase. The mandolin phrase also contains secondary elements of great importance pivoted around the tritone (whole-step and tritone, tritone and half-step). The nine notes of the mandolin and harp fill the chromatic space between C and A♭. The next phrases, which begin by adding the missing B♭, A, and B, center on tritones with the attached whole- or half-step; i.e., the opening three notes of the trumpet's phrase are an arrangement and transposition of the opening mandolin notes; the final D of the trumpet phrase and the two notes of the trombone phrase are an arrangement of the second through fourth notes of the mandolin phrase. Similarly, the following F♯ in the harp and C–D♭ trill in the clarinet, as well as the subsequent E–F in the celesta and B in the mandolin (the same B–F relationship that began the trumpet phrase, now associated through timbre with the opening), are related figures. The final violin phrase, beginning with a major seventh (i.e., whole-step inverted) and a tritone, is a synthesis of all the basic elements of the opening.

a. Interval structures.

EXAMPLE 5-1. Stravinsky, *Symphony of Psalms.* Copyright 1931 by Russischer Musikverlag; renewed 1958. Copyright and renewal assigned 1947 to Boosey & Hawkes, Inc. Revised version copyright 1948 by Boosey & Hawkes, Inc. Reprinted by permission.

A specimen analysis of a "neo-tonal" work.

The *Symphony of Psalms,* scored for chorus and large orchestra without violins or violas, uses excerpts from the Vulgate Latin version of three Psalms; Stravinsky specifies that they must be sung in Latin. The work opens with an E–minor triad, spaced, scored, and articulated in a very characteristic manner (a). The short, isolated, mezzo-forte sound, which recurs half a dozen times in precisely the same form, strongly emphasizes the minor third between E and G, one of the pivotal relationships of the work. The figurations that follow are based on arpeggios and scales that refer to E♭ and C, two of the principal tonal areas of the work, themselves separated by a minor third. The piece, as it turns out, is in a kind of super C, compounded out of the related keys and triads of C minor, E♭, E minor, and, to a much more limited degree, G. We might represent this tonality or polar center like this:

At the outset, however, E minor dominates, with a secondary tendency to move towards a G₇ and through a flat area. At ④ the altos enter with a "thematic" idea—nothing more than E's and F's—over a version of the arpeggio figure now slowed up to eighth notes and including a new figure based on minor thirds a half-step apart (b). By ⑤ the impulse has carried the music to a G area (the omnipresent thirds are D and F in the soprano voice); the figuration remains stable although expanded. This impulse is checked by the ambiguous, compound harmony and instrumental melodic figuration at ⑥, and ⑦ is a return to point zero, but now more developed and intensified. By ⑨ the piece is heavily settled on the basic E and it remains so right up until the end of the movement, where the E to F melodic motion suddenly carries up to G while the bass struggles down through a B♭ and an A♭ to come to rest on its own G (c).

a. First movement, opening measures.

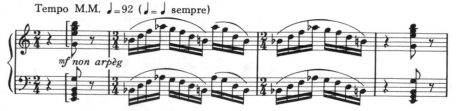

b. First movement, thematic idea.

c. First movement, closing measures.

     The second movement begins with a long woodwind fugue in C (minor) with a theme based on the pair of minor thirds a half-step apart already heard in the first movement (C–E♭; B–D) (d). The chorus enters in E♭ minor with its own fugue subject, which is developed over the continuation of the original woodwind subject (e). There is a brief *a cappella* stretto, a pause, a very intense compound of the main material, and then a very quiet final few measures in which repeated choral E♭'s hover over a harmonic and contrapuntal complex which ends the movement and implies the next (f).

d. Second movement, opening of instrumental fugue.

e. Second movement, opening of choral fugue.

f. Second movement, closing measures.

The third movement opens in a modified C with a strong infusion of E♭'s (and B♭'s) (g); at the cadence, this E♭/B♭ turns to a clear, bright C. The last time this C comes around, it does not shake off the B♭, which remains as part of a long pedal around which appear C major punctuation in the horns (with the familiar E–G at the bottom), a little half-step plucked figure centered on G, and a melodic line rising from G through A♭ and B♭ to C (h). The pedal sound pushes up to D and E, the bass picks up the G to C movement, then drops through the flats back to G and down to F at a big moment of climax. The climax is built on E and A triads with a bass that centers on F and G♯ eventually dropping through a long chain of thirds down to C. The E–G relationship of the opening movement is echoed by a C–E♭ relationship here, while the half-step melodic figures of the opening are turned into whole-steps. With the rhythmic, repeated-note "Laudate dominum" at [8], the chorus returns to the pivotal E, and the continuation at [9] takes off from a very subtle extension of the basic E–G relationship, now clearly connected with the C–major seventh chord that is so characteristic of this movement. After the opening "Alleluia" recurs, the quick tempo returns with repeated E♭'s and then a modified restatement of "Laudate Dominum" on the repeated E–G minor third and later another one on a B♭ triad. At [20], the movement and tempo settle down briefly in G over an ostinato which at first consists of a G major triad but later turns into a big trio of fourths under a simple melodic ostinato based principally on the notes E♭–D–C at [22] (i). This E♭ sound is the solid and static state of the piece until the very last measures, when only the B♭ of the ostinato remains in the bass. The "Alleluia" returns—the top is suddenly discovered to come right out of the long "Laudate" that came before—and the E♭–E♮–G ambiguity is definitively dispelled in the final C with its E♮ on top.

g. Third movement, opening measures.

h. Third movement, orchestral interlude.

i. Third movement, at 22 .

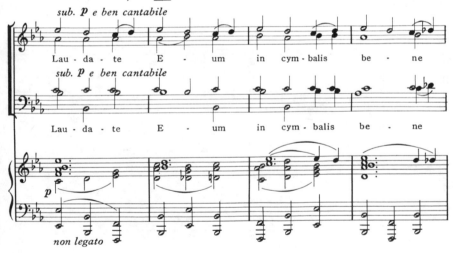

EXAMPLE 7-1. Hindemith, *Das Marienleben,* "O hast du dies gewollt"; 1922–1923 and 1948 versions. Texts by Rainer Maria Rilke. Quoted by permission of B. Schott's Söhne, Mainz.

The "softening" and regularizing of Hindemith's style illustrated by a comparison between the original and revised versions of *Das Marienleben.*

a. Comparison of opening measures.

b. Comparison of closing measures.

EXAMPLE 8-1. Bartók, String Quartet No. 4, First Movement. Copyright 1929 by Universal Edition; renewed 1956. Copyright assigned to Boosey & Hawkes Inc. for the U.S.A. Reprinted by permission of Boosey & Hawkes, Inc. and Universal Edition.

Intervallic structure in Bartók's music.

The basic intervallic content of this movement can be described as a half-step plus a whole-step. These elements, which have obvious parallels to traditional scale patterns, are used here in a very different way, to generate larger melodic and units and harmonic relationships. Thus a harmonic half-step plus a melodic half-step (two melodic half-steps) creates a harmonic whole-step; half- and whole-step melodic sequences fill out and define minor thirds; similarly, a cluster of harmonic half-steps for the four instruments fills in a chromatic minor third. Adjacent whole-steps—melodic or harmonic—create and define major thirds. Thus intertwined melodic and harmonic steps and thirds (it is almost impossible to tell where "harmony" leaves off and "melody" begins) fill out defined segments of the chromatic spectrum—most significantly, the regions between from C up to E♮ and, inversely, from C down to A♭. These intervals imbue the entire work with their characteristic sound and ultimately shape the entire harmonic and melodic invention. All of the elements are present in the figure in measure 7 as simply an extension of everything heard previously. The close of the movement (b) is a summation of the harmonic and melodic (and rhythmic) energies of the piece.

a. First movement, opening measures.

b. First movement, closing measures.

EXAMPLE 8-2. Bartók, *Music for Strings, Percussion, and Celesta*. Copyright 1937 by Universal Edition; renewed 1964. Copyright and renewal assigned to Boosey & Hawkes, Inc. for the U.S.A. Reprinted by permission.

Examples of the accommodation of intervallic chromaticism to modal/tonal music in Bartók's music.

The *Music for Strings, Percussion, and Celesta* begins with a rather dense chromatic fugue built on one of Bartók's most characteristic melodic types: a succession of ascending and descending half- and whole-steps contained within a very small compass (a). Locally this movement does not sound tonal at all, but its broad structure which departs from and closes finally on A through harmonic and melodic cycles of fifths suggests a chromatic interpretation of long-range tonal organizations.

a. First-movement theme.

The big A-major finale, based initially on a folkish theme (b), rounds off the entire work with a notable technique of re-interpreting the earlier chromatic sounds and types in diatonic and triadic-tonal terms (c, d, e).

b. Main theme of last movement.

c. Chromatic material in last movement.

d. Diatonic expansion (last movement).

e. Development of diatonic figures.

EXAMPLE 10-1. Row forms used in Schoenberg, Piano Piece, Op. 33a.

Note that the retrograde and retrograde inversion forms read from right to left. Together with the original and its inversion, these forms may be transposed to any of the other eleven degrees of the tempered chromatic scale (the inversion and retrograde inversion above are given at the transposition of a fifth—"I–5" and "RI–5"); the internal relationships —the intervals—remain constant and all twelve pitches appear once and only once.[2]

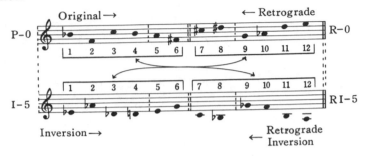

EXAMPLE 10-2. Schoenberg, Piano Suite, Op. 25. Quoted by permission of Mrs. Gertrud Schoenberg and Universal Edition.

Early use of row technique in Schoenberg's music.

a. The row, in all the forms used in the suite.

b. Präludium, beginning.

[2] Some commentators and analysts prefer to regard the first pitch as the zero point from which the series or row departs; thus the twelve notes are numbered from zero to 11. This has analogies to mathematical operations and presumably facilitates certain procedures. Nevertheless, the other common method—numbering from 1 to 12—may be clearer in an introductory description of the method. In any case, the spelling-out of the row and row-forms in analyses and discussions should be considered only a helpful abstraction, valid only as far as it is useful. Some of the technical problems associated with the development of twelve-tone and serial music now seem of greater historical than current technical interest.

c. Gavotte, beginning.

Etwas langsam (♩ = ca 72) nicht hastig

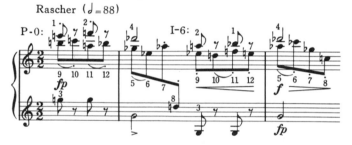

d. Musette, beginning.

Rascher (♩ = 88)

e. Intermezzo, beginning.

(♩ = 40)

f. Menuett, beginning.

Moderato (♩ = ca.88)

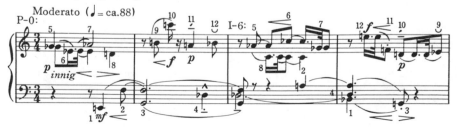

g. Gigue, beginning.

EXAMPLE 10-3. Schoenberg, Piano Piece, Op. 33a. Quoted by permission of Mrs. Gertrud Schoenberg and Universal Edition.

Brief analysis of Schoenberg's use of row material to generate harmonic and melodic elements of a piece.

Example 10-3 shows how the row material of Op. 33a is used musically. The basic units are the three four-note chords at the beginning (a); they color the entire work.

a. First subject.

Only later, as the piece develops and unfolds, are lines extracted. Note the close relationship between the phrasing and structural articulation of the piece and the twelve-tone groupings; this kind of phrasing is particularly clear at the start and at the main points of articulation. The first three chords present a harmonic arrangement of the original form of the row; the second three, the retrograde inversion. In the next three measures, the arrangement takes the form of a succession of pitches with one form of the row (the retrograde inversion) in the upper register, and another (the retrograde) in the lower parts; measures 6 and 7, however, develop the pitch material of measures 1 and 2 in the original order. The following measures again present different forms of the material in "contrapuntal juxtapositions"; notice the important use of repetition as an extension device in measures 8 and 9 and in the new section beginning at measure 14. If the independent use of registers is kept in mind, it is not difficult to follow the twelve-tone thread through measure 20. In measure 20, however, the first "irregularity" occurs: the final two notes of both the retrograde and the retrograde inversion do not appear; instead, the music seems to reverse its steps so that the return at measure 21 to the outline shape of measure 14 begins at the middle point of the rows.

b. Second subject.

It is clear that from measure 14 onwards (see b), the basic arrangement of the row material is no longer in three groups of fours but in two groups of sixes (subdivided into smaller units of threes). If the given rows are examined, it will be seen that the collection of the first six pitches of the original contains the same notes (although in a different order) as the first six pitches of the retrograde inversion; and, of course, the same is true of the last six pitches of each form. Thus if the original is presented simultaneously with its inversion (at the given transposition), the first and last six notes of each form combine to produce new, complete twelve-tone combinations; this remarkable fact, carefully calculated by Schoenberg, provides the structural basis for the music as it evolves from four-note chord sounds towards the arrangements in six-note groupings. Beginning at the end of measure 27, there is a kind of development section (continuing the development that began in measures 21 and 22) in which the pairs of three-note groupings began to appear transposed onto different levels (up a step and then down a fourth, first presented in complementary six-note groups and in complete transposed rows). The re-establishment of the original row material at the original levels after the *fermata* in measure 32, the return to the conditions of measure 14 in measure 35, the unified arrangement of complete rows in short descending and ascending phrases in measures 37 and 38, and the final re-interpretation of measures 1 and 2 at the end can be easily traced.[3]

---

[3] The attentive score-reader—perhaps even the alert listener—will find, in addition to the above-mentioned omissions at measure 20, a note taken from the lower register and substituted for a missing note in the upper in measure 22, exchanges of note order in measures 29 and 37, and a clear misprint in measure 35.

EXAMPLE 10-4. Schoenberg, String Trio, Op. 45. Quoted by permission of Mrs. Gertrud Schoenberg and Universal Edition.

Later evolution of row technique in Schoenberg's music.

This is the opening of the work, showing how the pitch groups of the row are revealed gradually. In measure 1, the total chromatic material is presented, divided into two groups of six notes, with the distinctive feature of a half-step trill. In the second measure, the pitch content of these groupings is established: B–C–G♯–F♯–G–F for one "hexachord"; the inversion (transposed) produces the other six notes. A primary order form of this material is revealed only in the fifth measure, first in groups of two notes divided between the violin and viola, then in a strictly linear form in the viola (accompanied by harmonies made up of complementary forms of the same material transposed to fill out the twelve-note groupings). In measures 6 and 7, the same material re-appears now in four-note groupings. In measures 8–13, there is a systematic presentation of the material in three complete rows—taking off from the basic form of measure 4—out of which the violin extracts a new line which in itself is a new grouping of twelve-tones.[4]

[4] Later in the work, secondary row material is formed by permutations within the "hexachords"; the pitch content of the hexachords, however, remains constant.

EXAMPLE 10-5. Berg, Violin Concerto. Quoted by permission of Universal Edition.

Synthesis of row technique and tonality in Berg.

a. The row.

b. Solo violin, Introduction to First Movement.

c. Opening of Andante, First Movement.

d. "Viennese" themes, Allegretto, First Movement.

e. Carinthian Folksong, Allegretto, First Movement.

f. Bach chorale, Adagio, Second Movement.

EXAMPLE 10-6. Webern, *Concerto for Nine Instruments,* Op. 24. Quoted by permission of Universal Edition.

Reduction and rationalization of row elements in Webern's twelve-tone music.

The twelve-tone row of the concerto is shown below (a). The basic intervallic units are the same as those of the *Bagatelle* mentioned in the text: major third and minor second. The row itself further breaks down into four groups of three notes, the last three of which are transpositions of the other forms of the original—retrograde inversion, retrograde, inversion; also the retrograde inversion of the whole row of the given transposition preserves the pitch identities of the three-note groups. Here are a few measures of the realization of this concept (b). The actual structure of the row is crucial; in the second movement, for instance (c), the groups of threes are formed by single tones in the "melodic" instruments complemented by two-note harmonic groupings in the piano. The solo line consists of the initial notes of each three-note group of the row, which themselves form other transpositions of the identical three-note group. The interlocking of these groupings is carried out systematically. Transpositions of this material are chosen which produce further relations and further identities. Certain pitches and certain groups of two and three notes re-appear in different forms and transpositions of the row material, and these relationships are exploited in terms of register, tone color, position in the phrase, and so forth; non-pitch aspects of the music are thus brought into close relationship with the twelve-tone material.

a. The row.

b. First movement, meas. 1-5.

P-0 RI-1

c. Second movement, meas. 1-18.

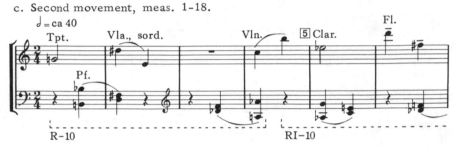

R-10 RI-10

R-6 I-5

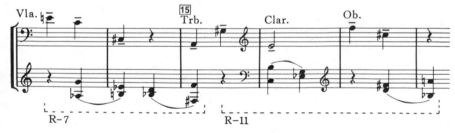

R-7 R-11

EXAMPLE 12-1. Ives, *The Unanswered Question*. Used by permission. Copyright 1953 by Southern Music Publishing Company.

Layering, juxtaposition of diverse elements, and symbolic reference in Ives.

This is an excerpt from the middle of the work showing the tonal string chorale, the questioning "expressionistic" phrase in the trumpet (or English horn or oboe or clarinet), and two of the dense, cluster-like woodwind "answers."

EXAMPLE 12-2. Varèse, *Ionisation*, © 1934 by Edgard Varèse. By permission of Franco Colombo, Inc., Publisher.

New approaches to the use of rhythm, timbre, and frequency bands in an all-percussion work by Varèse.

    This is an excerpt towards the end of the work, showing the structurally important entrance of piano and bells, the use of a low and high siren, and some of the important rhythmic motifs as well as the general variety and lay-out of percussion instruments. Note that the siren permits the use of pitched sound on a continuum while the writing for piano and bells uses clusters and harmonic aggregates, creating a very distinct point of arrival in the piece.

EXAMPLE 12-3. Cowell, *Tiger*. Quoted by permission of Associated Music Publishers Inc.

New keyboard techniques and notations: tone clusters and harmonics in Cowell's piano music.

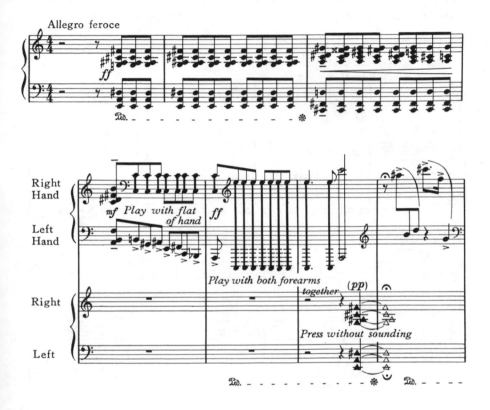

EXAMPLE 14-1. Babbitt, *Philomel,* excerpt. Quoted by permission of Associated Music Publishers, Inc.

Serialism with live performance and synthesized sound.

The score of Babbitt's *Philomel* shows the carefully notated solo voice part with a cue-score notation of the tape part, which is an amalgam of electronic music and electronically altered vocal sounds.

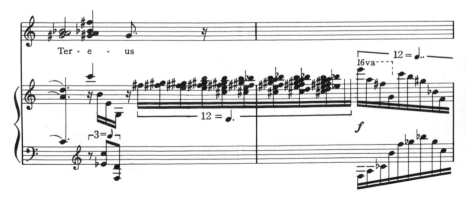

EXAMPLE 16-1. Brown, *Available Forms 2*. Excerpt from Orchestra I score. Quoted by permission of Associated Music Publishers, Inc.

Example of open-form notation with elements to be ordered in the course of performance.

Three out of five possible "events" on a page of score for one of the two orchestras. The conductor of each orchestra successively selects various events during the course of the performance and indicates his choices to the musicians by holding up the fingers of one hand.

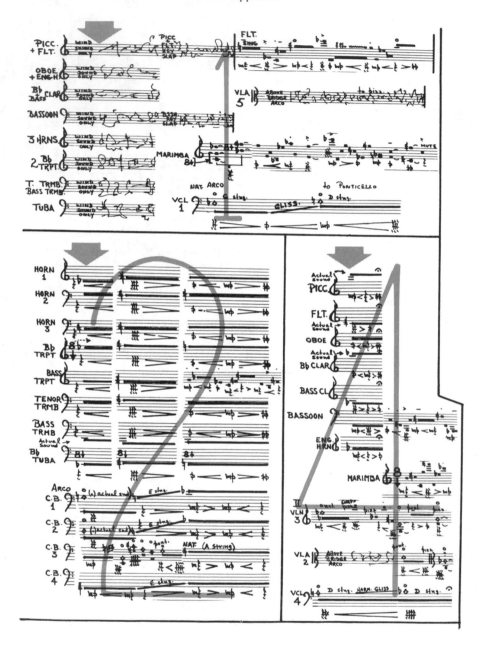

INDEX